Travels
with Artsy
and Twinkle Toes
on the A.T.

Travels With Artsy and Twinkle Toes on the A.T.

Twinkle Toes

To order additional copies of this book, contact:
Xlibris Corporation
1-888-795-4274
www.Xlibris.com
Orders@Xlibris.com

19052

To Mark Grove —

Come travel with us as we

Travel along the A.T.

Meet some of the charming

people that we shared our

experiences with.

Twinkle Toes
&
Artsy

5

PREFACE

The basic purpose of this book is to inform my friends and relatives of my hiking experiences on the Appalachian Trail. There were many times when I thought that my trail hike was over, that I would never see the A.T. again, and many times when I did not *want* to see it again. However, the lure and magnetism of the Trail can be spellbinding so that it keeps drawing one back to it. Possibly, this lure will be felt by others so that they, too, will be able to experience the thrill and adventure of hiking part or all of the A.T. For those adventurous souls, I wish them the best and hope that this book will give them an idea of the sights, smells, and tastes of a great hiking experience that may await them.

INTRODUCTION

Who are Twinkle Toes and Artsy? Where did they come from, and why those funny names? You first must understand some of the "rules" of Appalachian Trail hikers. Most hikers rarely go by their given names. They are not secret; they just lose some of their significance on the Trail. There may be many Bills, Joes, Janes, and Jills. However, there are very few Stump Stomping Bills, Wild Man Joes, Jitny Janes, or Jittery Jills. With rare exceptions, your Trail name is yours alone as not many others will have one like it.

On my first hike, several of us were talking around the campfire one night, telling what other things we liked to do. I mentioned that I loved ballroom dancing, and one other hiker remarked, "You're a real twinkle toes, huh?" The name seemed as good as any, and I kept it.

My hiking partner who joined me after several years is a retired high school art teacher and quite an artist in her own right. The name, Artsy, seemed quite fitting and appropriate.

"Twinkle Toes" is really David S. Swan, Jr., a retired CPA born in 1930 who loves the outdoors and the activities that can be performed there. While I work inside, I really like to play outside. Hiking and backpacking are just two of the outside pursuits that I enjoy.

"Artsy" is really Mina A. Swan, a retired art teacher who also loves the outdoors. Before we were married in 1999, we talked about the various kinds of activities that we enjoyed and were amazed that we liked to do so many similar things. Many of the activities that one of us had experience in, the other had always wanted to do. As a result, we now share our hiking, backpacking, scuba diving, bird watching, and travel experiences.

Will Artsy finish the Trail? That is a question that we do not have an answer to yet. I have promised to help her finish if she so desires just as she helped me. She has the ability and has already completed some of the toughest sections. However, she has so many interests that our allotted time just may not permit it.

CHAPTER ONE

As a prelude to my tale of my hike along the Appalachian Trail, I early on decided to keep a daily log of my travels and experiences. In writing this, it would serve at least two purposes. First, it will keep the memories fresh of what I did and, second, it should keep me from ever trying to do it again! Later on, my children would sometimes ask me, "Dad, don't you ever read what you have written?"

May 10, 1991

The southern terminus of the Appalachian Trail is on the peak of Springer Mountain in northern Georgia. This is not an easy spot to reach. The 8.8-mile approach trail from Amicalola Falls State Park is reported to be rough. In fact, it is *so* rough that some hikers give up their dream of hiking the A.T. rather than going through more of it further on in the Trail. Knowing this, I wanted somewhat of an easier start so that I could prepare myself for the tough sections ahead. A little research allowed me to find another way to the summit of Springer Mountain.

The bus and I left Clearwater, Florida at 6:00 P.M. on the way to Gainesville, Georgia. I shared the seat to Lake City with a big black dude who talked the whole trip. He *never* shut up—and I got no sleep! From Lake City to Atlanta, the seat was shared with an overweight black girl who promptly curled up to sleep. With her curled hot rump on one side of me and the air conditioning going on the other side, the contrast in temperatures kept me awake the *rest* of the trip to Atlanta.

The connections were on time, and I arrived in Gainesville, Georgia at 9:00 A.M. I was right on time, but my scheduled ride

was not there! I waited half an hour and called him just to get a
recording. Finally, I asked the clerk if anyone had called in that
day in reference to me, and she said no. After another half hour of
waiting, the clerk informed me that someone had come the day
before looking for me at 9:00 A.M., had waited a while and then
left. Fortunately, she had kept his name and telephone number. A
call woke Jack who stated that the man who was supposed to pick
me up got another trip of three days and had asked Jack to meet
me *Friday*! Jack came to the station in another hour and was able
to take me to within half a mile of the start of the Trail. The last
twenty-three miles of driving were on forest roads and the recent
rains had not helped them at all. It was *not* the kind of road that
you would want to take your family car on. At 12:45 P.M., I started
on the Trail in a steady rain.

May 11, 1991   Hawk Mountain Shelter
                            Trail Distance: 7.5 miles

Steady rain made the Trail muddy, slippery, and not very
pleasant. There was fog (clouds) with the rain and a high humidity
made eyeglasses useless. For the first three miles, I felt strong, the
next three miles, I felt adequate, and the last two miles, I was
exhausted. A few miles after starting, I passed through a stand of
very old evergreens, reverently referred to as the Cathedral Hemlocks.
This section of forest was too remote to be harvested many years
ago and remains as the only virgin timber to be seen on the A.T.
until the Smokies are reached. To envision what this long stretch
of forest looked like in colonial times, you are asked to mentally
double the height and triple the girth of every tree that you see
and fill all of the cleared land with similar forests. It makes for a
fantastic mental picture!

The planned shelter at Hawk Mountain was arrived at about
5:00 P.M., but it was full. A party of four had taken all of the spare
room. In addition, an older man had commandeered a section of
the shelter and had already been there for several nights. He was
"hiking the Trail" but could not get past the first shelter. Although

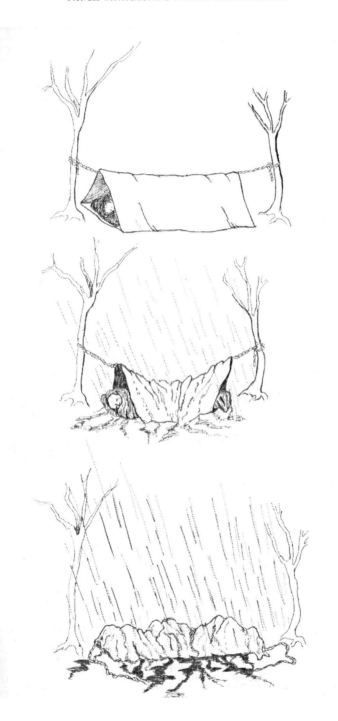

the shelter was designed for six sleeping bags, those five had stretched themselves to take all of the room. Rather than starting an incident early on in my hike, I elected to use my emergency tent, and it was no fun.

My tent was set up in the rain, and there was no place to shelter anything. The rain slowed up enough to cook dinner but started immediately after. I was already wet to the skin but was able to get my sleeping bag set up in the tent. I had a rain cover for my pack but could not get anything out of it without getting it wet. The result was I went into the tent wet, it had a head room of only about two feet, everything came off wet, and I crawled into the sleeping bag with soaking wet underwear. I was able to keep most of the bag dry, but the tent kept peeling back so that rain would fall in my face. I finally just undid the thru-rope and let the tent fall on me. It was not a pleasant night, but I *did* get some sleep. The moisture condensing on the inside of the tent left it as wet as the outside. The dry bag did get my underclothes dry so that I woke up dry and warm.

May 12, 1991   Gooch Gap Shelter
                              Trail Distance: 8.7 miles

There were three young men sharing a two-man tent in the area where I had my tent. They were all from Pennsylvania, going in the same direction as I, and left a few minutes before me this morning. We all had planned on stopping to the Gooch Gap Shelter for the night giving us a hike of about 8.7 miles. I did not feel strong! My wet boots had started a few blisters, and it was a rough up-and-down day. My pack with wet clothes in it felt ten pounds heavier, and my feet felt like lead. Again, the last three miles were a nightmare. When I finally reached the shelter by one path, the party of four had reached it about the same time by another path. Fortunately, the three young men had reached it much earlier and taken most of the room. I immediately asked if there was room for one more, and there was. They had "saved" a spot for me. There was *only* room for four, and we had a pleasant, dry evening.

I took a two-hour nap as soon as I came in and got set up, awoke at 6:00 to fix dinner, and joined it with two bowls of soup and lemon pudding. By 9:00, it was dark and we sacked out and all slept until 6:00 the next morning. It really felt luxurious! We had heard that this shelter had mice in it, and was later to learn that *all* shelters had mice. We purposely left some food out for them. In the morning, the food was gone and our packs were safe. I took the extra precaution of leaving open my pack and leaving open a bag of mothballs that I carried. I continued to do this every night, and my food was never disturbed. I also hung my pack up as high as I could.

May 13, 1991   Neels Gap Hostel
                                  Trail Distance: 3.7 miles

We all arose at 6:00, and had our respective breakfasts, all different. Mine was dry cereal with powdered milk prepared the night before. After using the milk, I immediately made another half a pint for my instant pudding for dinner time. Although my meals do not leave me hungry, it is obvious I am not eating sufficiently for the exertion that I am doing. On this day's hike, I felt immediately tired and hills, while not steep, took much effort and a lot of resting. A young couple passed me like I was standing still—which I was at the time! I had planned to hike to Woody Gap where Georgia State Road 60 crosses the Trail. It is about two and a half miles to the town of Suches, Georgia, where, I had been informed, there was lodging and a trail outfitter.

Reaching Woody Gap at 10:15 A.M., my feet felt like they could not take another step. I waited thirty-eight minutes for the very first car to pass and, fortunately, it stopped for me. An elderly couple took me to Suches, where no one knew of any motels. The single grocer in town knew of none closer than Dahlonaga, Georgia, and I had passed through there on my auto ride to the *start* of the Trail. The couple thought that they knew of another motel nearby and drove me there. By sight, it was obvious it had not seen service, except as a chicken house, in many years. I asked directions to

Neels Gap, which is on the Trail and has a hostel. They could not just give me directions but *drove* me there. This was the shelter that my three friends of the night before were aiming for. It was a fourteen-mile hike including a climb to the top of 4,400-foot Blood Mountain. They all made it including the one with the blistered feet. Were they surprised to see me?

The accommodations at the hostel including a full dinner, full breakfast, plus a towel for a shower cost a total of $23.50. We completed our spaghetti dinner, and each left enough food to more than fill another person. An enormous helping of spaghetti with meat sauce (full of meat) came with a mixed salad, two loaves of homemade bread, a huge piece of chocolate cake, apple juice, coffee, and a gallon of milk to be shared with six men. We were hungry, we ate like pigs, and *no one* cleaned his plate. Also, in reference to the two loaves of bread, one remained untouched! My plans were to rest up a day in a motel and get my clothes washed and dried. (I am sure the wet clothes that I am lugging around add another two pounds to my pack.) My feet are in worse shape than yesterday, and I am planning on staying another day here to bring order out of things. The feet *must* be in good condition to continue. Although I did not consider myself as bringing any extras, common sense dictated that I lighten my load. Therefore, my binoculars, bird book, edible plant book, plus a few other odds and ends (five pounds total) got UPS'ed back to Clearwater. It may not sound like much but every little bit helps. One hiker claims to have cut two inches off his toothbrush and cut the labels out of his clothes to save weight. The experienced rule seems to be to carry no more than four days food supply *unless* there is no store on the way to replenish. I think that it has lots of merit and will be something to pass on to others.

It is interesting to note that the Trail passes right through the hostel at Neels Gap. There is a covered driveway between the hostel and the store and the trail sign is right on the corner of the drive. Hikers *have* to pass through!

We haven't seen too much animal life. The Rangers are training in the forests and the sounds of rifles, machine guns, and high explosives probably have all animals hiding for dear life. Last night, I went to sleep with the sounds of barred owls and whippoorwills trying to have an endurance contest. I saw a pair of goldfinches today (beautiful birds) and the sounds of pileated woodpeckers are constantly in the air. Although heard all through Georgia, the sounds gradually diminished until heard not at all in the Smokies and I *never* got to see one. Most of the bird life could be heard but not seen. The dense foliage, rain clouds, and fog made visual sightings rare. Some of the hikers saw some but not me. And I have seen only two pileated woodpeckers in my life!

May 14, 1991   Low Gap Shelter
Trail Distance: 10.6 miles

The breakfast at the hostel was just as fantastic as the dinner. I hated to pass up the homemade cinnamon bread, but there was just no place to put it. I felt better and decided not to take another day off. Everyone left at his own time, me being about the third out. Six of us made it to the Low Gap Shelter where we were joined by two others, one a young lady hiking alone. I was impressed by Margaret. Long, lean, and lanky, I was to find out the next day that she could set a pace that none of the men could match. That girl could move!

This shelter could hold only six people, but two of the men had their own tents and, even though early arrivals, preferred to set up camp away from the shelter. There was no problem with physical privacy. By 9:00, it was dark and I could not tell what anyone wore or did not wear to sleep. By 6:00 in the morning, it was still fairly dark but the young lady was already up and dressed. I have no concern for her safety. She was probably safer "sleeping" with five men on the Trail than if she had been alone somewhere in a motel. A resident of Maine, she had already walked a few hundred miles of the Trail in prior years and was now walking home. I say, "More power to her!"

May 15, 1991   Helen, GA
Trail Distance: 9.4 miles

Today was supposed to be an easy day with nine miles of relatively flat terrain. Well, it was easier than some, but it still took its toll on me. I was immediately tired and the plan of doing fifteen miles was soon enough shortened to about ten. I was planning on setting up my emergency tent midway between two shelters to be alone with nature. *However*, plans got changed. Around noon, about a mile from one shelter, it started to rain again—out of a seemingly clear sky. And it rained! It was back to my rain suit and wet boots within minutes. I could feel the new blisters starting, but couldn't do a thing about it. I made Unicoi Gap and State Road 75 about 2:00 P.M. and decided to stop in Helen, Georgia for the night to get dried out and take care of my feet. It took over an hour to get a ride and I did not try or expect to get a ride in a car. My wet pack and the wet and muddy "me" were just not "car" dressed. A pickup finally stopped where I could dump my gear in the truck bed and he took me right to the Days Inn in Helen. The hot shower and shave again felt good.

In the early morning while filling my canteen from the stream running right by the shelter, the cap somehow came off and was lost in the fast moving current. It was still fairly dark, and I never saw the cap again. There was much searching for it when it got light but to no avail. A wadded handkerchief became my cap. This was replaced by a cork in Helen. Whereas the day before, I found no water in the last eight miles of hiking, on this day I counted fourteen springs and water sources within the first two hours. It seems that some mountains are dry and some are gushers. It is very obvious that the Trail was not intended to be easy or short. There is a clear resemblance to the old childhood game of connecting the dots to form a picture. In this real life situation, the dots represent mountain peaks, and the Trail is the lines connecting the peaks. Where there is *any* kind of a rise, a hill, or a mountain in front of you, you can be assured of going to the very top. As examples:

May 11	Springer Mountain	3,782 feet
	Hawk Mountain	missed summit
May 12	Sassafras Mountain	3,336 feet
	Justus Mountain	3,224 feet
May 13	Ramrock Mountain	3,200 feet
May 14	Levelland Mountain	3,942 feet
	Cowrock Mountain	3,842 feet
	Wildcat Mountain	3,700 feet
	Poor Mountain	3,650 feet
	Sheeprock Top	3,575 feet
May 15	Blue Mountain	4,025 feet

Between the peaks, the lands dips to an average of about 3,000 feet, sometimes higher, but never lower than about 2,500 feet. Even the level areas can be exceptionally rough. Just try walking on a few hundred yards of irregularly shaped boulders that no vehicle and few domesticated animals could traverse. And yet, there was a blind man with a seeing-eye dog who did the full trail in one year! Another man with multiple sclerosis did it on crutches. To me, those are unbelievable feats. This Trail is a nightmare, but I am beginning to like it and thoroughly respect it.

After coming into Helen and seeing my feet, I decided to stay another day. As much as I tried to get into shape, the old body is just not there. And I'll be d— if I will admit to being too old for this kind of fun. I had a super supper at "Mamios" and set my boots to dry under a lamp set of the floor. After that, I slept like a baby.

May 16, 1991   Helen, GA
Trail Distance: 0.0 miles

My boots dried, and I tried them on to find them uncomfortably tight. My feet must have swelled, and the blisters did not help. Many of the blisters, and the most uncomfortable ones, are on the tip ends and the end tops of the toes. The trails are often so steep, going straight up or straight down, that you have all of your weight on your toe tips as you are descending. There is just no way that you can pre-condition yourself to this kind of pressure. Your boots either protect your toes or they do not. Mine did not!

After a light breakfast, I went looking for new boots. I must admit that I like the boots that I presently have. They are light weight, soft and comfortable, and are great "rock" boots. But they are no good on muddy leaves, no good at going down hills, and *no* good at keeping out water. A "Bass" store was nearby, and they had just one pair of hiking boots my size. You have to remember that Helen is a town of less than three hundred people so the "shopping malls" are on the micro size. I really hate the thought of breaking in a pair of new boots on the Trail, which is madness itself, but I want dry feet. I have the boots doctored up with mink oil, gave the old boots another coat, and will give it a whirl. If nothing else, I will have a pair of "uphill" boots, the old ones, and "downhill" boots, the new ones.

It has rained once today, looks like more is on the way, and is predicted through the weekend. This is one wet place!

May 17, 1991   Addis Gap Shelter
Trail Distance: 10.8 miles

I had a most difficult time sleeping last night, and this is most unusual for me. I probably did not get more that about four hours rest and was hoping for nine hours. After checking out, I tried to get a ride to the intersection of the Trail with slow results. I had my little sign indicating that I only wanted to go to the Trail, but dozens of cars and pickup trucks passed me by. Finally, a young man in an old Dodge van picked me up and took me to the Trail. It was out of his way, but he said he was also a hiker. I started out today feeling very fresh and strong. However in the first five miles, I had to crest two mountains, and these really took the wind out of my sails. The new boots did a great job, no problems, but I am wondering if *I* am going to get into shape. I only went about eleven miles today, but the last three were pure agony. My pack cannot seem to get adjusted properly, and my shoulders are taking a beating. The pack should be adjusted so that the weight rests on the hips, but I cannot seem to get it to stay that way. Today, I passed and saw only one person, and he was heading in the opposite direction. I am at the shelter alone, and the bugs and gnats are about to carry me off. I like company, but they are just the wrong kind!

The first mountain I crossed today was full of wild turkeys, and they could be heard in all directions. I must have startled one because he took off close by, giving me a real bawling out in turkey talk. The second mountain was Tray Mountain, a difficult climb, but with fantastic views in all directions. For a while, it was clear and not raining. I had my lunch on top of the rocks, but couldn't stay long as the thunder and lightning began to take over. Fortunately, I missed the rain today. It was a 0.3-mile walk from the Trail down to the shelter. There was plenty of fresh water, but the shelter was kind of lonesome as I was the only one there. I was in my bag at 8:30 and arose at 6:30. Those ten hours were solid sleep, and nothing bothered me. I sprayed myself at night with insect repellant, ringed the top of my bag with mothballs, and left the open bag of mothballs in the top of my pack. So far, no mice or other little critters have visited. (And they never did visit my food or me the whole time on this part of the Trail.)

May 18, 1991   Plum Orchard Gap Shelter
Trail Distance: 9.6 miles

I was up at 6:30 and on the Trail by 8:00. This was a better day for hiking. I did about ten miles and did *not* feel exhausted. Tired, yes, *very* tired, but I thought that I could live. I came into the shelter about 5:00 P.M. and found one other man there. He looked neat enough, but I did not see a backpack. So, I asked him if he was packing. He said yes at about the same time I saw a huge pistol on his other hip. I told him that perhaps he misunderstood and was he *back*packing? The answer now was no. He was out hog hunting (illegal) and was not staying at the shelter. I thought that I would be alone again for the night, but five more eventually came in singly and in doubles. Most of us were in the bag by 9:00 and slept until 6:00. One of the southbound hikers thought that everyone should be up early and made enough noise that we had no choice. He was hiking with a young female dog that was really still a pup. That pup was very nice and refined. She made no sound—until 2:00 A.M. when she set off barking like a storm. We never found out what it was, but she protected us.

May 19, 1991   Standing Indian Shelter
Trail Distance: 12.4 miles

I was up at 6:00 and used the last of my powdered milk for breakfast. I *should* have measured my needs (one-half cup per day) rather than just taking a bag of powder. Well, I'm learning at lot. The first five miles today were really rough on me. These "uphills" still are tough. Other hikers do not seem to have the problem. Our age differential just may have something to do with it.

I entered North Carolina at 10:40 A.M., and it continued uphill. Eventually, we got to over four thousand feet of altitude, and it looks like we will be up here for a few days. The 12.4 miles were covered, and I came in tired at 5:15 P.M. Again, I was tired, but not exhausted. I feel certain that I could have covered a few more miles if it was needed. I would not have wanted to, but I could have. A couple in their 50s from Cincinnati were with me in the shelter last night and tonight. Our destinations seem to be the same each day, but they do move faster than I do. I guess experience in hiking does help. The couple's trail name is "The Seekers". He is a royal pain, an expert on everything, loves to lecture, and is impossible to carry on a conversation. On the other hand, the wife is very charming with a good sense of humor. She had no false modesty. When she needed to dress or undress, she just turned her back and did it. As a couple, they do not rest going uphill. I am envious and hope someday to match it.

It rained again today, and we stayed in the clouds all day. You cannot see anything around you except for the forest and the path. It sure gets discouraging! We had our lunch at a beautiful shelter at Muskrat Gap. (It was to become the prettiest seen.) It was built like a little "A" frame, could sleep twelve, and there was a mountain man (Frank) staying there for a few days. I would have really liked to stay for the evening and join him but needed to travel a few more miles. In the shelter this evening, we had "The Seekers" and a couple from Cocoa, Florida. We made a fine match, and all spent an enjoyable evening. Even the lecturer slowed up! We all bagged out at 9:00 and were up again at 6:30. The lady claimed that I snored a bit, but no bears came by.

May 20, 1991   Carter Gap Shelter
                                    Trail Distance: 8.2 miles

I felt ambitious today. The Trail ahead looked and sounded relatively easy. Hoping to do fifteen miles, I left before 8:00. Again, I was the first to leave. It was a relatively easy one hour climb to the top of Standing Indian Mountain. It was the first over-five-thousand-foot mountain that we have hit. I say the climb was relatively easy, but it left me pooped. My climbing muscles just have not developed yet. While we awoke to blue skies and an actual sunrise, it only lasted about ten minutes. Then the clouds came in again and stayed all day. When I say the clouds came in, we are *in* them. So, we had another day of fog, 100 percent humidity, and seeing nothing.

At the top of Standing Indian Mountain, it was pea soup all around. Others are also feeling the discouragement. It is no fun just to cover miles! I made the Carter Gap Shelter for lunch and decided to stay for the night. It was only 8.2 miles, but I was tired, my feet were sore, and my legs and knees have not loosened any. They are always stiff. Well, one of my earlier correspondents stated that it took him two to three weeks to get into shape, and he was the same age as me. So, I guess that I have only one or two more weeks to go. By then, I'll be back to a car.

It is now 7:40 P.M., and no one else has shown up. Dinner is over, a *good* dinner, dishes are done, and I am so cold that I'm hitting the bag just to get warm. This shelter is about 4,600 feet up, and that does make for some cool times. I have on my long pants, shirt, sweater, and windbreaker. I'm *still* shivering! Some of these shelters even come with a broom, and that helps. Sure hope that my mothballs continue to work. I'm calling it a day! I finally got my pack adjusted so that the weight is off the shoulders and on to the hips. It is a *great* help.

It had rained hard on the 19th and, once again, my boots and socks got wet. The combo usually makes for new blisters. This day, shortly after I decided to stay for the night, it started raining again and continued all night. *This* shelter just happens to have a corrugated metal roof, and it sang to me all night. I was a little apprehensive about staying here for the night. All shelters have little "log" books that hikers can write in. One of my earlier acquaintances had stopped here for lunch, and he was telling of a bear watching him eat. That bear gave him no problem and eventually moved away, but I was still a little nervous. What if the bear wanted to get dry in the night? There is no way that I can hang my food ten feet off the ground as recommended against bears. I would need a ladder, and the food would assuredly get wet. So I, and the others, hang it up on the walls of the shelters. I put my mothballs out and, so far, no problems from bears or mice. The constant rain did not allow me to sleep well as I awakened about every half hour.

May 21, 1991   Rainbow Springs Camp Ground
Trail Distance: 12.8 miles

I really did not want to get up today. I was warm, it was still raining, and the "thrill" of walking in the rain was losing its edge.

After getting dressed, I found that I could not get warm. Reluctantly, I then dressed for hiking knowing that the exertion would warm me up. After a breakfast of dry cereal (*very* dry as I was out of milk), I packed for the Trail. Almost immediately, it stopped raining. Still, I was in clouds all day and the Trail was quite wet and muddy. My boots were still wet, got wetter, and I eventually got a couple of new blisters. These things are really getting to be a pain!

Today, there were some nice hiking trails. Some were actually level, but most had either a slight rise or slight fall to them. The only really bad section was a few hundred yards short of the summit of Albert Mountain. There, the Trail simply climbed the cliff. You could actually stand upright and *touch* the Trail in front of you. A slip could have been very painful. Once on top, though, you tended to forget the climb up. With an accessible fire tower, the views were magnificent in all directions. Earlier, the Trail had skirted the side of a cliff for a couple of hundred yards where a slip could have meant a one-hundred-foot fall. I am surprised that more people do not get hurt on the Trail. The opportunities are surely there.

We had seen notices of hot showers, meals, groceries, bunks, etc., at the Rainbow Springs Campground. It was a mile off the Trail at Wesser Gap, and I needed all of the aforementioned items. The "meals" left something to be desired as you got microwaved food only. The hot shower and shave were worth it, though. The bunk with a mattress made for a great sleep. The bunkhouse was shared with two other men that I had met earlier on the Trail. There was Tony, who likes to pitch his own tent, and Frank, the local mountain boy, who just likes to live in the forests. Both were super nice. Tony will be heading my way but traveling twice as fast. Frank, who I had met earlier at Muskrat Shelter, had taken other trails to arrive at the campgrounds. I think he just likes to hike and camp out. With me, a double helping of microwaved chili and beans, a shower, shave, laundry, and I called it a day at 9:30 P.M.

May 22, 1991   Siler Bald Shelter
                                    Trail Distance: 6.9 miles

I had looked forward to those advertised cinnamon rolls. The store does not open until 8:30 so breakfast is going to be a bit delayed. After breakfast, the owners will then shuttle us back to the Trail, a mile uphill from here. I am planning on 6.9 miles today. It was that or twenty miles, as the shelters do not come where you may want them. The feet are now a problem again. I thought that I had that part cured but I guess my thoughts were a bit premature. Well, perhaps it will stay dry for a change and the feet will not get any worse. According to the weather reports, there is only a 20 percent chance of rain, but the weather here is fickle. Night before last, it rained all night and most of the prior afternoon. A couple of mountains away stayed completely dry. These hills *are* funny!

I think the Rainbow Springs Campground to be a bit over-advertised. The washrooms and shower are a good fifty yards from the bunk house, and the laundry and store are another twenty-five yards away. When I get up in the middle of the night, which I did, fifty yards is a far piece to go, *plus* it was cold! I don't know just how cold it got as I could not find a thermometer.

Those five-pound jobbies that they tried to sell me just would not fit into my pack. It was a good day for the Trail. It was cool, the clouds lifted, and the sun actually came out for a few minutes. I spooked a grouse today, and I did not know who was the more frightened. When he took off, virtually at my feet, the sound that he made really brought me awake. I had my lunch on a small stump and when done, noticed a snake lying behind it. Non-poisonous and only about eighteen inches long, it seemed completely unconcerned about me.

Oh, I was discouraged today. It had taken me two and one-fourth hours to go 2.1 miles, and I had *thought* that I was moving at least one and a half miles per hour. But then, the next 1.7 miles was completed in twenty minutes. It was simply a matter of the distances not being correct. That is fairly common here. Yesterday a scheduled one-mile walk had a sign at the end saying it was 1.7 miles back to where I had started. You just cannot trust the distances stated. I came into this shelter at 2:15 after starting at 9:00 A.M. All in all, it was a 7.8-mile day. I saw no other hikers on the Trail and was expecting to find the shelter empty, but two men were already there. They had been there for one night and were planning to spend a second. I am well rested, not tired, the feet feel fine, but I cannot get warm when I stop hiking. There is no problem when I am moving, but stopping for the evening means long pants, my sweater, windbreaker, and *still* I shiver. I woke up last night in my bag all wet. I guess the body so enjoyed finally being warm that I just lay there and sweated. I *did* get a good night's sleep, though. Tomorrow is a planned twelve-plus-mile day, and it does not look to be an easy one. We will flit back and forth from about 4,100 feet to about 5,300 feet. That will keep it cool.

This shelter is at about the 4,800-foot level as is the scheduled one tomorrow. I had a taste for sassafras tea again and could not find any sassafras here. In every place else, it was all over the place. It could be the altitude or maybe just the location, but the next time that I find some sassafras, it is going to be dug up. A good supper is planned for tonight. Last night was a disappointment, and I'm making up for it tonight.

We had a fine evening after a dry day. This was the third day of no rain. Ed (Toothpick) a retired 68-year-old dentist from Sarasota and Jerry (The Seeker) and I built a bonfire from wet wood, and that warmed us *and* the shelter. I had started a candle under a few wet twigs and they dried and started to burn. We put larger twigs on top of them and continued the process. In a couple of hours, we had a real fire going, and it did feel good. The fire probably lasted until midnight, but by then we were all warm in our bags. I never did find out much about Jerry. He talks so much that you cannot get any info from him. He carried on a travelogue for the better part of two hours. Toothpick listened to it all, but my ears got tired. All in all, it was a good day, great company, and topped with a good night's sleep.

May 23, 1991   Cold Spring Shelter
                                   Trail Distance: 12.4 miles

We awoke to the sound of rain, and got to listen to it all day. It wasn't a hard rain, just a steady drizzle. My boots are obviously not hiking boots as they were soaked within five minutes. I received no new blisters but it was no fun walking in thoroughly wet socks trying to keep them from getting a new blister. The Trail was not too rough today and I easily made the planned 12.4 miles to the shelter. I think that I will have it to myself. I passed no other hikers from either direction in the last three days. This weather sure keeps the day hikers at home.

Shortly after starting out this morning, I crossed over Siler Bald which is really bald. Some of the stated "balds" have forests covering them now. However, the U.S. Forest Service had restored this one to a grassy bald and it would normally give excellent views in all directions. Camping is permitted on the top but there is no water. A few miles further on, I crossed Wayah Bald, another grassy bald topped with an observation tower which would normally give great views all around. With solid clouds all day, I could only imagine the views. Hopefully, others will be able to enjoy them. This spot even came equipped with a privy and a small stream for any campers who may wish to stay here.

After a long day, I put as much hot food into me as possible. I'm still cold and will hit the bag by 8:00 P.M. I'm not sleepy but it is the only way to get warm. I plan on leaving the Trail tomorrow at Wesser (about eleven miles) and hitch a ride to Fontana Dam, where I am to meet Charles Wilson Saturday morning. The shelter at Fontana is supposed to be something special, and I do want to visit it. As far as I can remember, I have not seen a mountaintop since arriving in North Carolina. And that includes when I am *on* the mountaintop! For the past three days, except for a very few minutes, I have been walking in the clouds, literally. I sure miss Florida, among other things. I must give the North Carolina trail builders some credit, however. In Georgia, the Trail usually went straight up or straight down a mountain. At least in North Carolina, they had the sense to zigzag or dog-leg the Trail up the side of a mountain. It may be longer, but it is surely easier.

May 24, 1991   Fontana "Hilton"
Trail Distance: 11.6 miles

It was a peaceful night, and I slept like a baby, maybe *too* well! I had left my clothes and sneakers by my head. Some critter, mouse or ground squirrel, had eaten a three-inch hole in my sweater and the laces from my sneakers. My food, as usual, was untouched. We had a beautiful day, no rain, sunshine, great views, and I actually saw some of the scenery. Views from the mountain tops are something special. This was supposed to be an easy day, with most of it downhill. It was *supposed* to be! There were many ups and downs, and the downs were brutal. I really would not want to do it in reverse. I arrived at US 19 (Wesser, North Carolina) in midafternoon, immediately got a store bought hamburger with all the trimmings and hitched a ride to Fontana Dam. It took a while, but the ride did come through. I then met Charles who had arrived a few minutes earlier. It was perfect timing!

In checking in at the Fontana "Hilton", I met four others that I had met earlier on the Trail. There were the three young men from Pennsylvania whom I had met the first night on the Trail and Margaret, the young lady from Maine who was walking home. They were surprised to see me but did give me a welcome. All four were going to stay an extra day at the shelter to rest up.

Re-sorting food supplies showed me over on some items and short on others. As the store will not open until 9:00 A.M. on Saturday, it looks like we will get a later start. Oh well, that is the breaks of the game. It will at least give me a chance for laundry and a good breakfast. I found out why this shelter is referred to as the Hilton. It is built like an old farm house where they have a porch running through the center of the house. On each side were two levels of sleeping space, the first about a foot off the porch level and the second about five feet off the level. There was room for six sleeping spaces on the each of the four levels. A very nicely constructed shelter, it was very roomy, and had larger than normal capacity.

May 25, 1991   Mollies Ridge Shelter
Trail Distance: 9.7 miles

Hiking in the Great Smoky Mountain National Park requires following a few more rules than were previously required. Foremost of these is the requirement that hikers must register and receive a permit to hike in the park. Self-registering is simple enough, and the permit slip must be attached to your pack at all times and be visible at all times. The thru-hiker permit for the park is good for seven nights and eight days and does not require the hiker to designate which shelter he or she will be staying at. This is unlike the day hikers who must state specifically which shelter will be utilized. There are a few more rules, but the rule regarding the permits is the most important to remember. The permits, or course, are free so this does not impose any kind of financial hardship on the hikers.

After getting re-supplied, laundered, and breakfasted, Charles and I were on the Trail at 10:30 A.M. From the start, we could see a fire tower on a distant mountaintop and never expected to be having our lunch there. The Trail goes from 1,800 feet to 4,000 feet in the first four miles. It wasn't brutal, but it *was* steady uphill, and it *was* rough on me. Charles seems to be able to chug uphill without resting. More power to him, but I am envious. There were some beautiful views today, especially from the top of Shuckstack, the mountain that we had seen from Fontana Dam. Of course, the fire tower on top added to the thrill. Yes, it rained again, and *again* I had wet boots and wet feet. Charles and I go at our individual paces; he is usually ahead of me as I take more time going uphill.

We came to our shelter for the evening at about 7:00 P.M. to find it packed. It is supposed to be reservations only in the Smokies, which we had, but we found the fourteen-person capacity filled. One lady agreed to double up with her husband, and somewhere another opening appeared so that both Charles and I had a spot to lay our bags. That place was crowded! There were packs and gear all over the place and for too many people to get to know anyone. Basically, I cooked in the twilight, sorted gear in the darkness, and it was little better in the morning. The people were nice and friendly, but there were just too many for one shelter. The shelters in the Smokies are a bit different than in other parts of the Trail. For one thing, they are larger and will accommodate from twelve to fourteen people rather than the earlier four to six persons. Here, the open side is completely enclosed by a chain-link fence that reaches all the way to the ceiling. The chain-link door is closed at night so that there is no concern about bears. They may come to the fence but cannot get through. I slept fitfully as no position was comfortable for long. I was sure warm enough, but my legs ached and my right knee was downright painful.

May 26, 1991   Derrick Knob Shelter
Trail Distance: 10.7 miles

No one in the shelter seemed to want to be the first up, so it was after 7:00 before we arose and 9:30 before we hit the Trail. On the first day with Charles, we did 9.7 miles, and this day 10.7 miles. Charles is younger and stronger, but it had to be rough on him going from sea level to over five thousand feet in just two days. It takes a few days just to adjust to altitude and he *had* to be feeling the adjustment. This was a dry day, my fifth, as I don't count it raining when it does so *after* reaching a shelter, which it did. We still did not reach the shelter until after 6:00 P.M. This shelter had room for twelve, but there were only seven of us there so there was plenty of room for all.

I saw my first deer on the Trail today, a little doe that did not act afraid of seeing me. The area around Spence Field Shelter has many grassy areas, and this attracts the deer. In the evening, there were three or four more does and a young buck that wandered all over the shelter area. You could get as close as about ten feet from them before they would move. They were beautiful, seemingly fragile animals but obviously at home in their environment.

After passing the Spence Field area, we hiked up to the top of Rocky Top, the mountain famed by the song. It was a mite rough going up but the fantastic view was well worth it. Wow, it was great! There were four young men there who had brought lawn chairs up by another trail and were just sitting and enjoying the view.

The day finished with a good supper, dry boots, a warm bag, and a fire in the fireplace. In the bag at 9:00, up at 7:00, I awoke a lot in the night but still slept well.

May 27, 1991   Double Spring Gap Shelter
Trail Distance: 7.1 miles

We had only a 7.1-mile hike planned today. We must stay in shelters, and they don't just happen where you may want them. For one thing, they are usually near a spring or running water in a creek. As the Trail through the Smokies usually follows the crest line, there are no creeks or springs at this altitude. As a result, the shelter may be down somewhat from the crest.

Well, I am glad that we planned on only 7.1 miles. We awoke to rain, and it rained on and off all day, although the really heavy stuff waited until we were safe in the shelter. Still, wet boots, wet feet, *cold* feet, but there were no new blisters for me today (there's no room for any more!). With a holiday weekend, that could account for the crowd the first night in the park. The rain could account for the scarcity of the packers yesterday and today. After all, there *are* some who have enough sense to get in out of the rain. Arriving at the shelter at about 1:15, there was plenty of time for a hot cup of tea, a big bowl of hot soup and catching up on my writing. Again, we are being visited by several deer that are not afraid of humans. I contrast that with the grand total of three squirrels that I have seen who seem scared senseless of humans.

We should have been having beautiful views. The Trail follows the crest line, which is also the Tennessee/North Carolina border, so we are on the top and can see nothing because of the clouds that we are in. Tomorrow, we are due to cross the very highest part of the whole Appalachian Trail, Clingmans Dome at 6,643 feet. For all of the day, we will be above the five thousand-foot mark. It will probably be the one chance in a lifetime for a view from up there. We are sure hoping for no rain, lots of sunshine, clear skies, and we may as well wish for a little more warmth. I still have to hurry and change clothes as soon as I get through hiking for the day. The chill sets in fast. I am sitting here now watching deer graze about fifty feet away, completely oblivious of me. The shelter last evening was infested with gnats and bugs that crawled, flew, and swam. This shelter seems to have none, and I am most thankful.

I still cannot say that I am having fun. It's an adventure, it's exciting, some of the views (when visible) are thrilling, but I still find it to be terribly hard work. You couldn't pay me enough to do this!

Eventually, we had seven people in the shelter—a young couple from Spartanburg, South Carolina; a father (61) and son from Baton Rouge, Louisiana; an elderly professor from Magnolia, Arkansas; and Charles and me. It was a great mix and much friendly conversation developed, some quite funny, and it continued after bagging out. The rain, which had intensified in the afternoon, continued all night.

May 28, 1991   Icewater Spring Shelter
Trail Distance: 13.2 miles

The day started with a light rain, just enough to keep everything wet. But the continual rains have left the Trail a muddy quagmire. Again, no views, wet boots, and the Trail is a glorious mess. The flat areas are deep in water and mud, and the ups and downs are small swift moving streams. It is now 8:30 P.M. and raining steady. Charles has indicated that he is going back home tomorrow. All of his clothes are wet with no chance of drying, and his feet blisters are a real mess. I do not blame him and just may join him. If it is raining tomorrow morning, I think that I will throw in the sponge. Fifteen days of rain out of eighteen days is enough for me. I met a young man and his bride on the Trail today, and he is from

Shreveport, Louisiana, my home town. They were honeymooning in the Smokies and were just taking a short walk. We had a long chat. When I finally reached the shelter, there were four young men from South Louisiana. They were planning on staying in the park for three days but got tired of the rain and didn't even stay the night.

We passed over Clingmans Dome, but all that we saw was the tower on the top. There were absolutely no views. True, it was a disappointment, but we are kind of getting used to those. Perhaps some day, we will be able to drive back and get a good top view of the mountains that we have traversed. We crossed the highway at Newfound Gap, and it was an interesting spot. This is the only road that crosses the Smokies so it gets more than a little visitor traffic. There is a large parking lot for the day hikers to use, and there seems to be quite a few cars there.

The next shelter is less than three miles from Newfound Gap, and it gets more than a little use. In *this* shelter, *we* are the guests. The shelter is owned by a young lady who just happens to be a very pretty, full-grown, fully powered, and very independent skunk. Priscilla tolerates visitors *provided* they treat her as the lady she is. *No*body insults Priscilla! We treated her with respect, and she did the same for us. We understand that sometimes she is visited by a gentleman friend, and the same rules apply. Knowing that she craves salt, I had been given some salty wheat crackers earlier in the day and passed some on to Priscilla. She took them as was her due. I had a food wrapper lying down, and she promptly "stole" it. All in all, she nosed around, but we kept our food up, and she gave us no problems. There was a father-son that joined Charles and me for the evening, and they insisted that Priscilla was crawling all over my bag during the night and that I just kept snoring away. Now, how many people can say that they slept with a skunk—and that the skunk smelled better?

I am down to one pair of short pants, one tee shirt, and one pair of socks. Everything else is wet and, in this 100 percent humidity, they will not dry.

On the Trail coming up to the shelter, I met some ladies coming down the Trail who had camped out one night, were going home, and had food left over. They offered, I accepted, and wound up with cheese and crackers, raisins, candy bars, Gatorade, and miscellaneous other stuff. I believe them to have been two mothers and two daughters. We had a long talk on the Trail, and they were planning on coming back in a couple of weeks for a week of hiking. The Louisiana boys had left me a meal also. Now, I am well supplied. Again, we have deer but no bears. Night has come, it's raining harder, and we are locked in for the evening.

I finally felt today that the body was getting into shape. I had the pack on for over five hours, feeling no need to take it off. I hiked from 7:15 in the morning until 12:30 without feeling the need to stop and rest at all! Then, I stopped for lunch, but not because I was tired. My hill climbs were non-stop although admittedly very slow. At any rate, those "leaning stick" stops every fifty feet were not needed.

May 29, 1991   Homeward Bound

I awoke to a beautiful sun, few clouds and a cool day. Too late! I don't trust the weather, and I have no more desire to wade through more mud and water. And it could be raining again within the hour. We will go back 2.9 miles to Newfound Gap and try to get rides back to Charles' car. Hopefully, we can!

After breakfast, Charles and I hiked back to Newfound Gap. Most of the water was gone from the trails, but it was still quite muddy in spots. At least, I was able to keep my newly dried boots dry. Clouds were already coming into the shelter by the time we left. There were quite a few tourists at Newfound Gap when we returned and hikers receive a lot of attention. Many people will come up to you with questions, comments or just to talk. For about half an hour, I was the center of attention. While there, I met Margaret again who was traveling north. She was alone having outdistanced the three young men that she had been with. When I told her that I would be leaving the trail three days early, she requested that I join her for the three days as she wanted company.

I reminded her that she moves *much* faster than I do. She was planning on doing about fifteen miles this day and twenty miles the next. That girl can move! She hopes to complete the whole Trail by October 14. I am betting that she does. At any rate, she promised to contact me and let me know the outcome.

After about four hitches, Charles and I made it back to his car. Looking back to where we had been, we could see a huge thundercloud forming. We would have been rained on again! After a shower (much needed) and shave, we left the park and made our way home. After weighing myself the next morning, I found that I had actually gained half a pound. I am thinner and leaner and obviously react favorably to my own cooking. Also, my blood pressure dropped thirty-five points, and this was *without* medication. I sure hope the future memory dims the misery and increases the fun of this hike. I do want to go back someday and complete the missed sections that I was not able to complete.

Total Trail Distance: 165.3 miles

Other mountains crossed:

May 17	Rocky Mountain	3,960 feet
	Tray Mountain (beautiful view)	4,430 feet
May 18	Kelly Knob	4,276 feet
	Powell Mountain	3,850 feet
May 20	Standing Indian Mountain	5,499 feet
May 21	Albert Mountain	5,250 feet
May 23	Siler Bald	5,120 feet
	Wayah Bald	5,342 feet
May 24	Copper Ridge Bald	5,200 feet
	Wesser Bald	4,540 feet
May 25	Shuckstack Mountain (great view)	3,995 feet
	Doe Knob	4,520 feet
May 26	Devils Tater Patch	4,775 feet
	Rocky Top (best views of all)	5,441 feet*
	Thunderhead	5,527 feet

May 27	Cold Spring Knob	5,240 feet
	Silers Bald	5,607 feet
May 28	Clingmans Dome (no views)	6,643 feet
	Mount Collins	6,188 feet

*   This is the mountain that the song *Rocky Top* is named for. It is a beautiful peak, well worth the climb, and the song does it justice.

EPILOGUE

After returning from the Appalachian Trail, I had some experiences that were not exactly normal. With one exception, I did not tell my friends and family as I did not want them to be concerned, to worry, or to visit. Before anyone gets concerned now, let me say in all honesty that I am perfectly all right, there is nothing wrong, and that I need absolutely no medical attention. *I am healthy and feel fantastic!* I *did* tell my son, Steven, of my continuing condition as I wanted *one* person to know of the possible consequences and that person to be reachable day or night. There was no need for others to be concerned as they could no nothing about it.

May 30, 1991—I came back from the Trail feeling tired but relieved to be back home. I felt in super physical condition and would have given long odds that there was nothing wrong with me. My strength and stamina continually increased on the Trail to the point where I really felt rather proud of the old body.

May 31, 1991—I had my first "spell" where it felt like someone was squeezing my heart. This was accompanied with shortness of breath, clammy skin, being a bit nauseated, and feeling exceptionally weak. It only lasted a few minutes, but it got my attention. At first, I thought that it was some "bug" that I had picked up on the Trail. There are some exotic ones there, and they are no fun to deal with. There was just no way possible that the "spell" was caused by my heart. I was too strong and healthy.

June 1-2, 1991—The "spells" continued once or twice a day and appeared to be getting worse rather than better. Never lasting longer than about five minutes, the last one on June 2 felt like a heart attack was supposed to feel like. And, believe me, it was no fun!

June 3, 1991—I called my regular physician and got set up with his earliest appointment on June 6. His office manager had asked me if it was urgent, and I had replied that it wasn't but was probably just a "bug" that I had picked up hiking. Not satisfied with my reply, the doctor called me back within a few minutes and asked me my symptoms. On hearing them, he immediately cancelled my appointment with him and set me up with an appointment with a cardiologist on June 5.

June 5, 1991—My exam with the cardiologist went smoothly, my heart sounded normal, and the EKG showed no abnormalities. In addition, the doctor complimented me on just how strong the heart sounded. However, I was put on a portable monitor to wear for twenty-four hours. I was to note the time that any subsequent "spell" came, note when I ate anything, when I went to the bathroom, and when I went to sleep.

June 6, 1991—I had two more "spells" while wearing the monitor, and these were minor compared to some of the prior ones. At any rate, something was wrong, and the monitor was sent to the hospital for analysis.

June 7, 1991—I again met with my cardiologist who reported that the monitor did report my two "spells", that something *was* wrong and that they did not know just what it was. A catheterization was suggested whereby dye could be inserted into the heart arteries so that a definite diagnosis could be made. This sounded OK with me, but I still *knew* that there was nothing wrong with my heart.

June 11, 1991—The catheterization was performed in the Largo Medical Center, and I could see the results from the dye. I did *not* like what I saw! The doctor did not have to tell me that I had blockages as they were obvious. There were two on the left artery, one 60-80 percent blocked, and the other 40-60 percent blocked. There had been no damage to my heart at all, but I was only a heartbeat away from having a heart attack that *could* do damage. When the doctor heard that I had been backpacking for three weeks without any symptoms, that the symptoms started when I returned, and that the symptoms usually occurred when I was at rest or sleeping, he could hardly believe it. He must have pointed his finger at me a half dozen times to remark, "You are one lucky man." Finally, he pointed his finger up and said, "Someone up there must really like you, for you are *one lucky man!*"

At any rate, we now had the problem localized, and the question was what to do about it. I didn't like any of the options. The first option was to do nothing, control my diet, watch myself, take life very easy, and take the chance of having an attack at any time. The second option was angioplasty, a procedure in which a narrowed artery can be widened by the inflation of a balloon-tipped catheter. My blockage was so close to the main artery (the aorta) that this procedure was too dangerous, and they would not even attempt it. The third procedure was atherectomy, a procedure in which a little machine is inserted in the artery and the fatty deposits are shaved off. However, this procedure is relatively new, is done in only a few hospitals in the country, and is not available in this part of Florida. The fourth option was open heart, double bypass surgery and this was the recommended route. I had to lie on my back for six hours after the catheterization, and this gave me time to get used to the idea of the surgery. They did not have to convince me of the problem; I could readily see it. When I was discharged that evening, my tail was really dragging.

June 13, 1991—My cardiologist phoned to officially go over the results of the cath exam and to discuss the options. I told him that if he was in full agreement with the cardiologist who did the cath exam, to go ahead and set me up with the hospital for the surgery. *However,* I would first like to be sure that some other place in the country was not available for the atherectomy. To this, he heartily agreed and further agreed to do some phoning. Within a half hour, he called back with the word that Emory Hospital in Atlanta, Georgia, would like to review the video of my x-rays. He asked if I could pick them up and air-express them up there. I did not have to be asked twice!

June 14, 1991—With due haste, I picked up the videos of the x-rays and mailed them to the doctors at Emory Hospital.

June 18, 1991—After waiting several anxious days without

hearing anything from anyone, I telephoned Emory Hospital and asked the status of my request. When the lady there stated that a letter had been prepared and was being mailed out, I requested that she fax me a copy and I would hand deliver it to the local cardiologist. This was done! The letter stated that I met the conditions for their procedure and could phone and set a time for admission to the hospital if all concurred. My doctors had already agreed and I immediately phoned. When asked how soon I wanted to come in, I stated, "Yesterday!" She replied that the nearest they could come to that would be the next Friday, when a prior appointment had been cancelled. Without further ado, I made the appointment.

June 21, 1991—Airfare on short notice was $565 roundtrip, and this did not make good sense. I left on a bus Thursday, had a good night's sleep, had quick transportation to the hospital, and was able to check in at 8:30 A.M. They allowed me to use a room for a shower as I really needed it. Being the last one on the appointment list, I was taken last and did not get my atherectomy started until 4:45 P.M. It lasted two and a half hours and was most interesting. I will not bore you with the details, but I was awake and watched the process. If you can visualize the heart's arteries and veins looking like a road map, the blocked areas looked like secondary roads (gravel) before the procedure. When completed, it all looked like "Interstate"! Gee, it looked pretty!

The attending doctors, pioneers in the field, were very well pleased with the results, as was I. All of this was done without surgery and without any stitches. I was bruised! My groin looked as if I got hit by a truck, and it was a bit tender. The insertion of all of the equipment was through my leg artery in the right groin. I had a small local anesthetic, and it was all painless. The truly uncomfortable part was lying on my back for twenty-six hours waiting for my blood to thicken a bit before they could take the shunt out. It normally would not have been so long, just four hours to remove the shunt, but I was late in the evening and had to wait all night. Then there was another six hours after the shunt was removed to give time for the artery to heal. All in all, it was twenty-six hours that were not fun! But I had a smile the whole time because it was "over", and I had *no scars on my chest!*

June 22, 1991—I spent the whole day on my back, could not turn, and would *not* have wanted visitors. I know that some people would have wanted to visit, but believe me, they would not have been welcome!

June 23, 1991—After final exams by everyone involved, I was released at 11:00 A.M. This was a super hospital. From the highest ranking doctor to the lowest orderly, they were, without exception, friendly, helpful, and available for any question. Well, maybe the kitchen staff could take a few pointers! Unfortunately, I do have to watch myself in the future. A diet low in fat and cholesterol should be easy enough to come by. I already meet all of the other conditions. I will have a checkup in about six months to see if any of the buildup has reoccurred. It does in about 30 percent of the cases and it has to be redone. It rarely needs to be done and redone again. And if it does not come back in six months, it probably will not. But I would rather have this every six months than go through the open-heart routine.

— — — — — — — —

It is now thirteen years later, and regular stress tests show absolutely no problems!

CHAPTER TWO

September 14, 1991   Wesser, North Carolina
                       Hostel
                       Trail Distance: 10.7 miles

The Trail from Woody Gap to Neels Gap was a section that I had missed in May for various reasons. On this day, I hiked the section without a backpack, in dry boots, and on a dry trail. This was a rather popular section of the Trail for short timers to hike as I saw thirty-seven people in the ten miles. The most popular aspect of the Trail, Blood Mountain, had beautiful views and interesting rock formations for the younger ones to climb. I was able to see one doe (my only deer sighting in the two weeks on the Trail), very few birds, and heard few. The quietness was a dramatic change from May. It was an easy day of hiking, but the knees really hurt. I had left my car at Neels Gap and hired a ride over to the start of my hike. So, the car was there when I completed the hike. I then drove the sixty-six miles to Wesser, NC, rented a hostel room, left my pack off, and drove to Fontana Dam where I left the car. After walking a mile back to the highway, I had no luck in getting a ride to Wesser.

The cars were very few and very full when they passed. After forty-five minutes of trying and it getting dark, I walked back to the car with the intention of driving back to Wesser, doing my three day hike to Fontana, and then worrying about getting back to the car. As it happened, just before reaching my car, I passed a young man obviously just back from a hike getting into *his* car, and I started talking to him. It turned out that he had done in one day the hike that was going to take me three, *but* he had done it without a backpack. He had started at Wesser and left his car there;

another friend of his had started at Fontana and left *his* car there. They had hiked toward each other, swapped keys in the middle when they met, and continued on their ways. It still took him twelve hours even without a pack and he does this rather frequently. I had also told him what I was trying to do and got a ride all the way back to Wesser as he was going through there on his way back to Atlanta. He was one of the volunteers who worked on the Trail and stated that he had the responsibility to keep up, maintain, and repair three miles of the Trail near the start in Springer Mountain. So now, the car is where I want it to be, I am in Wesser, and hope to see the car in three days.

The restaurant in Wesser had closed for the night by the time I got back to town but there were still people inside. I went in anyway, told them that I was hungry and could eat anything. In the end, I got a huge bowl of chili, a small loaf of homemade bread, much cheese, and iced tea. It was super!

September 15, 1991   Sassafras Gap Shelter
Trail Distance: 6.8 miles

I had a fine night's sleep. I shared the hostel (a former hotel room) with two other men who were there for the river rafting. I was out and on the Trail by 8 AM and saw and met no one. By 1:35, I had reached the shelter and had to admit to being very tired. The Trail was not nearly as tough as I had been told and had expected. It was strenuous as it was all uphill but was not too bad. I had seen *much* worse. I saw no animal life, heard few birds, but *did* see a couple of Piliated Woodpeckers while writing this. I have heard a few but these two were silent, just searching the tree trunks, making no sound.

It certainly feels better hiking in dry boots on a dry trail. This was the second day without rain! It may not continue. It is 3 PM, getting dark, and I hear thunder. That is *not* a good sign. This shelter even has a privy———a real one with four sides and a roof! For most of the Trail so far, hikers are required to carry a small spade, told to use it, and to dig deep.

These past few days have been much warmer than in May and I really go thorough the water. This place has some nuts around that I have not seen before. I ate a couple and saved a few to take back *or* to test if I get sick. They have a bitter aftertaste; perhaps roasting will take that away. They look like what I think chestnuts should look like. Somebody should know. I saved a few of the nuts just in case I get a reaction to them so that someone could find out what I had eaten. (And it began to rain———gently so far)

I have pulled up a load of firewood and have it set to light when it gets dark. I just may have to leave it to dry out for the next guests. The gnats, mosquitoes, and flies were bad today. My "Off" stays on just long enough to sweat it off. Tomorrow is not be a "fun" day. It's fourteen miles to the next shelter and I guess that's the really rough part of the Trail. The six miles today were really tiresome, and I have the feeling that I may have to use my emergency tent tomorrow, but, hopefully, *not* in the rain.

September 16, 1991   Cable Gap Shelter
                                Trail Distance: 14.6 miles

There was a lot of small creature night life that sang all night. It was no problem though———they just sang me to sleep. My knees still bother me some at night as I can't lay straight and sleep. They have to be curled up. The day started with a mile hike to the top of Cheoah Bald, billed as beautiful views in all directions. I got there before the morning fog had lifted and could see about 20 feet in all directions. I was into the Trail about two hours before the rough stuff started and it was not as bad as billed. It was brutal enough but Georgia had some worse. Or did the fact that it was dry just make it feel better? The rain did not come last evening as it just threatened. At any rate, there were about nine miles of Georgia style ups and downs, and no fun. Fortunately, it got better by midafternoon or I would not have been able to make it to the shelter. As it was, I had trouble *finding* the shelter. It was supposed to be .2 miles from a particular point. I went at least ½ miles past, saw nothing, dropped my pack, and retraced my steps to see if I had missed it. I found nothing and continued on beginning to feel just a bit nervous. I had almost run out of water today, was low again, and the only water for miles was supposed to be at the shelter. I finally came to it a good ½ mile from the place where it was supposed to be. It *did* look good and there *was* water. I didn't get there until 7:30 PM and I was beat.

It's fairly dark by 8 PM as the shelters are usually down the mountainsides and very well shaded. Supper was cooked by candle light and really tasted good. I am not sure what I ate as it was too dark to see. Today, I was able to see another Piliated Woodpecker, one rabbit, and two turkeys. The wild life is not very visible and the birds remain scarce and silent. It is one quiet forest!

I still sleep fitfully as the sleeping bag and lack of good padding take some getting used to. This shelter is unusually dark at night. It was so dark that I could not tell which side of the shelter was open—--every side was black. Flashlights do come in handy at times.

September 17, 1991   Fontana "Hilton"
Trail Distance: 7.9 miles

This was supposed to be a relatively easy day. It was to be only a bit more that seven miles and all down hill. It didn't quite work out that way. There were a *lot* of "ups" and they were tough. The "downs" were not much better. Between yesterday and today, I was able to pick up three blisters and on the same toes that took such a beating in May. I arrived at Fontana about 12:45 and had time to shower, shave, do laundry, eat a good lunch and plan on the next four days with my hiking partner, Charles. I am due to meet him tomorrow in the middle of the Smokies and complete our trek through there.

Yesterday, I met two pairs of men hiking south and they were planning on taking four days for the section that I did in three days. I was at the shelter alone for the past two evenings, passed no one today, and realize that this part of the Trail is not well traveled. Its reputation gets around! I will be staying at the Fontana Shelter tonight and again, it would appear that I will be alone.

48 TWINKLE TOES

I was wrong about tonight! Two young college girls were day hiking in the park and stayed at the shelter with me. I must have really looked out of place to them as they seemed rather nervous. I first introduced myself and explained why I was there. That broke the ice. They then became very friendly and talkative, and we had a pleasant evening together. They had taken a semester off from Calvin College in Grand Rapids and were seeing the country at no particular schedule. With names and addresses of friends across the country, they were going all over and having a ball.

While doing my laundry in Fontana, I met a couple from Ohio down for a square dance convention. They identified the nuts that I had saved as Buckeyes and stated that they were *not* edible. I had to agree with them as the after taste took several hours to go away. (I was to learn later that the nuts were poisonous!) For me, the good meals, nice shower, clean clothes, and a smooth shave made for a good nights' sleep.

September 18, 1991   Icewater Spring Shelter
Other Distance: 2.9 miles

I had already rearranged my pack and gear the previous day so that this day I packed quickly and hit the road early. It was quite a few miles to where I was to meet Charles, and I wanted to be on time. I did have time to again try the scenery from Clingmans Dome and, again, found it socked in the clouds. I still made Newfound Gap at 10:30 and literally met Charles's pickup truck coming in the parking lot from the opposite direction so that we both got to a parking space at the same time. Talk about timing! (He *did* allow me to get the space.)

It took us until 4 PM to transfer his truck to the end of the park and get back to Newfound Gap in my car. It was far more miles by road than it is by Trail. We were on the Trail by 4 PM for the 2.9 mile hike. Almost immediately, we began to hear thunder. Remembering May, we could just hope and move as fast as we would. As it turned out, it actually started a light rain about fifty yards from the shelter and came down very hard just as we entered the shelter. Just seconds more on the trail and we would have been soaked. Three others were already there so we will have company in the evening. The rain stopped after about an hour, but tomorrow is scheduled to be a really wet one. All I can do is hope for dry walking. Good food, good company, and a warm bag made for a great evening.

I was wrong about the rain last evening. By nightfall, it started and came down about as hard as I have ever seen it rain. It lasted on and off for a few hours but stopped by morning. The trail was super wet the next day but we decided to chance it anyway. During the night, the shelter leaked all over, and people were continually moving around swapping places for hours. *My* spot was dry but the many flashlights looking for dry spots kept shining in my face.

September 19, 1991   Tri-Corner Shelter
                             Trail Distance: 12.3 miles

It got super foggy and had really cooled off when the cold front went through. I awoke with no desire to leave the warmth of the bag. It was a scheduled twelve mile hike and we did not want to do it in the rain. It threatened several times during the day and sprinkled a couple of times but did not get serious. It was a *long* day and I came in fairly bushed. Charles has more stamina and reached the shelter 1 ½ hours before me.

It stayed foggy all day so we saw nothing of the mountains. This was a big disappointment as we had been looking forward to the great noted views from Charles Bunion, an exposed rocky knob close by the Trail. It did not make any sense to go to the knob when the only thing that you could see would be more clouds.

When reaching the shelter, I had to quickly get into long pants and sweater to try to get warm but it didn't work. It was a long wait for darkness when we could legitimately get into our bags. We were alone in the shelter and it was not a favorite one. Whoever constructed it had built it below ground level so that the dirt floor was half covered with water. Still, it was a welcome sight after the hike.

September 20, 1991   Cosby Knob Shelter
Trail Distance: 7.6 miles

We awoke to a rather cool, clear morning with no fog and no clouds. As we were scheduled for only a seven and one-half mile hike, we took the time to see some beautiful views. I took a side trip to hike to the top of Mt. Guyot, which is the highest point along the Trail other than Clingmans Done. As you may recall, Clingmans Dome was *always* soaked in clouds. The hike to the top of Mt. Guyot was billed as a rough climb and that was an understatement. It was brutal! To top it off, you could see nothing from the top. The peak was so full of fallen trees, undergrowth, live trees, and a general jungle appearance that no view from any direction was possible. It was two hours wasted and no views at all for it. However, I did get plenty of scratches and cuts from the bushes, limbs, and briars. My legs are really a mess. It was not a complete waste, through. I found some blackberries and gooseberries so I had a free snack.

When we reached the shelter, Charles and I expected to be alone so we kind of spread out. Charles had reached the shelter first and had a fine collection of firewood already collected. As we made our fire, people started to come in. There was a party of six men north-bound, one man south-bound, and a couple (man and woman) on horseback. The shelter sleeps twelve and we had eleven in it. Just before the horse-packers came in (they were rather late), we spotted a bear near camp and all were out watching him and taking pictures. *That* picture was when my camera decided to start acting up. No one tried to get close to the bear and all stayed about twenty-five feet away. The bear seemed completely unconcerned about us or the flash bulbs. He appeared rather bored by it all. With the eleven in the shelter, we had a friendly evening and the fire did warm up the shelter even with its open side. The south-bound man slept next to me, *really* slept, and snored all night with his volume turned up. Happily, it was another day without rain.

September 21, 1991   Davenport Gap Shelter
                      Trail Distance: 7.0 miles

This day was not quite so cool although I did wear my sweater for the first two hours. The party of six were leaving the Trail for home at Davenport Gap. Charles had decided not to stay overnight in the shelter, so I have it to myself so far. I collected enough wood for a fire so I will have that. We arrived here by noon after an easy seven mile hike that was mostly downhill. There was really no reason for Charles to stay when he could be home by breakfast time. I had left my next week's supplies in his truck and he had hiked down, got them, and brought them back to me. That was about an extra four miles for him and it was appreciated. I leave the Park tomorrow and will continue to straddle the Tennessee/North Carolina border for a few days. It's about three days to a town and I'm ready for it. I could use a shower badly and to think that I have to wait three more days for it. You *do* have to change your social customs and requirements some when hiking and be able to accept the limitations. It is early, only 3 PM, and the writing will slow up while a nap is taken.

The nap was short, awakened by seven students from the University of Tennessee. There were four boys and three girls looking for a place to camp for the evening. I offered the shelter but I guess the thought of having to share it with a dirty old man (literally) did not appeal to them. They claimed that they were going to party late and didn't want to disturb me. They seemed like a nice bunch, but they kept looking. I had a good fire going for the evening and had it to myself. When I left the Park boundary the next morning at 8:30, the young people had three tents pitched and one boy was sleeping soundly outside the tents.

September 22, 1991   Groundhog Creek Shelter
                      Trail Distance: 10.6 miles

I got up at 7 AM, daylight, for an early start. I had expected this day's hike to take longer than it did. As it was, I made the shelter by 2:30. I had about five miles of continuous uphill. It wasn't tough, but it was constant. For a while, I was thinking that I had developed fatigue until I remembered that Charles had brought me my next week's supply of food and my extra clothes. I was probably carrying 10 pounds more than the day before. My back didn't notice the extra weight but my legs sure did.

About midway through this days' hike, I missed a good view of Snowbird Mountain. It is noted for its "hum". There is an FAA transmitter on the summit that gives the appearance of a spaceship and it gives out a distinctive humming sound. We can't see and hear everything and this one was passed up.

Arriving at the shelter for the evening, I was pleasantly surprised as it had recently been remodeled. It has a rain gutter on the roof, a new privy, a couple of cords of firewood had been cut, and it came with a new picnic table. I preferred my own wood, found plenty, and had the friendly fire going for the evening. My supper consisted of Chicken Soup, Rice and Gravy, Beef Stew (all hot) along with hot tea and Chocolate Pudding for dessert. My, this trail life is rough!

We saw no deer in the Smokies on this trip. In May, there were dozens of sightings. I cannot explain it.

September 23, 1991   Walnut Mountain Shelter
Trail Distance: 13.1 miles

Physically, this was a full day of hiking. The morning wasn't rough, just a lot of tiring ups and downs. The afternoon started well with several miles of either level or moderate grades. The first mile, however, was a real stinker, all up, and I came in bushed. I had passed one shelter, about two miles back, built by the Mountain Marching Mamas, a group of ladies from the Sarasota, Florida area. It was the neatest shelter that I have seen. There was room for three bags on each side of a divided shelter, with a table in the middle for writing or cooking. It had a skylight, plenty of hanging pegs, an outside grill, table, and was right by a flowing stream. I would have liked to have stopped for the night, but tomorrow is going to be long enough without adding a couple more miles to it.

The shelter for the night is kind of a bummer. It was built by the Civilian Conservations Corps in 1938, as were many of the shelters. However, this one especially leaves a bit to be desired. I think a blowing rain could reach all corners, it sleeps five on rather weathered boards, it *looks* like it was built in 1938, and the spring is seventy-five yards downhill, a *steep* downhill.

I saw a young couple on the Trail yesterday, recent grads of Eckerd College in St. Petersburg, Florida. Becky and Matt are heading for Damascus, Virginia, are camping out rather then using shelters, are taking their time, and I assume that they are now behind me. I saw no one today, and at 7 PM, I have the shelter to myself. Well, as far as humans go, I am alone. But the resident animals must love this place. From the age of this place, I would say that it has been their home for a couple of dozen generations. In the night, a mouse (?) tried to get warm by crawling by my neck. There were plenty of shelter noises but none from the forest. In the bag by 8 PM, I didn't get up until 7 AM. I still do a lot of tossing and turning and sleep fitfully but figure that I must get nine – ten hours of sleep a night. I am really looking forward to tomorrow evening for a clean shower, clean clothes, clean shave and a clean bed. It is so easy to take all of those things for granted.

September 24, 1991   Jesuit Hostel—Hot Springs, N.C.
Trail Distance: 12.4 miles

The day started with a one and a half miles hike to the peak of Bluff Mountain. From then on, it was mostly downhill to Hot Springs, North Carolina. The "downs" must use a different set of muscles and can really get painful. And I must have stepped on too many rocks as the side of my left foot is most tender. I got to

Hot Springs about 3 PM and the very first building off the Trail
was the Jesuit Hostel. It is very informal, completely open (and
stays open all night), unattended, with a box with a suggested
donation of $9 for the night. That includes bunk, shower, towels,
writing room, T.V. and kitchen use. Not bad! I went up to the
main house to visit the resident priest, had a nice chat with him,
and donated $20 for either two nights or a contribution for the
work that they do. If I *do* stay two nights, I will up it some.

It had started raining lightly about two hours before I arrived,
and if it continues tomorrow, I'm not moving! There is only one
other man here and he is the one that I met in May who talked so
much. He *still* does not have a job, is out of money, and spends
much time on the Trail looking for "something". He stated that
this is the fifth time that he has visited the hostel this year, and I
think the priest is getting a little sick of seeing him.

The laundry, phone, and café are a bit further away, a good
quarter of a mile. I had to visit them even before taking a shower as
I had no clean clothes to put on. I am sure that the townspeople
have had plenty of experience with "ripe" hikers. I feel that I have
four days to cover three days of hiking so I have an extra day. If it is
still raining Thursday, then I will plan on going home. Well, I got
my laundry, shopping, shower and shave in that order. The only
telephone that I was able to find (it's just down the street!) was by
the laundromat (also right down the street) and both were a good
quarter mile away. Everything seems to be "just down the street"
no matter how far down the street it is.

I had a good meal at the local café and feel much better. It is
now 9 PM, much later than I normally stay up. I sure hope that I
can sleep as well as I plan to. I tried to keep away from Jerry "The
Pilgrim" as much as I could and to not let him get started. He has
been on the Trail since March 25th, just going back and forth, and
up and down. As he explained it, he had no job, no home, no
money, but he was *free*! I suppose it makes sense to him.

September 25, 1991   Spring Mountain Shelter
                           Trail Distance: 11.2 miles

I awoke to an almost dry day. It wasn't raining, but there was just enough moisture in the air to rust things. Here in Hot Springs, the Trail goes right through town, with the Trail markers on the downtown telephone poles. It *is* a small town and I stopped in the local café for my first hot breakfast in a week. By the time I had finished, it had started a light drizzle. The weather report claimed that it would stop in the morning hours and clear by afternoon. So, I decided to chance it and go on. The rain stopped at 2 PM, the sun peaked out at 3 PM, and it started raining again at 3:15 PM. So much for the weather report! I didn't reach the shelter until 4:15 and by then I was cold and wet. I am in dry clothes now, all that I can put on, and I am *still* cold. I mean fingertip numb kind of cold! It's only 6:30 PM, supper is over, still raining, and I am going to have to bag it just to get warm.

Hot Springs was a nice, pleasant town, but I believe that almost everyone smoked. I never saw anyone, except kids under the age of 4, who did not have either a cigarette in hand or in the mouth. Everyone in the café was smoking, even the serving waitresses, and *all* were complaining about the high cost of cigarettes. To top it off, I never saw anyone who looked like they could *afford* to smoke.

Back in May, the hostess at the first hostel that I had stayed had lost her father to a heart attack on the Trail in 1983. Today, I passed the memorial stone where he had died on the Trail. He was only 62 (one year older than me) and trying to hike to Maine. It was kind of sobering to be at the spot.

The shelter tonight is kind of small, another CCC venture built in 1938. That seemed like a good year for construction. This one, also, has all kinds of resident creatures as noises come from all over *and* under.

September 26, 1991   Jerry Cabin Shelter
Trail Distance: 15.3 miles

The rain stopped during the night, the moon came out and really lit things up, and that old cold wind started. I was seeing my breath all day, and my hands took turns warming up in my pockets. This was one of my longer days and I didn't reach the shelter until 5 PM. I didn't expect to reach it until 6 PM so it came as a relief.

There was another view that was missed because of the weather. A side trail went to the White Rocks Cliff with a stated view of Mt. Mitchell. I so thoroughly enjoy the views that I *do* see that I shouldn't complain about the ones that I miss.

A person just has to chuckle when he arrives at this shelter. It is maintained by Sam Waddle, a Trail volunteer. He obviously takes pride in his work and I love his offbeat sense of humor. This shelter has electric lights, a telephone, and a mail box. Of course, none of them work, but you just *have* to try them——just to be sure! However, the privy *does* work! Most of the shelters now seem to *have* a privy and most appear new. I know that some are recent additions since May. This shelter also has a thermometer that works and it was reading 50 when I arrived *and* I thought that it had warmed up in the afternoon. By morning, it was to read 38 degrees. At any rate, it called for a fire, and I built one *before* I prepared supper. I was cold! I got a good fire going and I *kept* it going until I sacked out at 8 PM. This fireplace was built into the shelter and did take some of the chill off.

I had earlier found a bandanna that had snagged on a briar bush along the Trail. I kept thinking that I may meet with its owner. I didn't meet him, got the bandanna washed, and started wearing it on my head at night while I slept. It *did* make a difference! The nights were cold but the "bare" head kept warm. This shelter seemingly has no resident animals or else they slept at the same time as me. It was a quiet, peaceful, though cold night.

September 27, 1991   Hogback Ridge Shelter
                         Trail Distance: 14.2 miles

At 38 degrees, you dress quickly, move quickly, eat, pack and move out as quickly as possible. I wore everything that I reasonably could and *still* shivered. By noon, I had made the next shelter and was able to take off the windbreaker and change to short pants. The wind continued cold and was particularly noticeable when hiking the crest line. This was a slightly shorter hike than the day before but proved to be tougher. The easy part was in the morning when I was rested. The tough climbing didn't start until about 1:30 and I had about two hours of steady, steep, uphill hiking. And just before I got to the shelter, there was another steep uphill. The shelter was not reached until 6 PM and it *was* a relief.

The guide book had already warned me that the nearest spring was ¼ mile away so I filled up on water and replenished every chance that I got. I had plenty for supper and to get me started the next day, but the dishes did not get done. (And they didn't get done until I got back to my home in Clearwater.) The night was cold and there was frost on the grass this morning. It did not feel as cold as the last morning but it did make for some cool hiking. I scared up a flock of about six grouse today. I have been sighting about one a day and this was the first time that a whole flock took off. Those birds could take some pointers from the Piliated Woodpeckers. They would then have a much better chance with the hunters. The woodpeckers start cackling when a person is fifty yards away and will fly away, still cackling, when he is still twenty-five yards away. The grouse will stay well hidden until a person is only about 10 feet away and then, fly away with a roar. This was my last shelter on this hike and it was a very nice one. I didn't try to start a fire; I just cooked, ate, and sacked out.

September 28, 1991   Back to the Car
Trail Distance: 2.1 miles

I arose a little later than normal. It was chilly, I was in no hurry, and I didn't have much further to go, only a couple of miles. I met a couple of squirrel hunters who agreed that there was not much wild life around this year. They said that last year, the forests were teeming with squirrels.

I reached US 23 at the North Carolina/Tennessee border at about 9 AM. I had made up a sign stating "A.T. Hiker—Back to Car" thinking that it would really help in getting a ride back. By now, I was about one hundred fifty miles away from the car. After about an hour, a van stopped and I found out that they were waiting for their son-in-law to come off the Trail. He had driven to a spot earlier that morning about seven miles away and had hiked it, without a pack, just for the exercise. He arrived shortly and I was invited to join them on a circuitous ride to his car and back to Ashville, North Carolina. They were all a very friendly bunch. They drove me to the bus station in Ashville to see if there were any buses to Cherokee (there were not), and then drove me to the highway that I was seeking. I had no luck in getting a ride even with my sign, and eventually walked about four miles to the outskirts of town and to the entrance of I-40. Many hours and several rides later, I finally arrived at my car. Night was coming before I got my last ride out of Cherokee and I was thinking that I would have to spend the night there. That was not a happy thought as there were literally thousands of motorcyclists having a convention there and *no* rooms of any kind were available. Fortunately, that last ride came through. It was in a van with a husband and wife with seven children in a seven passenger van. Again, they were most friendly and talkative. It was almost dark before they picked me up and it was 8 PM before reaching my car. It was interesting that as they parked next to my car, one of the sons remarked that it was in the same spot that they had earlier parked to have lunch as he had remembered my car.

Back in my car, I put on the heater, stopped at the first KFC that I came to, got a good meal, and started back to Clearwater. It really felt good to be in the warmth and security of my little Thunderbird.

After arriving back in Clearwater and checking my Edible Plant Book, I found that the Buckeyes that I had eaten were not only inedible, they were poisonous and displayed with a skull and crossbones. Fortunately for me, I had absolutely no reactions. No, I will *not* try them again!

Total Trail Distance 311.1 miles

Other Mountains Crossed:
September 14 Big Cedar Mountain 3,737 feet
Gaddis Mountain 3,545
Blood Mountain (great views) 4,461
September 15 Cheoah Bald (solid fog) 5,062
September 19 M. Sequoyah 6,000
Mt. Chapman 6,250
September 20 Mt. Guyot (no views) 6,621
September 23 Max Patch (fine views all around) 4,629
Walnut Mountain 4,280
September 24 Bluff Mountain (no views) 4,686
September 27 Lick Rock (no views) 4,579

CHAPTER THREE

May 15, 1992   **Start of Hike**

I drove to U.S. 23 on the North Carolina-Tennessee border to start my hike where I had left off the prior September. Arriving in the area at 7:00 A.M., I had to wait a while before any of the local houses showed any activity. There was no town, no businesses, and few residences in the area. I needed a place to leave my car for a couple of weeks, and I knew that I could not just leave it on the side of the highway. I wasn't being fussy but wanted a place that would be reasonably safe. One young man had about two acres of side yard filled with abandoned cars but did not want mine parked there. I thought that mine would improve the appearance. A nearby elderly lady was happy to let me park by her house. Possibly, the appearance of another car would give her a sense of additional security.

May 16, 1992   **Bald Mountain Shelter**
                                           Trail Distance: 7.1 miles

I started on the Trail at 8:00 AM and was expecting to just have lunch at the first shelter about noon. Arriving there at 1:30, I decided to stay for the day. The Trail was rough, not brutal, but I was not in shape. I was not only carrying a full pack *but* was carrying fifteen extra pounds on me! The combination really makes a difference. The Trail was dry; there were some rain threats, but no rain. There was no one else on the Trail until I reached the shelter. Then two men stopped by but continued north. A third man, friend of the first two, decided to stay for the night. He had foot problems and is a bit slower than his friends.

This shelter is a fine shelter with good water nearby, *plus* it has a privy. It's funny how some simple things in life can be appreciated. You must remember that only a few of the shelters come with privies. At one time, none did, so things are improving. This shelter is also one of the highest on the whole Trail, and *that* will make for a cool evening. About a mile before reaching the shelter, I passed over Big Bald with beautiful views including that of Mt. Mitchell, the highest peak east of the Mississippi. A person can try to commit some of these views to permanent memory, but there are just too many views. For most of the views, it is a case of present enjoyment to be soaked up knowing that it will not last.

My shelter-mate, "Rainmaker", was on the Trail earlier in the month when the big snow fell. He stated that his part of the Trail got a foot of snow, other parts two feet, and some parts of the mountain got four feet. He was on the Trail during the storm and got lost and had some concerned moments. He was in a "whiteout" and saw just how easy it was to lose the Trail even with the many markers on it. Some people have memories that I have no wish to share! He was good company and it kept me from having to have my first night on the Trail alone.

May 17, 1992   No Business Knob Shelter
Trail Distance: 9.6 miles

We did have a cool night. This being a mile high really does make a difference. We had both sacked out about 8:00 P.M. as there was nothing to do and the bags were warmer. I slept most of the night and awoke about 7:30 A.M. I awoke a few times during the night mostly because I was cold. Unless you mold the sleeping bag to your neck, it slips open, cold air comes in, and you wake up dreaming of being frozen alive. It is rumored that the second day of hiking is usually the roughest, and today tended to prove it. On the Trail by 8:30, I was exhausted by 11:00 A.M.

Today saw all aspects of Trail conditions, from being very easy to being downright brutal, with about equal parts of each. It started easy enough with the path going through tall grass, grass wet with dew. My boots with five applications of water repellant, stayed dry for about three minutes. Well, so much for the repellant! Fortunately, by day's end, the boots were almost dry again.

There were some excellent views today of the surrounding mountains. Sometimes you have to take a few minutes extra to hike to the best viewing points, but it is usually worth it. After all, you are seeing something from a vantage point that few others can share. And photographs can never catch the full impact of a genuine view.

"Rainmaker" was going to the same shelter as I was, but he was way ahead of me. He is younger, about forty-five, retired, and trying to do the whole Trail this year. I wish him the best and hope that he will be able to complete *his* dream.

I had a little mishap on the Trail, and that could have been much worse than it was. "Rainmaker" had already passed me on the Trail and had no reason to come back for me. I was trying to do my contribution to the Trail by breaking off branches that could catch a hiker in the head. It's not much but it all counts. As I tried to break off one branch, the whole branch came loose. It got me off balance, and I grabbed another branch which promptly broke off. My trusty hiking stick was thrust behind me for support, but it sunk in a pile of loose leaves on the side of the Trail. By that time, I was off balance with forty odd pounds on my back, falling backward off the Trail, and helpless to do anything about it. I could hear branches breaking, but going backwards, head first, I could do nothing but go along for the ride. It was a relatively deep ravine with rather steep sides, but the dead branches thrown off the Trail plus some nicely placed trees broke my fall. I fell only about six feet, landed on my back with my pack beneath me, and landed head down with my feet straight up in the air. After determining that nothing was broken and the cuts not serious, I then had the job of getting out. I first wadded some toilet tissue (biodegradable) behind my ear to stop some bleeding, and then had to get out of my pack to regain my feet, and try to climb out. I could not get my pack out without putting it back on and literally climbing out. I was fairly exhausted before I fell; I was zapped by the time I got back on the Trail. My glasses had been knocked off,

scratched but not broken, and it took me a few minutes to find them further down the ravine buried beneath some leaves. My first concern of breaking them turned into a real concern of just finding them. It did take some searching. When I finally reached the shelter, "Rainmaker" took one look at me and remarked, "Well, it looks like the Trail won today". I had to agree. He also stated that he was getting concerned and was seriously considering going back to look for me. I guess that my little exercise took quite a few minutes, probably much longer that I had estimated.

There is much less bird life than I noticed last May in Georgia, probably only about 10 percent as much. I cannot explain it. The songs I hear—they are mostly strange to me, but they are distinct— follow a definite pattern, and I feel sure that a true "birder" would be having a ball. There have been a few squirrels, only one rabbit that came up to about five feet of me to get a better look, and nothing else. Fresh meat around here is not meant to be on the menu.

May 18, 1992   Maple Gap Shelter
                                   Trail Distance: 10.0 miles

You may note that many of the shelters and place names have the word "gap" in them. In some parts of the country, this term would be known as a "saddle". When you go from one high ridge or mountain over to another, you have to go down and cross over on a section of land that sometimes appears to be a high earthen dam with drop-offs on each side. This is referred to as a "gap". It keeps a hiker from having to go all the way down to the bottom of a valley before starting up the other side.

This was another good day on the Trail. It was dry again but a bit on the warm side. I made Irwin, Tennessee, and was able to get a shower, shave, but no store bought food. The nearest café was closed at lunch time, and I did not feel like waiting for dinner. Nor did I feel like going all the way into town for anything. This was a rather dull day on the Trail. A fellow hiker coming behind me spotted a four-foot rattler on the Trail that I guess I luckily missed.

I got to thinking today that this whole hiking business is nothing less than a self-ordained and self-inflicted torture, and the only reason that I can think of doing it is because I have always *wanted* to. When I am "committed", perhaps my shrink can find an answer to that one. I could have stayed at the hostel in Irwin but did not think that I had "paid my dues" yet. Perhaps in a couple more days, I may feel different.

This is an OK shelter with a good, close spring. I will be sharing it with a 76-year-old *very* talkative man and a very quiet younger man. Rain keeps threatening, but so far it is good and dry. I'm still very tired and really feel the last few miles of hiking today. Tomorrow is due to be twelve miles plus, and most of it is uphill. We will see if I have been broken in yet. Sure hope so, but there is no alternative. The forests are still very quiet. The bird life is really zilch! Where can they all be?

About 5:30, a young lady stopped by just to have a peanut butter and jam sandwich before continuing on the Trail. And I thought that *I* used a lot of peanut butter. "Running Bonnie" was a cute little thing, looked about 24, found out later that she was 36, and was planning to do the whole Trail in 1992. To top that, she is already making plans to come back in 1995 and *run* the Trail in order to be the fastest woman to cover it. Other than that little quirk, she appeared quite normal.

May 19, 1992

Cherry Gap Shelter
Trail Distance: 12.2 miles

The threatened rains finally came with a vengeance. I got about two hours of it and was thoroughly soaked. It was a warm day so I did not even try to put on rain gear. I would have gotten just as wet plus getting a lot hotter. When I reached the shelter, there were a few people inside including three tenters. I told a 61-year-old Rhode Island couple that I was wet, getting cold, and that I was stripping. At that, the lady politely turned her head. (She may have peeked once.) With dry clothes on, I joined the others in watching the rain, listening to the thunder, and seeing the mess that it was making to the Trail. When you are on *top* of the mountains, you find that the lightning does not have to go all the way to the valleys. It hits much closer to the mountain tops! It was a very interesting evening. Wet leaves and wet mud make for some slippery times, and I had fallen at least three times prior to reaching the shelter. When I did, I just stood in the rain and rinsed off—I was a mess!

The elderly man that I had met yesterday, Mac from DeRidder, Louisiana, was about three hours behind me, and he stated that he had gotten hail in addition to the rain. This guy comes in talking and *never* shuts up. After twice trying to tell him that I was also from Louisiana and getting interrupted both times with his babble, I gave up trying. *Man,* he likes to hear himself talk!

This shelter leaked in spots but we found places for four of the sleeping bags. The three tenters insisted on using their tents. And I found out later that "Running Bonnie" gave up her idea to "run the Trail". According to her, she was in the lightning for a total of eight hours, both hiking and tenting, and she "freaked out". She had no idea that the bolts would be that close and often and there was "no way" that she wanted to go through that again, alone.

May 20, 1992   Clyde Smith Shelter
                                    Trail Distance: 8.7 miles

It did not rain today, but the Trail was still quite wet and slippery in spots. The sun never came out, and it was a case of being in the clouds all day. Even though several summits were crossed, there were no views at all and even the birds were walking. Today was purposely short as the next shelter from here is 5.4 miles, and it is all uphill. I'll try it in the morning when I am fresher and hope to skip it and go on to the next. I was looking forward to some of the anticipated views today, but am getting used to being disappointed.

It is an enjoyable evening at the shelter this evening with "Reno" (he was with us last evening) and "Rainmaker" who took a day off the Trail and caught up to us. Both are rather quiet, excellent company, and we will probably see each other in the days to come. "Reno", at least, has indicated that his next two days are scheduled to be the same as mine. And that is a planned overnight stay in Roan Mountain, Tennessee, for a hostel, laundry, telephone, food, and another shave and shower. It's funny what a short life a good shower has! Fortunately for my fellow hikers, they are in the same boat.

We now have a good fire going, it has warmed up the shelter, and we go for long periods of silence broken every few minutes with just a few words. The evening is coming to a close and light is gradually fading out of it. It's time to bid goodnight to all including the birds and animals, wherever they may be. That does not include the owls and whip-o-wills that are just waking up.

May 21, 1992	Overmountain Shelter
	Trail Distance: 11.6 miles

I am sitting in the open door of the second floor of an old barn enjoying some of the most beautiful mountain scenes in this part of the country. You can almost taste the beauty! Several birds are singing unfamiliar songs. A ground hog just came around to size up the company. The nearest house is probably many miles away, and that is good. Any hint of civilization would spoil the area.

Three of us started out this morning for the shelter before this. I usually leave first from whatever shelter that I am in. My breakfast is always cold, already prepared, and I am up and out in forty-five minutes. Most cook their breakfasts or prepare coffee, and that takes additional time. At any rate, I leave, then "Reno" and "Rainmaker" leave when they are ready. They always catch up and pass me before noon. All three of us had planned on stopping at the last shelter, but it was so dismal that we all individually decided on going another two miles to this one. It is unusual to have shelters so close, but I suppose when the Council acquired this land, the barn was on it and it really gets used. There was a house at one time, but it is not there anymore. The barn is stated to sleep as many as twenty on the second floor, and I have no doubts that it could hold them. We three have it to ourselves.

The barn is purposely airy with cracks intentionally put in the walls and floors. The roof appears good and rainproof. Whoever constructed this building did a masterful job. In the time that we were in it, we did not hear a single creak, groan, rubbing or *anything* from the barn. It was solid! Put together with pegs rather than nails, I could only marvel at the carpenters.

When "Rainmaker" started to put his boots on the next morning, he started laughing. Mice had filled one of his boots with nuts. I suppose that they thought they had found a good place to store them. I thought that it was funny until I examined my pack and found that the nuts came from *me*! It got funny again when I started to put *my* boots on and found half a dog biscuit in one of them. I guess the mice figured that was a fair swap. (I left the biscuit for the next hiker.)

The morning started with a climb to the top of Roan Mountain, the last six-thousand-plus-foot mountain that the Trail has until New Hampshire. It was a rough climb, and it sure took its toll on me. From the shelter to the top was only six miles but it took me six hours to do it. It was not that difficult—I was just bushed. I am now in the shelter, it is chilly and windy, and my bag will surely feel good. Unless the temperature goes up, I am going to have a hard time *getting* up.

May 22, 1992   Roan Mountain, TN
                                   Trail Distance: 8.3 miles

This was a rather unusual hiking day. For over four miles, we were hiking over mountains with no trees. We were not above the tree line; there just were not any. There were places where we could look back for over a mile over trails that we had covered and look forward for over a mile on trails yet to be covered. This section crossed a highway and parking area so that there were a few hardy souls day hiking on it. As some of the Trail included ascents and descents, they were not always welcome. The view from one spot today made this whole trip worthwhile. Hump Mountain is not the tallest, but it has the best view of any other place visited. It has a rounded top about the size of half a football field, no trees, with a panoramic view of 360 degrees of just mountains in all directions as far as the eye can see. Visibility was great, and the views were simply fantastic. These views are reserved solely for hikers; there is no other way to the top.

This was a day that we had waited for. I was the last of my bunch to reach U.S. 19 and hike another 0.8 miles to Judy's Café where we were to phone for a ride to the hostel. We will have five to the room. There's "Reno" and "Rainmaker" of course; "Beatin Feet", who stayed over for another night; and "Sooner Zoo Man", who caught up with us. They are all nice and congenial. We all had our supper together but will probably leave tomorrow at different times. I want to leave early.

This section of the Trail is one of concern to the Trail Council. It is thirteen-plus miles long, but some locals along the Trail are reported hostile to the Trail. They burned down a shelter along this section, and hikers are warned to *stay* on the Trail, to not camp unless necessary, and to not travel alone. I am sure of the initial reason for the concern. One story has it that a hiker reported some cultivated marijuana seen.

There are supposed to be some illegal bear hunts in the protected bear zones near here. I passed some old abandoned stills, and I guess some of the locals just do not like government men in uniforms. As far as I know, no hikers have ever been hassled. With five of us going through, I have no concern. Also, we are told that all of the water in this section is contaminated and not to be used *even* if boiled. Interesting!

Well, we five are sharing a motel room that has been converted into a hostel that would normally sleep six. I've had my much needed shave and shower, my clothes are all clean, my grocery shopping is done to the extent of the local limited supplies, and my fourth meal of the day was a rib eye steak sandwich, garden salad and my second large Dr. Pepper drink. My knees are not painful, but definitely are not in good condition. I walk like an old

man, *feel* like an old man, and simply am not comparable to the
other hikers. I honestly do not think that my knees will get any
better, *but* I feel that they are not getting any worse. My knee
"sleeves" seem to be doing the trick.

I'm usually in my sack by 8:00 P.M. Tonight I get to stay up
until 10:00 P.M. Some treat!

May 23, 1992   Moreland Gap Shelter
Trail Distance: 13.6 miles

On the Trail at 8:05 A.M., it was 6:45 P.M. before I made the
shelter. It was a real bummer of a day. What was thought by all to
be a rather long day of even country was a real roller coaster. We
must have crossed three dozen streams all requiring a climb down
to the stream, crossing it on rocks and logs (low water), climbing
back the other steep side, climbing a hill, climbing back down the
other side of the hill, meeting another stream and starting over. It
was constant, and we all agreed that it contained no fun. My knees
were screaming, my legs felt like Jell-O, and I was generally pooped.
The last one in as usual, I was a good three hours later than planned.
To add insult to the injury, we started the hike by crossing a rather
large and hilly pasture for cattle. Obviously semi-civilized, the
cattle used the Trail for going up and down the pasture. You can
just picture where they left all of their cow "chips"!

Virtually every day I pass some excellent campsites, some with
good forest views, and almost all with a good source of water. For
the hikers who prefer to tent, they will usually have more choices
than those of us who prefer to stay in shelters. I am sure glad that
the tenting sites are available as there will be times when I may
need them.

May 24, 1992   Laurel Fork Shelter
Trail Distance: 7.2 miles

This was a relatively easy day and a pretty one. We had six in
the shelter last night, four inside and two tenting out. One of the

tenters was gone early, but no one else was up before 7:30. We were all rather faded. On the Trail at 9:00, I made the next shelter at 2:00. I think only "Reno" and I will be here tonight. All of the others wanted to go further and tent out. I hope that they did all right as it started raining at 4:00 P.M., and *I* would not want to be tenting in it.

One fellow mentioned that there are basically three kinds of hikers—the speed demon, the party animal, and the nature freak. As I cannot be the first, too tired to be the second, I guess I must be relegated to the third category.

We passed over the White Mountain Fire Tower about a mile past the shelter of last night. It would have made an ideal shelter except for no water. The tower was open, unused, had two cots with mattresses, and plenty of reading material. On a clear night, I would believe the star sights would have been a real treat. I did not know of the tower beforehand or of what it had to offer and it would not have made any difference. I could not have made the extra distance even if I had known.

We are now in the Pond Mountain Wilderness Area, and it is most scenic. There is a waterfall about one hundred feet high cascading over rocks, a rather deep gorge, a noisy stream flowing out from the falls, and the only way to really see it all is to travel a brutal trail down and back up over lots of rocks. Many rock formations are in the area, and the local shelter is on top of one. There is a steep trail up to the shelter and at least a twenty-foot drop on all sides. It is no place for a sleep walker.

I waited until reaching the shelter before having lunch and cooked a hot one. After lunch, I went to the stream for my dishes and water, and it was a steep, slippery path to the stream. The stream is also really a series of small waterfalls. In the process of getting water, my second water container slipped and went swimming down the stream and waterfalls. Search as I could, I could not locate it. And going down the hillside was an exercise in agility itself. About the only time that I really need the extra container is at supper time or a day like yesterday when the extra supply was needed. I figured that yesterday I went through about three quarts of water, was always thirsty, and it got so bad that I could not produce saliva and got a good case of cracked and chapped lips from it. Yesterday was *not* fun! If the Trail people were not so neat, I could probably pick up a discarded pop bottle for an extra water container. As it is, I will have to wait until the Trail gets back close to civilization.

Today, I did meet quite a few local people day hiking. Without exception, they were friendly and congenial. Three young men stopped in the shelter to get out of the rain. They left when it slacked some, but there is no way that they could have made any other shelter before it started again. Well, "Rainmaker", "Beatin Feet", "Sooner Zoo Man", and "Cool Breeze" are up the Trail from us and hopefully dry. *We* are!

May 25, 1992   Watauga Lake Shelter
Trail Distance: 10.5 miles

We had met some locals yesterday who had warned us that the climb to Pond Mountain was a rough one. By A.T. standards it was a "piece of cake". "Reno" and I had both looked forward to the café that was supposed to be at U.S. 321. It was not to be! About one hundred feet before reaching the highway, the Trail took a steep descent, and it was nothing but slippery clay. I could see where others had slid down it. Try as I did, I could not stay on my feet and slid *off* the Trail down the hillside. Luckily, a tree stopped me. It smacked me in the face, and I grabbed it. Again, I lost my glasses and again, got them back unbroken. My face was not so lucky. My nose got gashed up some and swelled to twice its normal size. My lips got a couple of cuts and also were swollen. I got a cut on my right hand and I looked far worse than the damage actually done. To top it off, when I went to the local café to get cleaned off and get something to eat, I found that they had stopped serving meals a couple of years ago. I *was* able to get cleaned up a bit, and the owner got me a TV dinner heated up. His nursing care and band aids were very thankfully received. For a few days, I looked as if I had gotten mauled by a bob cat. There was no major damage done, and it all healed up. I will have to be careful of my right hand for a while and use the left hand for my hiking stick.

I'm in the shelter this evening with "Reno" and "Rubber Duck", a young man who had been ahead of us and got off the Trail for a few days. In solid clouds all day, the scenery was rather sparse. "Reno" likes a camp fire as I do, and he gets one going when he arrives. I just help with gathering the wood. It's a good arrangement for me.

I have reached the conclusion that I will leave the Trail at Damascus, Virginia. It's a well known point on the Trail, the whole town is Trail oriented, and it is a good place to start *if* I come back. To finish the Trail now is not a top priority with me anymore. This procedure of doing two weeks at a time is *not* good advice. It takes me that long for the body to get into shape, and the knees just never make it. Perhaps when I retire, I may have another go at it, but as of now, this is pure torture. But I do love the forests, the fellow hikers, the camaraderie at the shelters, and the scenery (when not in clouds).

May 26, 1992   Iron Mountain Shelter
Trail Distance: 13.0 miles

It started raining by the time that I got to the shelter last evening and it continued lightly all night. Three of us in the shelter, "Reno", "Rubber Duck", and I awoke to a cool, rainy day. We did not want to get out of the dry, warmth of our bags. Other hikers stopping by about 9:00 A.M. for a snack shamed us into arising. If no one had stopped by, we probably would have stayed in our bags until it stopped raining, whenever that may have come. As it was, we dressed, put on our rain gear, and were on the Trail by 10:00. This was not a day to start late. A planned thirteen-mile day on less-than-the-best terrain got me into the shelter at 7:15.

The Trail today crossed over the top of the Watauga Dam, a large earth-filled hydroelectric dam that just happens to be where the A.T. wants to pass. Dams are always interesting to me, and going over the top of one gives me a childish thrill. Further on, I passed the Vandeventer Shelter with stated excellent views of the Watauga Lake. With the rainy day, I did not even try to get a view.

The shelter for the evening sleeps six, and six were already in it. Fortunately for me, they all knew that I was coming and had already made room for me. So the capacity six fits seven very well. However, it *was* cozy. Five of the hikers were going to try to reach Damascus the next day and would have an early start. "Reno" and I stayed in our bags and let them clear out before we got up. The day before was exhausting for me. I came in cold, tired, and physically beat. My supper was made, eaten, and I hit the bag. My leg muscles cramped and I spent a rather limited sleep night. Funny thing, as much as I was awake and as crowded as it was, no one snored! Just peaceful, dead tired, sleeping men. It was so quiet it could have been a convent.

May 27, 1992   Abingdon Gap Shelter
                                Trail Distance: 16.2 miles

This was a nice day for hiking—cool, cloudy and the terrain was not too rugged. "Reno" is still with me, and we decided that if we made the first shelter by noon time, then we would try for the second shelter and make it a sixteen-mile day. The day turned out OK. I hit the Trail about 8:00 A.M. and arrived at the second shelter at 5:20. It was a relatively easy day, although a long one. By the time I reached the shelter, "Reno" already had a big fire going, and we had a young visitor stop in who was hiking south. We had a pleasant evening together with good hot food, good company, a good fire, and about the only thing missing was a privy. They *are* getting scarce. And some of the recent ones visited were little better than a log with just about as much privacy.

Our water supply here was 275 yards downhill, and I mean *down* hill. I made the trip only once. The dishes can wait until tomorrow. I had washed last night's dishes when I stopped at the first shelter today for lunch. Water there was only fifty feet away, and that is about as close as some kitchens.

I still get amazed at how different the mountains are. On some, there are streams every hundred yards, on others as many as six springs in fifty feet, and others are bone dry. In them, if you run out of water, it is just tough.

Even with the fire going, it was a chilly night, and we all hit the bags just to get warm. At least "Reno" and I knew that the next day would be short as we did not have far to go to reach Damascus.

May 28, 1992   Damascus, VA
                         Trail Distance: 9.8 miles

The day started cool and clear, and we all arose at 7:00 A.M. During the night, we remarked that we all had heard the same sound, something like a roar that a mountain lion would make. We had no idea what it was, and we never found out. As soon as I prepared for the Trail, it started to rain, and it rained all day. After thinking about it for a while, I finally decided to put on my rain jacket. It never rained hard—just steady. My boots and socks were wet within minutes, my pants took a little longer, and the rest of me stayed dry but never warm. This *has* been a cool two weeks. It will feel good getting to a lower altitude and a warmer surrounding. I just cannot imagine those hikers who started out in March or early April or those who stay at the shelters in every month of the year. They encounter temperatures much below freezing, snow in lieu of rain, and trails covered by ice and snow. The wet trails are a menace—the icy ones have to be deadly. And people think that we are having fun!

On the Trail at 8:00 A.M., I made Damascus by 12:45 and immediately checked into a Methodist-sponsored hostel. It sleeps twenty-eight in six rooms of an old two-story house, has two bathrooms, two showers, kitchen, and family room with a TV. Most of the bunks were full. The place is unheated, *no one* closes the back door, many windows are kept open, and I still cannot get warm. I *did* get a shower and shave, brushed my teeth with a replacement brush as I had lost my toothbrush again (lost one last

September, too), put on dry, clean clothes, and actually look halfway presentable if you did not notice my nose and mouth which are still kind of a mess.

The hostel is so full because some of the people here will not go on. The cost is only $2 per night, strictly voluntary, and I feel some are taking advantage of it. There are people here who passed me two days ago and others who were so far ahead of me that I never met them. Still, it's a friendly group, albeit a rather large one, and there is always room for one more. Unless it stops raining or slows up a bit, the hikers here may have to sleep in shifts. Some have been here five days and will not leave until the sun comes out.

Some of the hikers are that in name only. They'll skip some hard sections, bypass others, catch rides to go further up the Trail, and generally "miss some markers", as the saying goes. Others, most I believe, are obsessively keen on doing the Trail by the letter! These, I respect the most!

I crossed the Virginia line a few miles prior to reaching Damascus and that was a milestone. Anytime that you cross one state and enter another, you get the feeling that you have accomplished something. More often than not, the scenery does not change, and you keep seeing what you saw in the last state.

Well, I have reached Damascus, Virginia, and have strong doubts as to whether I will go any further. The Trail is rough on me, or to be more correct and honest, my legs and knees just are not up to the strain and physical demands required. Funny thing, the backpack or weight of it seems to have little or nothing to do with the strain. I can go up a hill without a pack and *still* pant and strain and have to rest every few yards. Others do not have this problem, or if they do, are sneaky enough not to show it. These legs could match the younger ones in biking, but much older legs than mine put these to shame in hiking. It's just a fact of life, and I wish that I were smart enough, honest enough, or mature enough to accept it. If my Trail days are behind me, at least I have accomplished part of my goal. Springer Mountain, Georgia, to Damascus, Virginia, covers some of the toughest parts of the trail.

The next comparable portions will be the mountains of New Hampshire or Maine. I won't say a definite no—just a long maybe. I may come back some day and do parts of Virginia. It's pretty and much more sane than the Trail further south. So, this chapter ends. If I'm lucky, so does the book!

Total Trail Distance: 448.9 miles

Other mountains crossed:

May 16	Big Bald (beautiful panoramic views)	5,516 feet
May 17	Little Bald (wooded and no views)	5,185
	High Rocks (rough climb but good views)	4,280
May 19	Beauty Spot (fine views)	4,437
	Unaka Mountain (wooded and no views)	5,180
May 20	Little Bald Knob (limited views)	4,459
May 21	Roan High Knob (limited views)	6,285
May 22	Hump Mountain (*best* views of any seen: 360 degrees panoramic)	5,587
May 24	White Rock Mountain (fine views from tower)	4,105

CHAPTER FOUR

June 12, 1996   Preliminary to Hike

After a few years of not hiking, I thought that perhaps my legs and knees would have forgotten some of their past problems. At any rate, I decided to try it again. After all, Virginia was supposed to be "easy", and I would hate to think that this little Trail got the best of me. Thinking of some of the real old timers, who have done the Trail in just one year, gets me kind of embarrassed. So, here I go again!

I drove to Damascus, Virginia, where I had last left the Trail several years ago. It is a neat little town, not large by any means, but a focal point on the A.T. As the Trail goes directly through the town, a hiker does not have to leave the Trail in order to get supplies, use the Laundromat, have a good meal, or enjoy one of the best hostels on the Trail. While the town is not large and is not that well known outside of the immediate area, it *is* well known to hikers. Many plan their hikes to either start here or end here.

I was able to enjoy the accommodations in the hostel and to start out with a nice shower and clean clothes. The area around the town is a favorite for both hikers and bikers. There are old abandoned railroad beds that make it ideal for both. Those are some of the favorite hiking paths. The grades are always so gradual that you do not mind the ups and downs. Several persons in the hostel are hikers in name only. They may hike a little, come back to the hostel, and then get a ride further up on the Trail. *They* usually look well fed and well rested!

June 13, 1996   Start of Hike: Saunders Shelter
Trail Distance: 9.4 miles

The Trail started out nice and easy following some of the abandoned railroad beds near to the town. A little tricky part encountered was when the Trail followed a highway out of town and turned off into the forests. I missed the marker indicating the turnoff and continued for another quarter of a mile. What a way to start! All in all, it was a fairly easy day. I had brought my knee braces along and had them on without waiting for the knees to ask for them. It was a dry, warm day and made for nice hiking. However, the 9.4 miles were on legs a little out of practice, and it was a tired hiker coming into the shelter.

Food on the hike is consistent with past practices. Breakfast is Grape Nuts with powdered milk prepared the night before. If you prepare the milk a few hours ahead of time, it allows it to get a more natural flavor. It was suggested that it be refrigerated during this time, but that is not quite allowable here. Lunch is the Mt. Adams Logan bread along with a helping of gorp. On this trip, the bread could have been cooked just a few minutes more as it was just a bit undercooked. It is still good, though, and will not go to waste. Supper consists of a hot beverage (usually tea), a hot soup, rice or bean-based main dish, and a pudding for dessert again prepared with powdered milk that was prepared after breakfast. Food is sufficient, and I do not have to worry about putting on weight. I can eat as much as I want and will still lose some weight at the end. I ate my meals today alone, as the shelter has no other visitors.

June 14, 1996   Lost Mountain Shelter
Trail Distance: 6.0 miles

This should have been an easy day of hiking. However, my left leg started acting up and is really not very comfortable. It feels like

I pulled a muscle. Fortunately, the terrain was relatively easy to hike, and I did not plan on going too far this day. I crested Lost Mountain (elevation 3,400 feet), but the views left something to be desired. At least, it was then downhill to the shelter. There were a couple of other hikers in the shelter going the same direction as I am, but they are moving much faster and going further each day. I will probably see nothing of them tomorrow except their tracks. This is a nice shelter with plenty of water available, and I hope to rest myself and especially my legs. The knees let me know that they do not care for this type of vacation. Hopefully, my legs will not join the chorus.

June 15, 1996   Thomas Knob Shelter
                                 Trail Distance: 13.0 miles

This was really not a fun day. The knees now feel all right, but the left leg is downright painful. The day was long and the A.T. climbed about a quarter of a mile in altitude. There were many, many stops and rests along the way. The Trail came close to the summit of Mt. Rogers, the highest point in Virginia, but I passed up the opportunity to visit the summit. It is covered with dense spruce forests, and there are no views in any direction. For much of the day, the Trail goes through forests. As this shelter for the night is over a mile high, I expected and got a cool reception. I had the shelter to myself and preferred it that way. I just did not feel like company. My leg was really aching.

June 16, 1996   Old Orchard Shelter
                                 Trail Distance: 10.6 miles

At least, the day started out with some good views. There is a place on the Trail called Rhododendron Gap that is over a mile high and has some very nice views. These would be the last views for a while. Coming down from the mountain, the Trail goes into forests and gets kind of boring. A person can enjoy just so many views of trees, rocks, and paths. On one of my many rests today, I swear that if I could have called a cab, I would have! Whatever I pulled, it is not getting any better. Unless something magical happens tomorrow, I will leave the Trail the first chance that I get. Once the pack is off in the evening, things get somewhat better. Hopefully, the leg will straighten itself out and I can continue. It really feels like this is going to be a long time to cure.

June 17, 1996   Dickey Gap, VA
Trail Distance: 10.6 miles

There were several parts of the Trail that used old logging roads, and these made for some better hiking. In a normal hike, this could have been considered as a fairly easy day. However, the decision has been made to leave the trail at Dickey Gap and try to get back to my car. Hiking on the A.T. has never been considered as "fun", but *all* enjoyment is out of it now. I did make Dickey Gap in the early afternoon and had a bit of trouble getting a ride. The local store at a nearby intersection was closed permanently, and the outside telephone was not working. After about two hours, a young black man in a pickup gave me a ride all the way into Damascus. He was a very friendly fellow who was going to Damascus to do some biking in the area. For the whole trip back, he kept up a running recap of "black" jokes. These were funny, and I could not stop him. Each time I would ask him to stop, as I was embarrassed, he would say, "Oh, I've got one more for you". Then, he would be off again. Once in Damascus, I invited and he accepted to have dinner with me. We both enjoyed the spaghetti dinner with all the trimmings.

I am spending the night in the hostel. At least, I will leave tomorrow clean and somewhat rested. Will I come back to the Trail? I keep saying "no" and keep on coming back. I'll just say, "Probably not unless I can get someone to come with me and share my misery!"

CHAPTER FOUR—
POSTSCRIPT

While I had not done any hiking on the Trail in a few years, I still belong to the Appalachian Trail Conference and get the monthly newsletters. Each year, there is always a request for volunteers to help with repair work on various portions of the Trail. In early 1999, Mina and I volunteered for selected trail work. Our first choice was in the Smoky Mountain National Park, and we were accepted. Neither of us had to be too concerned about the part that required parental consent.

We really did not know just what would be expected of us. We knew that we would be doing repair work on the Trail in the Smokies and that it was to be "the hardest physical work that we would ever do". It sounded like a real experience, and we had the time to devote to it.

Our time to join the work crew coincided with the arrival of Hurricane Floyd on the east coast of Florida, so we left a day early to try to get ahead of the expected exodus of residents on the Atlantic coast. It seems like the exodus came a day early as the residents there wanted a good head start from the hurricane. We went up U.S. 19 north along the western coast of Florida, and every motel and rest area was packed. They were parking along side of the highway as the rest areas had no more parking places. We just kept going until we came to a small town in Georgia that had a Wal-Mart with a sign inviting travelers to park in their lot, as Floyd could not reach them there. This we did! We laid our sleeping bags out in the rear of the station wagon and had a fairly comfortable night's sleep. In the early morning, we were awakened by a rap on the window inviting us to have coffee, juice, and donuts with the compliments of Wal-Mart. It was a pleasant surprise, and we did enjoy their hospitality.

Getting back on the road, we had the time and we stopped at Andersonville. This is a "must" for anyone who has not visited there. After a long memorable visit at Andersonville, we continued on our way and made the check in at the crew house where we would spend the night. They served us our supper and gave us instructions as to what we would be doing and where we would be doing it. Rather than doing repair work, we would be part of a crew that would be building a new trail around the top of Little Baldy in the Smokies. Through the years, the hikers and horses had made the old trail somewhat dangerous. After instruction from our "trail boss" we gladly tried out the crew house accommodations. This would be our last night in a bed for ten nights so we did try to get a good night's sleep.

After a good breakfast in the early morning, we drove our car to the starting point. The others went in a van, but it did not have room for all of us and all of our gear. At the parking lot, we all donned our backpacks, loaded up with water, and started a five-mile hike *up* to our campsite. The site was near to the Russell Field Shelter, and that was over four thousand feet up. Packhorses had earlier brought up the heavy supplies and equipment, so we had only to bring ourselves. There was a tent where all of the supplies were kept, where we had our meals, and where we gathered whenever we were not in our tents. Everyone had their own tent, some singles and some doubles, and these were scattered over the top of the hill. Ours was a fairly large double, and it served our needs very well.

The area had been in a drought condition for several months so water was rather limited. The spring near the shelter had practically dried up, and water had to be obtained several hundred feet more downhill. We had a couple of backpacks fitted with five-gallon containers, and *all* of our water was brought up in these. This was one where we let the "young bucks" do the work. Getting and bringing the water was hard work. By the time each day was done, we were both bushed. The water did have to be filtered and

to this David helped. We were all to help with the cooking, the cleaning, and the general chores around the camp.

The toilet facilities consisted of a trench dug a couple of hundred feet from camp in a secluded area. We had a system to let persons know if the "trench" was in use. Normally, the work crew consists of both men and women. However, for this trip, Mina was the only woman other than our camp "mother". They were all younger than we were, and some were younger than our children! We did fit and got along very well.

Getting started on the first day was a two-mile hike to the starting spot. This was on September 17, 1999. The prior crew had worked the new trail up to a particular point. We were to continue it. With instructions and demonstrations, we got underway. Basically, we were to cut a new trail along the side of the hill. This was known as "side cutting". The crew leader had marked out the proposed trail with flags stuck into the ground every few feet. He tried to keep the flags going up at no more than a 10 percent grade. We understood that this would be for the benefit of the horses that are allowed on the A.T. in the Smokies. A worker would pick a couple of the flags and do his side cutting between the chosen flag area. Our basic tools consisted of pickaxes, Pulaski hoes, shovels, axes, winches and shin guards to protect our shins. We would mark the lower portion with a line drawn with our hoes. We would then extend the hoe far enough up the hill so that if we then cut down at about a forty-five-degree angle, we would be able to leave a path at the bottom about four feet wide. It sounds simple enough, but trees, rocks, brush, and roots had the habit of just getting in the way. Some of the obstacles were small, but some required much muscle to move or to cut through. There was always someone willing to help you if you got into trouble, and at times we all needed some help. We could rest whenever we wanted. No one timed us or tried to make us go faster or criticized our work. Our team leader had a very nice way of letting you know that your work may not be quite up to "acceptable". Even so, by midafternoon, I was on the verge of exhaustion. This *was* hard work! It also gave us a sense of accomplishment as we could see the progress that we were making on a day-by-day basis.

After a breakfast that usually consisted of dry cereal but sometimes hot meals, we prepared sandwiches for lunch, and these were augmented with cookies and fruit. Supper was usually a one-dish hot meal with rice as the base. It was not gourmet, but we ate well indeed. No one went hungry, and we all had healthy appetites. There was not that much to do in the evenings, and we were too tired to do anything that would take any effort. We all usually went to our tents early.

As water was scarce, showers or baths were out of the question. One time, and one time only, Mina and I took a couple of inches of water in a bowl, went down the hillside, and tried to wash off somewhat. That water turned black fast! About halfway through our "bath", we heard talking nearby and found that we had gone to within about twenty feet of a portion of the A.T. We easily saw the two hikers going by, and they could have seen us had they glanced up.

Each day was much like the last. We hiked to the work area, did our work, and hiked back. As the work area kept getting farther and farther from our campsite, the daily hikes kept getting longer. Fortunately, we were not carrying backpacks for this, so all that we got was some good leg exercises each day. We took pride in what we did and enjoyed seeing it "all come together". The Conference will allow the new trail to "age" for about a year before it is opened for general use. This will allow the soil to harden and make it less prone to damage from the hikers and the horses. Mina and I really do not want horses to use the trail that we helped build. They can really tear up any trail, and the horsemen do not help in maintaining any part of the trails in the park. After seeing just what the horses' hooves can do and hearing some horror stories, I let it be known that we would not be doing any more repair or maintenance work on any trail that allows horses. They may have a right to be in the Smokies, but I do not wish to share any trail with them.

We did not see any bears in the area, but they did leave their droppings on the Trail. They just let it be known that they were in the area. We heard coyotes almost nightly but did not see any. The lack of water at our altitude probably kept most wildlife at a lower level.

I had promised Mina that when we finished our trail work, we would hike to the top of Rocky Top, the mountain memorialized by the song. The plan was to take an extra day when we finished our work. We had not realized it, but our work was within two miles of Rocky Top. We had all been making better time than had been anticipated and were well ahead of schedule. Some of our crew had taken off early one day and hiked to the top of Rocky Top. At the time, we did not have our camera with us and opted for the next day. No one else desired to go with us so we went alone. It *was* a nice hike. Although we did not have a backpack on, we knew that we were doing some heavy-duty hiking. The trail to the top is steep, and horses are not allowed up. It would be too much for them. We got to the top, had a snack, and sang "Rocky Top". We had earlier gotten the words and music from one of our fellow workers. There was no one else around to hear us, and that disappointed us as we thought that we did pretty well. At any rate, we gave ourselves an "encore" and sang it again. All three verses! It was dark when we got back to camp as we had over a four-mile hike back. Supper was saved for us, and we needed it. Needless to say, we slept well that night.

Our crew actually finished the section of trail around the top of Little Baldy ahead of schedule. We were not expected to finish, so we still had a couple of workdays ahead of us that could not be wasted. So, our leader had us start on another new trail around the top of a hill about half a mile south of our base camp. Our other work had been north of the camp. This new trail required a steep hike down hill and obviously a steep hike back to camp after the day's work was done. It was a shorter walk but still involved some panting and sweating. We got a good start on the new trail but will leave most of it for some future workers. Now I would like to come back to this section in a couple of years just to see the condition and the results of our labors. It should be interesting.

Saturday, the 26th, saw the end of our work. I believe that we all felt a sense of accomplishment. It was a new type of work for most of us, and now we could say with a degree of pride that we were experienced side-hill trail builders! I must say that I would not want to have to do it for a living. It was something that I would do for "free", but you couldn't pay me to do it!

After breakfast on Sunday, we broke camp. This meant taking down and storing all of the sleeping tents and putting away all of the cooking supplies and equipment. Our campsite was not in view of the Trail or the shelter so there was little chance that anyone could come upon it. Primarily, the concern is for the benefit of any local bears or other animals that may come around. We had a "bear-fence" around the cooking tent. This was a low metal-grid fence that would be hooked to a battery when we were not around. The voltage was low, and we could touch it without any problems. However, it would startle any animal that came into contact. In the time that we were there, nothing was ever disturbed. It either worked, or we did not have anything that interested any animals.

Packing up and hiking down took some time. It was five miles down hill, but it took some time with a full pack. Even when we reached the first camping sites at the lower level, we still had some walking to do. The result was a tired bunch of hikers coming back to the cars. We nicknamed the campers that we saw the "round" people. They were all round and some rounder than others! It was good to get back to the lower base camp and get a shower. We could have stayed for supper and stayed for the night, but we opted to get on the road as we had a long way to travel. One of the last "official" things that we did was to stop at a good restaurant and have a full meal with all of the trimmings. We treated ourselves!

Mina did not mind the backpacking or the tenting out. She saw what a shelter looked like and what some parts of the Trail looked like. It was good experience, and it gave her a chance to do some practice hiking. She indicated that she would be agreeable to do some actual hiking on the Trail, so we just may do it next year. From where I left off in Virginia, the rest of Virginia is supposed to be relatively easy hiking, so we will give serious consideration to hitting the Trail again. I believe that it would be much more enjoyable with Mina along. We shall see!

CHAPTER FIVE

July 14, 2000   Preliminary to Hike

Mina and David Swan drove to Pearisburg, Virginia, with the idea of finding someone to drive them back to where David had last left the Trail a few years earlier. For this time on the A.T., David both had a partner and had been working out to try to get in better shape. His exercise machine gave him the ability to strengthen his legs, and the regular walking each morning with scuba weights had to have helped with the legs. At least, he felt that he was in fairly good shape to try the Trail again. We tried a motel in town and later felt that it would have been more comfortable to have slept in the car. It was noisy with various people talking and making noise until almost daybreak. At least the motel manager was able to get us in contact with a hostel manager who was agreeable to drive us back some one hundred miles to where David had earlier left the Trail. Bill Gautier was a retired Army man and did a bit of volunteer work around the hostel including being in the process of building a deck at the back of the structure that would overlook some of the Virginia mountains. Our transportation fee would go to purchase more materials for the deck.

July 15, 2000   South Fork of Holston River
                          Trail Distance: 6.5 miles

Bill Gautier drove and led us to the local hostel that we had not known about. It was a nice one. We parked our car nearby, and Bill then drove us back to Dicky Gap, a spot on the A.T. about one hundred miles south. We started hiking and stopped for lunch at Trimpi Shelter, about four miles in the hike. After lunch, we then hiked another 2.5 miles to a nice camping spot near the south fork of the Holston River. The nearest shelter was reported at fifteen miles away, and we knew that there was no way that we could make it. The weather was nice, the spot clean, and our tent fit very well. The trail varied between easy and moderate, but we were both tired and had cramped muscles. No matter how one may prepare for the trail, it will always get to you. In addition, David's pack was some six pounds more than it should have been, and the water canteens brought them both to a higher level. Once we knew what our water requirements would be for the day and the distance to the next water location, we could better judge the amount of water that we would have to carry. The extra weight does add up. Each day that we hiked, the weight of the packs would go down, so the first day would be the heaviest. It was a pleasant first day, and a good night's sleep was ahead of us.

July 16, 2000   Partnership Shelter
                                    Trail Distance: 8.0 miles

Waking up, we both felt fine. There were no muscle pains or cramps. David had thought that his knees would be acting up, as they have done in the past, but they surprised him by giving him no problems. We had met two south bounders yesterday after we had tented, and they told us of a new shelter eight miles further on. Even if we had known about it earlier, there was no way that we could have made it yesterday. The "out of practice" legs would not have allowed it. We had a relatively easy day and made the shelter with no problems. It was a real joy to behold. Complete with hot and cold running water, a shower, laundry tub with hot and cold water, and a "state of the art" privy, it was "one of a kind". It was constructed by the family and friends of a Thomas R. Baldwin, in memory of the 34-year-old who loved the local mountains. It was by far the nicest shelter that has been visited on the A.T. on any hike. We had a good meal and were able to wash all of our clothes. Unfortunately, the shelter did not have a dryer, and the clothes stayed rather damp. We had taken a nap when we first arrived at the shelter and were awakened by the visit of Jane, who had been our cook and "mother" on the prior years Trail Crew work that we had done. It was a surprise by all of us to meet as we did. Jane was working with another trail crew nearby and had just happened to visit the shelter. We saw a deer today and birds that could not be identified. Each day, our packs get lighter and we get in better shape. The trail today varied from easy to moderate.

July 17, 2000   Chatfield Shelter
Trail Distance: 6.8 miles

The distance covered today was only 6.8 miles, but it felt like a few more. There were many ups and downs, some easy and some rather difficult. Most of the day, we were in deep forests so the views were a bit limited. We reached the shelter before 2:00 and had a nice nap. The mosquitoes were out, and bug spray was a *must!* Again, we were the only ones at the shelter. For some reason, there are just not that many hikers out. We have seen only two, and they were headed south. Nearby is a small stream, so water is plentiful. We strain most of our water. The little that we do not strain, we purify with iodine tablets. In the past, David had not filtered water taken from springs. On this trip, it all gets purified.

July 18, 2000   Davis Path Shelter
Trail Distance: 7.3 miles

This was a fairly easy day. About four miles into the trail, we passed a limited supply store where we were able to stock up on soup, gorp ingredients, and energy bars. The store had no powdered milk and no main meal supplies. Well, so much for the trail guides that promised groceries. It was a nice day, and we had nice hiking. We stopped at a spring about a mile from the shelter and filled up all of our water containers. Another hiker, an elder black man from New Orleans, stopped at the shelter later and had missed the spring. He had an 8-month-old Labrador and was short on water. We had enough to share, and the dog was mighty thirsty. Our guidebook indicated the spring but promised a non-existent pond. The dog was very friendly, too friendly, and really should not have been on the trail. The trail is *not* dog friendly. We were glad that we had filled everything at the spring as we had sufficient to share. This shelter is an oldie but nice. The next shelter is about eleven miles, and tomorrow promises to be a long day. The plan is to start early and try to make it. We always have the tent if we cannot make the full hike. Today, we saw a four-foot Black Racer, and tested the blackberries, the blueberries, and the briar tips. There were some raspberries that are not quite ripe. All in all, it was a nice day.

July 19, 2000   Knot Maul Branch Shelter
                                Trail Distance: 11.9 miles

The hike today seemed like twenty miles. It rained most of the day, and we were both pretty exhausted at the ten-mile mark. We stopped for an additional rest of half an hour and some food. That got us to the shelter after hiking up, WAY up, for most of the last 1.9 miles. This is the second night to share with Romalice and his Labrador, Boy. The first night had David wake up to find Boy sharing his sleeping bag with him. Boy is kept leashed now. They are good company, though. Romalice has a hammock of a rather unique variety that he uses and usually sleeps outside of the shelter. David cannot seem to get enough water today. He is always thirsty. Today, the trail took us over a private cattle field that was literally full of thistles. The thistles completely covered what trail there may have been. We had gotten to a marker in the middle of the field and could not find another marker and could not find any trail. Mina went one way, and David went another trying to find where the trail may have continued in the forest about another couple of hundred yards away. For about half an hour, we searched with no success. Finally, David went back to the marker in the middle of the field and noticed the next trail marker at about a ninety-degree angle from the direction that we had been traveling and partially hidden by the windblown thistles. We had been getting just a mite nervous.

July 20, 2000   Chestnut Knob Shelter
                                 Trail Distance: 9.0 miles

The hike today started fairly easy for about half way. Then, we climbed about two thousand feet in a four-mile stretch. Romalice and Boy decided to stay another day at the last shelter. Boy had injured a paw, and the rest may give him a chance to get healed. The rocks on the trail can be rather sharp, and it is a small wonder that only one paw was injured. The dog is only a pup, although a fair-sized one. He carries his own pack with his own food, and it comes to about ten pounds worth. Romalice had rescued him from a shelter, so the dog is better off with an owner who cares for him. Yesterday, there were many cattle stiles to cross, and these were bad enough with a backpack. There was concern and wonder as to how Boy got over the stiles. He is too big to pick up, could not climb them himself, and he could not get under the fences. It was later found that Romalice had to repeatedly go down the fence line until he got to a gate or a road to get Boy through. It was really a long day for him.

Arriving at this shelter, we were pleasantly surprised. It is completely enclosed with stone walls about eight inches thick. On top of a mountain, it can get quite cold at times. It was cool enough when *we* got there. Inside the shelter, it had to have been at least ten to fifteen degrees warmer than outside. It would have been ideal with a fireplace, but it had been walled in. The shelter is directly on the peak of Chestnut Knob Mountain. Depending on which source you search, the mountain is either 4,309 feet or 4,409 feet tall. At any rate, it is the highest one around, and the views are just great. Fortunately, the walls of the shelter retain heat, so we had a comfortable night. We did hear and see a couple of mice, but they did not bother the visitors. Probably the mothballs kept them away. Each night, David puts moth balls around the sleeping area and hangs the food from hooks to discourage mice. This is the only completely enclosed shelter that has been seen other than an old barn that is used further down south. Probably, the altitude requires the enclosure. A small spring fed pond was passed a couple of miles from the shelter and the prior nights dishes got washed and all water bottles and canteens got filled with water. It was an interesting little pond. In most cases, fish tend to hide when someone comes up to the edge of the water. These little fish, probably bluegill variety, came up to the edge of the bank. They were probably used to being fed as hikers cleaned their dinnerware. They were not disappointed!

Candles were put out, and the place looked downright homey. We had it to ourselves and preferred it that way. We are planning on leaving the Trail day after tomorrow afternoon to go into a nearby town for supplies and a motel room. We really could use a shower and a store-bought meal.

The views from the top are really fabulous. In one direction, we could count five mountain *ranges*! The views in other directions were of farms in valleys that were a good half mile below us. Some of the shelters do not have water nearby, and you have to stock up before you get there. The next shelter should be OK, so we will need to bring only enough to drink en route. Of course, that could easily be three quarts for the two of us. On top here, it is peaceful, there were a couple of deer checking us out, but no trees, no birds, and no birds singing. Being alone at the shelters is so unlike most of David's prior trips. Quite often, the shelters had other hikers and sometimes were full. Most of this hike has seen no one else at the shelters. This shelter does have a privy as have most of them so far. This privy, like most on the trail, has three half sides with no door and no front to it. You do get a good view of the surrounding countryside though. We are usually in our sleeping bags by 7:00 or 8:00, and it is now after 8:00 and the sun is still out. It does make a difference when you are on top of the mountain. Tomorrow appears to be a long day but not necessarily a rough one. We will wait and see.

July 21, 2000   Jenkins Shelter
                             Trail Distance: 10.8 miles

The late evening views from the mountaintop were truly beautiful but were surpassed by the morning views. Looking down

into the valleys shrouded in clouds with hill peaks peaking through was awesome. Several pictures were taken but could not possibly catch the full scenes. David did not read his trail guide closely so missed where we were supposed to find water. We had to leave the trail at a particular point to locate a spring and did not leave at the designated point! The result was a shortage of water for the day. We had the one chance about a mile from the mountain shelter and missed it. There were absolutely no other places that we could get water during the day. David still thought that we would have sufficient water to drink though. However, the hike was somewhat longer than we had planned. Toward the end of the hike, we were 2.7 miles from the shelter, it was mostly downhill, we were moving from two to three miles an hour, and it *still* took us two full hours to make it. David believes that some of the trail distances are guesses and guesses from someone that has not been there! That last 2.7 miles just did not make sense. By the time that we reached the shelter, we were both "bushed" and had run out of water an hour prior to finding new water. We were dehydrated and probably consumed well over a quart each when we had it available. In addition, we each had two servings of soup to bring our water needs up. A pint of water by our heads at night was emptied and had to be refilled.

Much of the trail today, estimated at 3.7 miles, was along the crest of a rock formation cliff that rises about fifty feet above the surrounding land. It would take a mountain climber to get down from the north side—a mountain goat could make a south descent. In places, the rock formation allowed some great views over a location called Burkes Garden. There were some memorable views, but the day found some memorable thirsts, and some dead-tired hikers. The shelter was really welcome. Water was close enough, so we were able to fill our thirsts and to get the prior day's dishes cleaned. For some unexplained reason, the privy was another three-sided structure, located at least two hundred yards from the shelter, with the open side facing down the trail. It was a most interesting location. As much as has been heard about the Virginia mice, only a few have been seen and heard. Sleeping is getting easier for both, and David's knees still do not bother him. Mina is beginning to have some problems with one of her feet. A nerve starts to act up after about ten miles of hiking and can get rather painful. More and longer rest stops seem to help a bit. We think that it is getting better. Time will tell! The night is dead quiet with no wind, no birds, and no animal sounds.

July 22, 2000   Bland, VA—Motel
                            Trail Distance: 12.0 miles

We knew that this would be a long day, so it was planned mathematically. It seems that no matter how fast we think we move, we actually move about one and a half miles per hour based on the A.T. guides. So, we planned on two-hour segments, with rest stops after two hours, lunch after two more hours, rest after two more hours, and reaching U.S. Highway 52 after two more hours. With the rest stops entered, we expected to reach U.S. 52 by 6:00 P.M. We reached it by 5:00 P.M., and there were these two happy hikers standing by the road hoping for a ride. Mina had never hitchhiked before, so this was a new experience for her. After about twenty minutes (there were very few vehicles passing), a young lady in a Camaro stopped and took us all of the way to the only motel in town. She was the daughter a man who did a bit of hiking and was most friendly. She told us that her parents managed the local grocery store, and we were able to meet her father there the next day. We do not see just how we all were able to fit into the Camaro, but we somehow managed. Ah, that ride felt good.

A restaurant was close by to the motel, and we gladly waited until a table was available. We think that we tried to eat everything on the menu *plus* a huge hunk of apple cake a-la-mode. We asked for and received extra home made bread and left our plates very, very clean. We think that we were able to prove to them that 1) we were hungry and 2) we really liked their cooking. We were the last patrons to leave the restaurant. David still can't imagine where Mina put it all. She ate every bit as much as David did, and David claims to have a hollow leg! Needless to say, he did not help her at all. David had thought that he may have received a bit of her apple cake, but no crumbs were left.

Today, we had gone through one little valley for 3.5 miles and were supposed to cross one stream twelve times. We lost count after fifteen crossings! However, it did make for some smooth hiking. Some of the views from the upper trails were really beautiful, but the views in the forests get kind of monotonous after seven days. It is different each day, but all you want is for the trail to be "level". The "downs" are almost as bad and as slow as the "ups".

There was no Laundromat in town. We were able to take our showers and were able to wash some clothes in the motel lavatory but were not able to dry anything. Hopefully, we will reach the next shelter tomorrow in time to get some things dried. Our washed clothes are basically clean, but you could not tell by looking. They have that dirty look! We are still thirsty and go through water by the glass full. Hoping to replenish our supplies tomorrow at a grocery store, we *must* have certain supplies for the remaining four days before we can reach Pearisburg and our car. It was a most welcome sleep, and we did *not* set any alarm clock.

July 23, 2000

Heavy's Mill Shelter
Trail Distance: 2.3 miles

Getting out of town was more difficult than getting in! We had walked a half mile to the local grocery store for supplies and had met the father of the young lady who had given us a ride the day before. We got our supplies and then tried to get a meal in town before we started back to the trail. Everything in town was closed, and we did not feel like walking back to the restaurant on the other side of town. We then tried to get a ride to the trail but without success. So, in the rain and for two and a half miles, we walked back to the trail crossing. It was not a bad hike, and we did it with no problems. Stopping halfway for our lunch, we just enjoyed the day. Getting to the shelter was relatively easy, but finding water was most difficult. Water was supposed to be nearby with a blue-blazed trail leading to it. The shelter was on the top of a small wooded hill, and the hill was literally crisscrossed with paths going in all directions. *None* of the trails was blue blazed! By reading in the shelter logbook, we could see from past hikers that some never found water and some found some with great difficulty. I finally started down the trail that looked almost as well traveled as the A.T. and located a small bit of water at the bottom of a debris-filled little creek about one-third of a mile from the shelter. It was so far down the hillside that it was almost dark there. We did get our water, though. For others, we left directions, and Mina drew a map showing how to get some water. There may have been some nearer, but we never found it. Again, so much for the trail guide promising water "near".

This evening, we had two counselors and twelve young boys tenting near to the shelter. I believe that the boys had been in various kinds of trouble, and this little adventure was a means of trying to get their lives straightened. For some, this may have been their last chance. I commend the counselors. The boys, without exception, acted courteous and respectful. Some really took to Mina; perhaps she was like the "mother" that they may not have had.

July 24, 2000   Jenny Knob Shelter
                          Trail Distance: 9.8 miles

It rained all day! We could not see anything. The rain, clouds, and fog made visibility zilch all day. It was fairly easy hiking except it was wet and cold. We were really glad to make the shelter. We found water, got into semi-dry clothes, and had a good, hot meal. It does make one feel better. More rain is promised for the next two days, so tomorrow is not looked forward to. David's knees are still feeling great, and he thinks that working with leg weights for the past year or so have really helped. He can think of nothing else that he may have done that would account for it. Mina's feet are still acting up. They are good for most of the day, but then start hurting after about ten miles.

July 25, 2000   Wapiti Shelter
                                 Trail Distance: 13.3 miles

Rain threatened all day, but very little fell. With rain jackets on, we were as wet inside as if it *did* rain. We could not see any views as we were either in clouds all day or the clouds were at our feet. It was a very long day for us. Mina's left foot really started giving her problems after about ten miles. The day was marked by frequent stops and frequent rests for her. David knows how she must have felt. He can remember some of his knee problems and his thigh muscle problems. None of them were any fun. He has twice left the A.T. early because of painful knees and leg cramps. If her pain continues tomorrow, he will insist that we leave the trail when we get back to the car. We had planned on about twenty days on the trail in total, but it is no fun when you must put up with constant pain. Being uncomfortable is one thing; being tortured is something else. Our hike today was long, and we wanted an early start. As it was, we did not get started until 9:15, about an hour and a quarter late. We were told of a cafe about half a mile from the trail, down one of the road that we would be crossing. We had expected a good meal, but all we were able to get was a super cheeseburger. It *was* good, though. As that put an extra mile into an already full day, we did not reach the shelter until after 8:00 P.M. Two other young men were already there, and a third joined us later. A few deer joined us and came as close as about fifty feet away. They did not seem afraid at all. We were told that one of the park rangers will park his car and let the deer stick their noses in the car looking for food. He will then punch them in the nose. It may seem cruel, but it just may save some of their lives. They were just too tame for their safety.

We look at some of the meals that we prepare, and it may seem to leave a little to be desired. However, compared to some of the hikers that we see, we eat well indeed. Breakfast for us is dry cereal with milk (milk prepared the night before). Lunch is a cube of Mt. Adams Logan bread and a handful of gorp, midmorning and midafternoon breaks are a handful of gorp and an energy bar. Supper may have a hot beverage (tea, coffee, or milk chocolate), a simple soup, and a rice-based dish. This is usually doctored up by Mina, and is accompanied sometimes with mashed potatoes and gravy and is finished with a pudding made with milk prepared in the morning. We see other hikers with oatmeal prepared with hot water, peanut butter sandwiches, pop tarts, cheese and crackers, and strange things that they cook up. Some really look hungry.

It was a long day, a dreary day, and we were both tired. On top of it all, we did not sleep very well. Most everything that we have is wet and has been wet for several days. The rain, humidity, and clouds just do not allow for drying.

July 26, 2000   Doc's Knob Shelter
Trail Distance: 8.4 miles

Our morning was an eye opener. We had to go up 1,500 feet in about a mile and a half. It actually looked rougher than it was. Most of the trail was gentler than we had been led to believe. Once we were at altitude, it was a case of fairly gentle ups and downs. We did start to encounter a fairly new problem. While it was not completely new, the amount of it caught our attention. Virginia has rocks, stones, and boulders. Invariably, these make up a large part of the A.T. Picture, if you can, stones and boulders varying in size from head size to desk size and in all kinds of shapes and configurations. Cover them with moss or slime and wet them all. Now, make the trail using about fifty yards of them, going up hills and down hills, and repeat this every hundred yards or so, and you will get an idea of just how some parts of the A.T. are constructed. It does make for some interesting hiking. There were falls, and a couple of them came close to doing some major damage. Fortunately, nothing was broken or sprained.

Tomorrow, if all goes well, we will get to visit our car. The decision has been made to leave the trail. Mina needs to have her foot looked at. Surprisingly, David has had no problems with knees or leg muscles. We had one incident today that got David madder the longer that he thought about it. There was some part of the trail that is on the side of a steep hill, and the trail comes over a large boulder down about four feet to the lower level of the trail. You can't go around the boulder. The top of the boulder is the trail, and you must come over it. Trying to work his way down over the wet rock, he first thought that a small bear was attacking him. Trying to get his feet back up and out of the "bear's" jaws, he slipped and fell off the rock down on his face with his pack on top of him. Then a voice said, "Oh, don't be bothered by him. He just barks but doesn't bite." David didn't think that he was injured and let the stupid remark pass. Once again, he was reminded that DOGS DO NOT BELONG ON THE A.T.! For the rest of the day, he could not get his pack straight on his back. It had got out of kilter somehow.

July 27, 2000   Pearisburg, VA—Car
Trail Distance: 7.8 miles

The day turned out nice and pleasant, and the morning had some fairly easy hiking. We were now in much better shape and kind of took the up hills in stride with much fewer or no rest stops. The views were rather limited in the morning as trees usually surrounded us. David's pack kept giving him problems, and it finally dawned on him that his head was over his right leg rather than over the middle of his legs. By taking his pack off and having Mina examine his posture, it was determined that his back was noticeably out of alignment. Basically, it was "S" shaped rather than "I" shaped. That d— dog had really put him out of commission. By holding to the top of the pack with his left hand, he was able to continue hiking. It was *not* comfortable. Now, we had to leave the trail. Mina's feet gave her absolutely no problems today, but *David* couldn't cut it. Planning on going to his favorite chiropractor as soon as he got back home, he was pleasantly surprised to find that after about two days, the back was almost back to normal and two more days brought it there.

There were some beautiful views from the top of the mountain west of Pearisburg. We had our lunch sitting on a rock overlook that was a good half mile over the valley below. Getting off the mountain was a job in itself. It was almost solid boulders, and these were treacherous. It was a long, rough, hike down, and David's back did not make it any easier. Finally reaching the street into Pearisburg, it was a great relief to get the pack off. Mina phoned for our ride, and it came within a very short time. We were to find that we had come off the trail only a very short distance from where we had spent the night at the motel on our first night in Pearisburg. We were taken back to our car and the hostel where we were able to take a much needed shower and change into clean, dry clothes.

We then returned my two-quart canteen that I had gotten from Wal-Mart. It had started rusting within a few days of use and the straps were already cutting through. It looked to be about ten years old when it was less than two weeks. We then found a Laundromat and started on all of our clothes. Next was a restaurant that we had visited a couple of weeks before and we, again, had a fine meal. We then dried our clothes and took to the road.

This will be the first time that David has ever said, "We shall return!" On this trip, he actually enjoyed himself, and we both look forward to a visit to the A.T. next year. He had expected Virginia to be relatively easy, and it was a bit more than he expected. As he does not expect to finish the entire Trail, we will pick some portions that are a bit easier or more scenic and not so rough on these "older" bones. It was enjoyable, and *we shall return!*

Total A.T. distance—David: 610.4 miles

Total A.T. distance—Mina: 113.6 miles

CHAPTER SIX

June 8, 2001   Preliminary to Hike

David and Mina Swan left Clearwater, Florida, at 7:30 A.M. and arrived in Waynesboro, Virginia, at 9:30 P.M. Rain followed us all of the way across North Carolina and southern Virginia. Rain always makes hikers a bit nervous. Luckily, we were able to stay in a motel directly across the street from the Trail. So, it was an easy start the next morning to get our gear together and start on our hike. The motel graciously allowed us to keep our car in their parking lot for the duration of our hike.

Although this is not where we had left off our hike a year ago, we decided to do an "easy" section of the A.T. as we were not planning on completing the entire Trail. So we picked Shenandoah National Park to do our "easy" hiking.

June 9, 2001   Calf Mountain Shelter
                                Trail Distance: 6.9 miles

We were both tired and sore after only five miles of hiking. On the way, we heard pileated woodpeckers and bob whites. We saw grouse and quail. On arriving at the shelter at 2:15 P.M., we both took naps. On awakening, we both felt refreshed and were able to welcome new arrivals as they came in. Gradually, twelve other hikers showed up in different batches. Two later left, and two put up a tent. It was a nice group that stayed. All were young, including three women who came with their husbands. There were no single women in the group.

The views from Bear Den Mountain were great. There were valleys and mountains in all directions. David kept waiting nervously for his knees to start acting up. They never did, but he was always on the alert for it to happen.

June 10, 2001   Black Rock Hut
                                       Trail Distance: 13.2 miles

This promised to be a long day, and we did not know if we could complete the required 13.2 miles. Hopefully, we could opt to tent out. We were to find out that there was no water to be had *until* we reached the shelter. Leaving us little choice, we made the effort and finally made it. David was dead tired at the end, and Mina was in pure misery for the last four to five miles. Finally, David left Mina 0.7 miles from the shelter, was going on to the shelter to drop his pack, and come back to get Mina's pack. She did not wait. After a short rest and a change of socks, she came on the path to the shelter. David met her 0.3 miles down and was going to carry her pack, but one of the men at the shelter must have seen just how tired David looked, followed him down and brought back Mina's pack. David did not argue.

It was a nice day, mostly smooth hiking with only a few rocks, but just long for the second day of hiking. This is a nice shelter, we have good company, and a nice spring is located nearby. The day was rather cool but definitely a "plus" day.

June 11, 2001   Loft Mountain Campground
                                       Trail Distance: 7.4 miles

Last evening, everyone seemed tired. Some had talked and joked the prior evening *after* they had hit their sleeping bags. Not so this evening! By 9 P.M., we were all in our bags and *quiet*! The first chuck-wills-widow opened up at about 9:10 P.M. from a distance of about fifteen feet from our feet. These birds are a little easier to take then a whip-poor-will but not much. After a half dozen calls or so, we frightened him off for a while. He came back about ten minutes later and sat about *ten* feet from our feet. *This* time, we all put up an uproar, and he moved for the night. During the night, we could hear several others "singing" in the distance. Again, no mice disturbed us. There *was* one rat that sounded as if he was trying to gnaw through the flooring under Mina's head. She peeked through the flooring and saw him peeking back. We are not sure just who frightened whom the most! He then left and kept quiet.

This was not meant to be a long day. Mina really needed to rest up from yesterday. As it was, we covered 7.4 miles, mostly rather level. Our plans were to go into a camp ground for water, a shower, and a promised restaurant. After looking it over and liking what we saw, we decided to spend the night. Our tent site was close to restrooms, we had plenty of water, we got our showers ($1 for five minutes), but there were no restaurants. The closest was a hamburger place a "little way" down the road. A lady whom Mina met drove us there and said it was half a mile down. When we got there, a sign said it was 1.3 miles *back*! After a bit of mix-up on which way to go, we fortunately got a ride back. It was another beautiful day, temperatures in the 80s, with a nice, cool breeze. A person can still build up a sweat doing the uphills. Even the basically level areas have *some* hills in them.

One fellow that shared shelters with us for the last two nights opted out of hiking today and hitched a ride out. The Skyline drive is always close and we crisscross it frequently. So, going to the road is no problem. Doug has diabetes, and it was acting up on him. We will miss him. He is a nice guy and was good company.

This was a relatively easy day, and Mina felt much better, even at the end of the day. We were able to get some laundry done and were able to see (at least for us) many new species of birds. With no bird book, we had no idea of what kinds they were. So far, there are no mosquitoes, but the gnats are really a pest. They seem to especially like David. Does he perhaps smell better than Mina, or is it the opposite? This was a nice day, a nice hike and a nice campsite. Things look good!

June 12, 2001   Pinefield Gap Shelter
                       Trail Distance: 5.8 miles

We think the short hikes are paying off. Mina is feeling much better, no more hip problems, and her state of exhaustion is much more acceptable. She gets tired, as does David, after even a short day of hiking. We left this morning at 8:15 and made the shelter at 12:20. We both could have gone further, but there was nothing to prove and there just may not be much, if any water, between this shelter and the next. The next shelter appears to have its share of "uphills", and that may be enough for us for one day. We have had some good level stretches, and they look like interstates to us. We are both feeling stronger, and the rest stops are getting to be fewer and shorter.

This is a very nice shelter, sleeps about fourteen, and we do expect company. We got in early and cooked a lunch rather than having our staple Logan Bread and gorp. Also, a nice nap helped the mood.

Some local hiking scouts called our attention to a bear in a nearby tree. When we inspected the site, we found two cubs in the tree and a mother with another cub in a nearby stream. Needless to say, we kept our distance. She later moved as later hikers reported that they had seen nothing. We feel that it is rather rare for a mother to have three cubs; I think that she had her "hands" full.

We *will* keep our food up a bear pole tonight. The bear pole is a new one for us. It is a metal pole extending about thirteen to fifteen feet high with four short metal prongs extending from the top. With another long pole with a "V" at the top, we can hang our food items out of reach of the bears. It can sometimes be rather a problem in getting the food up *and* being able to get it back down. It may sound simple enough, but handling twenty-plus pounds of food at the end of a twelve-foot pool does require a delicate balance.

This shelter is very near to two streams that meet, it has plenty of water, there are nearby prepared tent sites, and it comes with a lovely privy. It is strictly "three-star" quality.

We saw and heard two veerys today, David's first time seeing them. He had heard them plenty of times while hiking in the past but was never able to see any. Their singing also intrigues Mina. It is so different! Perhaps there are other birds that can harmonize with themselves, but these are the only ones that we have heard. They sound something like echoes in a spiraling drainpipe. It is really an intriguing and beautiful song.

The last shelter was another quiet one, with no mice and no snoring. Sure hope that it continues. We saw many deer including one doe nursing her young twins. We saw a couple that look like they may be 2-year-old fawns. They were not very small but not quite adults either. One hiker reported seeing a rattlesnake on the trail and took some effort trying to convince it to move. It was gone by the time that we passed. We assume that it was gone; we did not see it.

We passed some beautiful lookout points on the Trail. These are viewing spots that only a hiker can see. The road does have some nice ones, but the best are reserved for the hikers. Looking out over the mountains, we can see that they very much resemble the Smokies. They are hazy and extend as far as the eye can see (at certain locations). They may be two thousand feet lower in altitude, but you cannot tell that by looking down on them.

June 13, 2001   Hightop Hut
                          Trail Distance: 8.5 miles

We had a nice quiet night with no mice and no chuck-wills-widows and no night sounds at all. (Light snoring does not count). We do not know just how many there are sharing the shelter and the tents. We probably number sixteen to twenty in all.

As usual, we were the first ones up, 6:00 A.M., and wide awake. This was to be a relatively short day but strenuous. As it turned out, we hiked only five hours, including breaks and a lunch stop. We arrived at our selected shelter at 12:50 P.M., and others slowly joined us. Some just showed up for water and kept going. It is now 3:20 P.M., and Pork Chops and Cara, the two young women who were with us in the shelter last night, are here now taking naps. They may go on, but the current sound of thunder just may convince them to stay the night. They have a mutt dog, Frankie, that one of their friends had found on the Trail, and she fits in nicely. The dog is quiet and friendly and glad to have a home, such as it is. With her little backpack, she loves the Trail.

All of the shelters that we have encountered so far in the park have privies, and all seem to follow the same design. They are functional and welcomed. This is a far cry from the facilities that David found when he first started hiking on the Trail. At that time, privies were few and very far between. Everyone had to carry his or her very own spade and know how to use it.

We saw more deer today. Mina met a big buck in her path, but he did not argue with her. With no hesitation, he gave her the right of way! Other wildlife seems to be a bit scarce. The ticks, though, are a bloody problem! Every day, someone picks ticks off him or her. The dogs—and there are several that we have met—really collect them. One owner claims to pick twenty to thirty off her dog every day. And these are just the ones that she is able to find! With their hair, there must be more not seen. Some of these ticks are so tiny that they could hide almost anywhere on the body. These are the really dangerous ones. Deer Ticks are tiny, maybe one of the smallest varieties. Some hikers, even the careful ones, can come down with deer tick fever. It is not a nice thing to catch. We have been informed that a deer tick has to remain on a body for about forty-eight hours in order for the disease to be transmitted. Therefore, a close, daily inspection of all of the body is mandatory.

Tomorrow is scheduled for twelve and a half miles. We both feel that we are up to that now. Each day is easier, and each day the "ups" are easier to take. We still don't like them, but at least we can handle them.

Our meals are still basically what we have had in the past. Breakfast is "Grape Nuts" for David and "Total" for Mina along with milk prepared the night before. The morning break is gorp (many kinds of nuts, fruits, and raisins); lunch is a hunk of Logan Bread and more gorp. Supper is a bowl of Ramon soup frequently garnished with dried vegetables, hot chocolate and/or hot tea, a serving of rice and beans or mashed potatoes and gravy, and finished with an instant pudding. When we get a chance at a restaurant, we really "pig out". We know that we cannot eat more calories than we use. For anyone *seriously* considering loosing weight, we recommend hiking a few weeks on the A.T. It may be rough, but we guarantee you to lose weight.

Dave has picked up a hoarse throat in the past few days. The throat is not sore, but it sounds as if it should be. Mina is back in fine shape with no aches, no pains, and no problems. Neither has had any blister problems.

June 14, 2001   Lewis Mountain Campground
Trail Distance: 11.6 miles

We had heard some thunder late yesterday afternoon. Sure enough, we got some rain later in the day and evening. It was not much, but it did convince Pork Chops and Cara to stay the night in the shelter. There were only five in the shelter and three more tenting.

This was a good day for hiking. It was a bit cool and the ups and downs were not too bad. Still, the 11.6 miles began to get a mite long around the ten-mile mark. There were some fantastic views that only hikers can see. Autos have some good views, but the best are reserved for the hikers. Hightop Mountain had just super views. Sure hope the camera caught some of them. There were no deer today, and no night sounds last night. The bird life is songful, but the night birds are quiet. We did see a couple of mice just about the time that we turned in. We then shared our mothballs with all in the shelter, and no one was bothered by the little critters during the night.

We had noticed some sawdust in one corner of the shelter and swept it up. The next morning, there was a good one-fourth of a cup of sawdust in the spot that we had swept. We then inspected and found a colony of wood-boring beetles. At the rate they were going, they could consume the shelter in a season or so. We will notify the PATC as soon as we find out who and how to call. Something has to be done, but we do not know just what. Sure hope someone else does.

Rather than going on an extra 0.9 miles to the next shelter, we opted to rent a cabin in the campground. They had no cabins for just two people, so we had to rent a cabin with two bedrooms. It seemed a shame to just waste the extra bedroom so we offered it to Pork Chops and Cara. They were the two young women that we made reference to earlier. At no cost to them and no additional cost to us, they got a nice bedroom and indoor plumbing. This will keep them indoors tonight, and it may be a bonus to them. The next shelter is scheduled to be full, and we may get some more storms tonight. The wind has really picked up, and the sky is not pretty. They are both a delight to have around. Pork Chops and Frankie are planning to complete the Trail this year, and we do wish them the best. Hopefully, our paths will cross in the future.

The store at the campground left something to be desired. However, we were able to partially replenish our supplies. We will pass Big Meadows tomorrow and get more supplies. Hopefully, tomorrow will be a dry day. It is scheduled to be a long one and the next day even longer. We just take them as they come. They do get a bit easier.

As we deplete the food, the packs get lighter and easier to carry. That helps when the day's mileage gets longer. If we want a lighter load, we just eat more!

At least we do not have to be bothered by mice tonight, so we do not have to spread our mothballs around. That soft bed without a sleeping bag on it sure looks inviting.

June 15, 2001   Rock Spring Hut
Trail Distance: 12.3 miles

We knew that we would get rain eventually, and today was it! We had two hours of light to moderate rain and sometimes it got heavy. We did not put our rain gear on as it was not worth it, and we would get just as wet. After an hour or so delay, it started raining again, and we had light rain the rest of the day.

We made the Big Meadows Wayside at noon and stopped for a super spaghetti meal with soup, meatballs, and hot chocolate. A grocery store was nearby, and we were able to completely replenish our food supplies. We now have sufficient supplies to get us out of the park, which is scheduled three days from now.

Tomorrow is to be our longest day to date. It is 15.1 miles and is reported to be very rocky. I think that we are in shape or at least sufficiently to complete it. Today, we started at 7:20 A.M. and finished at 4:45 P.M. That included about two hours off at Big Meadows. We shall see what tomorrow brings.

Today, we saw and heard wild turkeys and saw another doe nursing her young. Seeing them in a zoo is one thing, but seeing them in the wild is a memorable sight.

This evening, two park rangers visited us. They were checking to make certain that every one had a park pass and were in the proper tent sites. Pork Chops got a warning, as Frankie was not on a leash. That dog is better behaved and better controlled than *any* dog that I have seen on a leash. The rangers were friendly, however, but insisted on "rules" being followed. They stayed to visit, and we all had long chats with them. We found them to be knowledgeable, conscientious, and most helpful. They had answers to most all of our questions.

This is another nice shelter, and we will have plenty of company this evening. Our wet clothes may dry out, but I doubt it.

June 16, 2001   Thornton Gap
Trail Distance: 13.9 miles

This was not a nice day! It was long, it was continually wet with heavy rain, and it was *very* rocky most of the way. These were fist—to head-sized rocks, and they *were* the Trail. There may have been times in the past when we may have had a few hundred yards of rocks, but today we had fourteen miles of them. David's feet got sore, but Mina got several blisters and a few bruises. Her soles on her boots were thinner than were David's and that made for some rough hiking over the sharp rocks. Normally, we could have had some good views, but the clouds completely socked them in.

As rough as the Trail was, we had to admire the work done just to *make* the trail. Without the help of the CCC boys back in the 1930s, this trail would have had many ups and downs as it wove around many rock formations at the crest level. As it was, the CCC had leveled out the trail by building it up with rocks so that the actual trail was fairly level. It had to have been hard, physical labor as in many places the built-up trail was as much as ten feet above the ground below. They did a beautiful job of making the trail level. They probably filled in the top of the trail with gravel and soil to make it smooth in addition to being level. However, time and foot travel has washed away the top of the trail, leaving sharp, pointed rocks to walk on. Looking at the degree of work that was done, we know the CCC did not purposely leave the sharp rocks on top that now remain. By looking and noticing, a person cannot help but admire the work done by the early CCC.

We had hoped to make the next shelter, but had to give up at Thornton Gap. The last few miles were especially rough on Mina. She was in constant pain but continued as there was just no place to stop. Finally arriving at Thornton Gap, we were able to get a good meal and, later, a ride to Luray, Virginia.

Being wet all day got both David and Mina a bit chilled. Dry clothes and a shower made us both feel better.

We got to see a young buck that didn't look to be older than about two, but he was sporting two very short antlers, probably his first. He seemed so proud of them.

June 17, 2001   Pass Mountain Hut
Trail Distance: 1.2 miles

After leaving the A.T. yesterday, we had thoughts of just quitting. Mina's feet are in pretty bad shape from wet socks and boots, and she is exhausted by the ten-mile mark. We did have a good night's sleep, visited the Laundromat and the pharmacy. We got some medications for Mina's feet and will try them out. David had been told of the Luray Caverns, which are located about two miles from the motel. We checked out, got permission to leave our backpacks at the motel, and hiked to the caverns. They were just fantastic and well worth the walk. Actually, we would have missed them if we had not been required to leave the Trail. These caverns are highly recommended to any who may be even remotely close to the area. Hikers should take a day off, get rested, and have a wonderful viewing experience.

After walking back to the motel, we collected our packs, crossed

the street, stuck our thumbs out, and the very first car that came
by stopped and agreed to take us to the main highway going back
to Thornton Gap. When he got to the highway, he did not stop.
Maybe he liked our looks or Mina's talking, but he took us directly
to the A.T. marker at the side of the road up at Thornton Gap. He
was a gem! Hitchhiking is new to Mina, but it is accepted practice
near Trail towns. Many drivers may pass David by, but they will
stop for Mina!

We then hiked up to the shelter which was not far *and* was
generally void of the kind of rocks that we had met the day
before. David had told Mina that if her feet did not feel up to
it that they would hike back down to the Gap and not continue.
It was a short and relatively easy hike to the shelter. With clean
clothes and feet feeling better, the decision was made to
continue the next day.

Later, a young man and his male friend stopped by and stayed
the night. The young man stated that he was getting married July 8
and was going to have a bachelor party at the shelter. He claimed to
have hiked the complete trail twice and wanted to celebrate amongst
the kind of people that he was familiar with. With the help of one of
the other men at the shelter, they walked back 0.3 miles to his truck
and brought back a big cooler of pop, beer, and wine. I do not know
just how much beer there was, but there were six liters of wine. As it
turned out, there were only six of us at the shelter *including* the two
young men with the cooler. They had also brought turkey sandwiches
so there was more than enough of everything to go around. This
night was another with no mice to bother anyone.

June 18, 2001   Gravel Springs Hut
                                Trail Distance: 13.1 miles

This was a beautiful day with some fine viewing spots and
beautiful scenes. By the time that we got to Hogwallow Gap at
7.4 miles, we were both tired and hungry. We opted to get some
cheeseburgers and fries washed down with iced tea. David took a
short nap on the grass before the hike was resumed.

It was still a long day, and Mina's feet really gave her pain again. Somehow, David pulled his back out of alignment, and *he* was in pain. We limped into the shelter about 7:00 P.M. and made a hasty supper. To top it off, we had a restless night and were pestered by some kind of biting insects. They did not seem to be mosquitoes as there were no buzzing sounds, but everything that was not covered got bitten. This included the hands, feet, and head. It was not a fun night!

June 19, 2001	Compton Gap Trail Distance: 7.6 miles

This was to be our last day on the A.T. as we expected to complete the park and leave the Trail by a highway into the nearest town. David's back acted OK, but Mina's feet were a real problem. She had blisters on top of blisters. When we came to Compton Gap, she asked to leave the Trail right then. It was another 4.5 miles to the road that we had planned on leaving by. So, we rested, had some water, went across the road stuck our thumbs out, and the very first car that came by stopped and was able to drive us over one hundred miles back to the spot where we had left *our* car. Our hosts were an elderly couple who were former hikers and we were really able to enjoy each other's company. We were really lucky. If we had gone on to the road that we had earlier planned on, we may still be one hundred miles from *here* trying to *get* here. It really was a nice day. Tomorrow or the next day, we will decide on whether to continue.

June 20, 2001	Front Royal, VA Trail Distance: 0.0 miles

We took the day off! Mina's feet were a mess, and we could not continue with them. A shower, nice dinner, and a good night's sleep readied us for a visit to Thomas Jefferson's Monticello. This place is a "must" for anyone, and especially any Americans, who can make it. David had known that Mr. Jefferson was a great man and multi-talented. He has to confess, though, that he had no idea of just *how* great and talented he actually was. We spent about five hours at Monticello and only got a glimmering of his talents. One of the things that David admired the most was his taste in foods. His favorite vegetable was English Peas, as is David's, but Mr. Jefferson grew twenty varieties of them! David would really like to try all of them.

Our initial plans were to finish hiking Shenandoah National Park and then go back to Pearisburg, Virginia, and complete part of the two hundred-plus miles of Virginia that we had not done earlier in the year. However, Mina made the comment that she had always wanted to hike on the A.T. to Harpers Ferry, West Virginia, the national headquarters of the Appalachian Trail Conference. Several years ago, she and her family had visited Harpers Ferry, and she had a picture taken of herself standing by an A.T. marker there. She then had mentioned to her daughter that she wanted to hike the Trail and her daughter commented, "Oh, Mother"! This gave us a subject to discuss, and the outcome was that if we continued hiking, we would *not* go back to Pearisburg this trip but would continue on to Harpers Ferry. Our available time should permit it.

After visiting Monticello, we drove to Front Royal, a small town near to the northern boundary of the Shenandoah Park. The idea was to stay another day in the area in the hopes that Mina's feet would get better. The outlook was scheduled rain, which it did! We relaxed, got our laundry done, had another good meal, and topped it off with another good night's sleep.

June 21, 2002   Front Royal, VA
                                 Trail Distance: 5.9 miles

Mina's feet were getting better. We had put enough stuff on her blisters to control them. As a test, we "slack packed" from the point where we had left the Trail up to a highway further north. The term "slack pack" refers to hiking *without* a backpack. It is easier and legal for true through hikers to do, but there is seldom the opportunity to do so. David drove Mina to the highway crossing of the A.T. and let her out. He then drove fifteen miles back to town and then up the Skyline Drive in the park to the parking area where they had left the Trail a couple of days back. David then hiked north while Mina hiked south. When they met, keys were exchanged, and David continued to hike north until he reached the highway. He had to wait only a short time before Mina came in the car to pick him up.

Mina's feet held up so the decision was made to continue hiking. Yes, it rained this night and the weather report indicated three more days of scattered thunderstorms and rain. We will wait until tomorrow to see if things look any better.

June 22, 2001 Manassas Gap Shelter
          Trail Distance: 10.8 miles

The forecast did not change, but the weather looked good. There was a shelter 5.3 miles up the Trail so we figured that if it started to rain, we could get an early shelter. Just starting out, the Trail bordered a four-thousand-acre wildlife preserve belonging to the Research and Conservation Center which itself belongs to the National Zoological Park, an agency of the Smithsonian Institution. At times, there are exotic animals to be viewed from the Trail, but none were visible when we hiked by. The weather continued to look good, although overcast, but it did start to thunder in the distance. We figured, "what the heck; let's go for it!" So we went to the second shelter. Our time was good and we made the shelter about 3:15 P.M.

There were several signs posted warning us of copperheads seen near the shelter including a sighting of three the day before. That was plural copperheads so we watched our steps and did some close looking. We did not see any, but we acted as if they were there and let them be. We have been told that copperheads love mice so they may not bother us tonight. Frankly, we would rather rely on our mothballs than a nest of copperheads to control the mice.

Today, we were hiking along the northern boundary of the area patrolled by the Confederate Col. Mosby, "The Grey Ghost". To tell the truth, we do not see why anyone would even *want* this area. It is wild! We have not seen any deer for a few days now. With us being out of the park and hunting allowed, deer just may be a bit more cautious in these parts.

About 4:55 P.M. the rain started, and it was wild and windy. It only rained until 5:30 P.M., but we were glad that we were in the shelter and cooking inside.

We planned out the next four days, and tomorrow is due to be a long one. Surprisingly, we have not seen any ticks for the past several days. There were so many in the lower Park and none in the northern part. Maybe we are just lucky.

June 23, 2001   Rod Hollow Shelter
Trail Distance: 13.6 miles

We had more rain last evening, and it continued on and off all evening. Neither David nor Mina could get much sleep. We just could not get comfortable. Then there was the guy next to David who snored, very heartily, all evening.

This day was a bummer! It started out cloudy, foggy, and threatened to rain. We decided to go on anyway but with full rain gear on. Sure enough, it started raining about a half hour after we started and continued lightly until early afternoon. We did make fairly good time at least until midafternoon. Then Mina's feet started acting up again. She is now good for about ten miles, and then the feet start to hurt. The mileage markers seem to be guesses. Today, we either hiked 13.6 miles or 14.2 miles or somewhere in between.

This shelter has something like thirteen people either in the shelter or tenting nearby. It is a neat shelter with a nearby privy and a very nice spring. But by the time that we arrived, we were both bushed. Our suppers are fairly standard but we really look forward to them.

Tomorrow may be a bit rough. It is known as the "Devil's

Roller Coaster". It consists of something like seventeen hills and valleys scattered over ten miles. Neither of us like the ups and downs. Tomorrow, we will have nothing *but* ups and downs. Sure hope that we can cut it as the next shelter is a hostel with a great reputation.

June 24, 2001   Bears Den Hostel
Trail Distance: 10.0 miles

Last evening was an interesting one. There were about a dozen people including a southbound honeymooning couple. In one of the posts holding up the wooden roof over the outdoors table, a wren couple had built a nest in a hole about two feet off the ground. At first, we just noticed the wrens getting close to us, and then we saw them go into the hole in the post. When they flew off, we examined the hole and found three young wrens inside. We then tried to give the parents a little room so that they could continue feeding their offspring. They were a very industrious pair and continued to work until almost dark.

The honeymooning couple had stated that they had started hiking with a seventy-five-pound pack for the woman and a nintey-five-pound pack for the man. Those are heavy packs! However, it did not take them long to discover that many of their "necessary" supplies were not quite so necessary after all. The recommended pack weights are no heavier than about one-fourth of a person's body weight. It would seem that if a person is overweight, then to the extent that they are overweight, that excess should be counted in their allotted pack weight.

The Trail today was not as tough as billed, but still rough enough. There were nine hills to go up and naturally go down. Some of the "downs" were rougher than the "ups". By the bottom of the approach to hill #9, Mina just ran out of steam. It was rough enough for David. When we saw the sign pointing to the hostel, it was welcome indeed.

This is by far the nicest hostel that we have seen or even heard of. It occupies a home that would be in the million-dollar range anywhere. It is a truly beautiful place! There are coed rooms plus separate dormitories for males and females. Fully equipped kitchen plus laundry facilities along with a nice dining room and reading room add to the amenities. Other hikers have left unneeded food here so there are plenty of snacks available. Two young ladies manage the place, and they seem to do a super job. The daily fee is $12 for A.T.C. members, and it is most reasonable. Although the hostel is owned by the A.T.C., it is available to others, and there were non-members using the facilities.

The name "Bears Den" refers to a site of many very large boulders making a place where bears could have easily "denned up" in past winters. Now, the boulders make a great viewing spot overlooking the valley below. This is very close to the hostel and well worth the time to visit.

The next two days are due to be somewhat more hikeable. Hopefully, the A.T. will run out of rocks. We both are sure tired of climbing up, over, around, and down rocks. This isn't hiking; it's a bloody obstacle course!

June 25, 2001   David Lesser Shelter
Trail Distance: 11.2 miles

We sure hated to leave the hostel today. It was really neat with a beautiful home, a truly gorgeous landscaped lawn, and everything designed for the hiker. Hikers leave excess food and local residents add to the offerings. We had not only our food but we were free to take anything in the "to share" shelves.

Hiking today was not too bad. The morning saw about three hours of up and downs, and the afternoon was relatively flat along with the standard rocks on the Trail. Early on, we came to Crescent Rock, a fine and interesting viewing point. Later, we passed the Devils Racecourse, a boulder field with a small stream running beneath the rocks. It was an exciting day.

This shelter was built in 1991 in memory of David Lesser. It is a nice shelter. However, the water is a quarter mile way down the hill. It *is* way down, and it *is* steep. We filled everything that would hold water so we would not have to make the trip twice. The dirty dishes will wait to get washed until water is closer.

Tomorrow will get us into Harpers Ferry and the end of the Trail for us. We will probably take an extra day to see the town before we try to get back to our car and the ride home.

This shelter has a privy with a bird's nest right on the side of the privy. Of all of the trees around here, these birds seem to want to build near people. Sure hope they can raise their three eggs without too much interference.

The nights still get rather chilly. By 9:00 P.M., when we generally turn in for the night, the warmth of the sleeping bags really feels good.

We are seeing and hearing very little wildlife. Even the birds are more subdued. Mice still have not bothered us. It is now 8:00 P.M., the light is fading, and David still has some chores to complete.

June 26, 2001   Harpers Ferry Hostel
                           Trail Distance: 11.2 miles

This is to be our last day on the A.T., and it proved to be a nice one. The terrain was relatively level and just a few simple "ups" and "downs". There was no outside scenery except for the relatively constant forests. The solitude and beauty of the forests are a joy. They are always there but in a constantly changing format. Sometimes you are in the middle of an oak forest, then in a black walnut forest, pine forests and a general mixture of them all. You do want more landscapes, mountains and valleys to view, rivers to see, and mountain balds to cross. In this part of the forests, there must have been some high winds when we had our recent thunderstorms. Several trees had blown down over the trail, and some still had unwilted leaves on them. They were fresh. So, almost daily, the part of the A.T. changes in order to conform to the blocked paths and to the whims of nature.

We easily reached Harpers Ferry by noon, signed in, got our standard pictures taken at the A.T. Headquarters, got Mina a

membership card, reported the wood-boring beetle problems, and chatted with the staff. We registered as section hikers as we still had not made a decision to finish the Trail. Nearby, we got another spaghetti-and-meatball dinner and later topped off with double dip ice-cream cones. That was probably our last ice cream for many moons to come. We just don't get any at home (not allowed). Surprisingly, we met up again with Pork Chops, her parents, and Frankie. She had taken a couple of days off from hiking, and her parents had come up to visit with her. After a short visit, she and Frankie continued on their way to Maine. We both do hope that they are able to complete the Trail. They have worked hard for the thrill of completion!

We are staying at the Harpers Ferry Hostel, which is a few miles from Harpers Ferry located in Sandy Hook, Maryland. It is a nice hostel but nothing compared to Bears Den. Arriving here was rather interesting. The path to the hostel crossed a railroad track as it has in many places. However, this track had a train on it! It was a *long* train, and we could not see either end of it. Standing there and looking puzzled, a man approached and said that if we wanted to go across the tracks, we would have to climb over the train. He said not to worry as a train is usually parked there and it "probably" would not move. That gave us some reassurance as we climbed over the cars with our packs hoping that we would not feel a sudden jarring of a moving train. It would have been rather exciting to hang on to the cars wearing our backpacks. We may not have looked too athletic, but we did get across. Oh, the places that David takes Mina!

We had earlier made arrangements with a man living across the street from the hostel to drive us back to our car in Front Royal. We feel sure that we could get a ride by "thumbing it", but there is a limit (really) to the things that David can ask Mina to do.

A shower and clean clothes *do* make a difference even after only two days. Actually, a hiker needs a shower at noon *and* before his supper. A person can really get sticky on the A.T. even on nice and level hiking days.

Where the A.T. came into Harpers Ferry, it paralleled one of the redoubts built by and abandoned by the Federals in our Civil War. A redoubt is a huge trench, dug something like six to ten feet deep in very rocky soil. That soil had to be 80 percent rock, and the rocks had to weigh up to several hundred pounds each. Somebody really had to work! It does not take too much looking to see many evidences of the Civil War. Much of the landscape has been permanently changed.

Our ride will be here at 8:00 A.M. and we must be ready for him. We both have the strong feeling that he will be going to "talk our ears off". Just to say "hello" to him took a half hour, and we *still* did not get a chance to say hello! At any rate, our little car will be a welcome sight. We were correct; he talked non-stop the whole way back. We do have respect for him, though, as he is honest, fair, and basically a truly good guy.

Mina got through today with no blister complaints and without feeling exhausted. She *is* getting into shape for the A.T. even if she does not feel it. David had gotten through with no blisters, no foot problems, and no knee problems. In general, he is feeling better on leaving the Trail than at any time in the past. He does not understand about the knees. They were always a problem in earlier years but absolutely none now! He does not understand it but sure does accept it. He will never be in super shape, but he does feel better, stronger, and healthier than he felt ten years ago. Prior preparation of the A.T. *does* have its rewards.

David total A.T. to date: 774.6 miles

Mina total A.T. to date: 277.8 miles

CHAPTER SEVEN

September 14, 2001   Preliminary to Hike

Plans that had been made weeks earlier had to be changed for this hike. David and Mina had plane reservations to fly to Baltimore on September 15. From there, arrangements had been made for a shuttle driver to pick us up and drive us to Harpers Ferry, West Virginia. That was the point where we had left the Trail earlier in the year. Unfortunately, the September 11 terrorist attack had closed the airports, and plane traffic was not back to normal. We were left with a choice of canceling the hike, postponing it, or driving to Harpers Ferry. Since this was the only feasible time to take the hike for this year, the decision was made to drive.

Mina had been ill for several days, and she was still not fully recovered. Fever and general weakness had kept her in bed for a couple of days. She thought that she was much better and wanted to proceed. Doing nothing for a full day should put her back into hiking order.

The weather was not really cooperating. Tropical storm Gabriel was due to come ashore a few miles south of Clearwater, and it was packing some heavy winds and plenty of rain. Some fast packing was done and the day that had been scheduled for making sure that everything was in order for the hike became the day that we started driving north very early in the morning. We really wanted to get ahead of the storm, as a delay would probably require us to wait until it had completely passed. It had already started to rain when we left, and the rain and wind were fast getting heavier. As it was, it rained all of the way to South Carolina, and it did make for some slow driving. The rain seemed to be in fingers of the storm. There would be heavy rain, it would slack off, then get heavy, and continued in that manner.

We had thought that we could make it all of the way to Harpers Ferry on this day, but the slow driving required us to stop in Virginia for the night.

Sept. 15, 2001   Ed Garvey Shelter
                                Trail Distance: 5.0 miles

We did not arrive in Harpers Ferry until 1:00 P.M. We finalized getting our trail supplies and checked into the ATC headquarters to get an update on the Trail. We found that there was a new shelter that was not listed on the maps, so we decided to stop there for our first night. We left our car at the home of a shuttle driver who had helped us in June. Our plans were to call him when we finished our hike and to have him drive up and bring us back to our car. He was agreeable to that as it gave him a little extra money and it would sure help us.

Mina was still not feeling up to par but thought that she could do the first days hike as it was supposed to be only about three miles to the new shelter. Actually, it turned out to be more like five miles. It was a long five miles as it took us four hours to complete. Mina was weak, had stomach cramps, and was generally not comfortable. The hike was easy enough for someone in good condition, but Mina overestimated her physical strength. She was just not up to it!

This new shelter was beautiful! It had an entirely different design, had two floors with the second story entered by stairs in the rear. As with several shelters on the Trail, it was constructed in memory of an avid hiker and enthusiast of the Trail. Later, two other hikers, both short-term hikers, and both leaving the trail the next day joined us.

Sept. 16, 2001   Rocky Run Shelter
                                Trail Distance: 9.3 miles

Normally up by 6:00 A.M., we stayed in our bags until 7:00 A.M. It stays dark longer in September than in June, and neither of us likes to get up in the dark. It just kind of dampens the whole day. Mina was still not up to par. We had stopped at a pharmacy in Virginia, and the medication did help. However, she still had periodic cramps. The Trail was still rather easy but very rocky again. I suppose that the Trail was smooth to begin with, but thousands of hikers plus rain just washes the soil away. It is just no fun hiking on rocks! We continued taking it easy with frequent stops to rest.

The Trail took us through Crampton Gap where General Lee's army tried to invade Maryland. One unusual aspect was a fifty-foot-tall stone memorial to Civil War newspaper correspondents. It was a beautiful memorial and the only one to our knowledge dedicated to those persons.

This shelter is most unusual. A person cannot stand upright in it! There is only room for six bags and woe befall the first person to try to stand in the middle of the night. "Head Room" is only about four-feet high with a low of about three-feet. The shelter is on a side path of about a half mile long. It took a little hike just to get here. There is a nice-flowing stream next to the shelter, so water is plentiful and close. Built in 1941, the shelter is beginning to show its age. The basic construction is solid, although odd, but the outside benches and woodwork have seen better days, many better days.

We see various birds along the Trail but hear little. They are here but do not advertise the fact.

This shelter is down in a little valley, and we had to pass what we took to be battlements from the Civil War. There were many stone barriers and, left undisturbed, will probably last indefinitely.

Mina is eating somewhat better, but our next couple of days are planned to be short ones. We are in no hurry, and there is no sense in pushing someone past their physical ability. The days have been warm with the night's cool. It makes for good hiking weather, and we are both hoping that it will continue. An early winter is not desired.

At this time of year, there are noticeably fewer hikers. We had only one other hiker stop for the night, and he will be tenting. After seeing this shelter, we really do not blame him.

Sept. 17, 2001   Pine Knob Shelter
                                  Trail Distance: 7.5 miles

This was to be a short day so we took it easy. Up late with a leisurely breakfast, we hiked 1.5 miles to a hot shower facility built strictly for hikers and located right beside the Trail. Maryland is neat! This was the first of its kind that we have seen. Believe me, it came in handy. After getting and feeling clean, we continued.

The A.T. went directly through the Washington Monument State Park and fine views were to be seen from the top of the massive stone monument. Built by local citizens in 1827, it has been maintained and restored to its original condition. Used by the Union Army in the Civil War for an observation post, it does give a super view of the surrounding countryside.

The going is still slow as Mina is still not up to par. She is weak and tires easily. A reader might ask, "Why don't you both quit"? David does not believe that Mina ever considered quitting. It is always, "Wow, I feel better. Let's go on"! We did continue to take many rest stops. We did decide to visit a doctor or a health clinic in the first town that we come to. That may be tomorrow evening. It cannot be any fun feeling less than good. The A.T. is rough enough as it is for a person that is feeling good. Anything less can be pure misery.

The spring at this shelter has just about had it! Someone dug a hole in the path to collect water, and it did collect some. That is correct; the water hole is directly in the path. This is one spot where a water filter is a must. Even so, we had to clean the filter twice before we got our supply of water for the night. The shelter is much like the last one. It is basically the same design but could be even older.

A young man is also here but will be tenting out. Many prefer to tent even when there is room in the shelters and the shelters are nice. Oh well, to each his own! This shelter is fairly close to the highway, and the highway noise is easily heard. This is rather strange as most shelters are far from any road. We do not think that it will interfere with our sleeping, though. It will take more than a little road noise to keep us awake.

Unlike our summer hiking, the days are much shorter. It gets dark sooner and it is noticeably cooler. Our sweatsuits really come in handy in the evening. We have not seen too many serious hikers. There are some, but not many. There are, however, many day hikers, some out for just the day and some out for a few hours. The A.T. welcomes them all.

We are not sure just where we will go tomorrow. The A.T. Data Book lists one shelter and our map shows a different one about a mile apart. Both the book and the map are current so we will just have to wait and see. Sometimes things get changed, added, or deleted, and it takes a while for the publications to be brought up to date. We have encountered several instances of this. It is just one of those things that we have to accept and live with.

Sept. 18, 2001   Ensign Philip Cowall Shelter
Trail Distance: 8.1 miles

Our 2001 Data Book was correct. Our map, although new, is out dated. The Hemlock Hill Shelter is no more. It has been replaced by the Ensign Cowall Sehelter as a memorial to that individual. A very nice shelter, it is hoped that it will provide comfort for many years to come to many thousands of hikers. It was a relatively easy day of hiking. The weather continues warm and dry. Even last night was relatively warm.

One of the nicest viewpoints that we have seen in several days was at Annapolis Rocks. We dropped our packs and walked down a quarter mile to the view. It was nice and well worth the side trip. Further on, we came to Black Rocks Cliffs, another fine viewing point. The big problem at Black Rocks Cliffs is the very rocky trail. Big rocks *are* the Trail, and these cover a good quarter mile. Difficult and treacherous, the rocky trail was no fun.

We met three ladies in our age group who were section hiking the Trail much like us. They said that there were six more of them, they had been section hiking for about fourteen years, and were close to completing the Trail. It was a pleasant meeting for all of us.

Mina had thought earlier that she might need to see a doctor.

As the day wore on, she felt better and better and decided not to. We were going into town anyway so it would not have been out of our way. We wanted a hot meal, restaurant style. Thinking that we could easily hitch a ride into town, we were disappointed and had to hike it. After about a mile, we came to a little deli and opted for a fried chicken dinner. The "sit down" restaurant was still 1.4 miles further on. Interestingly enough, when we finished eating, enough people had stopped to talk to us about our backpacking that we had several offers to bring us back to the A.T. We accepted from a lady who waited until we had finished eating and then drove us right to the A.T. It was then only 0.2 miles to the shelter. We began to notice that the few times that we could not get a ride into a town, we had no problem in getting a ride back. People want to talk to us and then offer to drive us back to the Trail. It was a nice evening not having to cook. But we went through the water. Both of us drank twenty ounces with our meal. Since, we have each consumed another quart of water.

Tomorrow, we have a choice. It has to be either 4.5 miles or 14.1 miles. We know that we are not up to 14.1 miles so we will have to settle for the short hike of 4.5 miles.

The weather is holding nice. This area has not had any appreciable rain in weeks. We know that it needs it; we just wish that when it comes, it will come at night. Neither of us is in the mood for a cold, rainy hike. We are feeling better and stronger and wish to keep it that way. In the afternoon, we had tried to take naps on the Black Rock rocks. Neither of us slept, but we did get some rest. Then, it was on to this very nice shelter.

Sept. 19, 2001   Devils Racecourse Shelter
                                     Trail Distance: 4.5 miles

We had forgotten to mention yesterday that we had come upon a copperhead snake right on the Trail. The Trail was only a few feet wide at that section and David was on the right side and was almost past the snake without seeing it. Mina was on the left side and called out to David about the snake. It was on the left side and would not move. It was about two feet long, looked well fed, and was really a beauty. To alert others, we built a tripod of sticks, set it in the middle of the trail, and hoped that others would at least notice and look around for something. Later, we asked other hikers who were going the same way as we, but faster, if they had seen the snake. All had seen the tripod, looked for something unusual, but saw nothing. The snake and hikers remained safe.

For this day, we had been previously warned about a nest of yellow jackets whose nest was a hole in the middle of the Trail. Several had been stung by them as they were quite aggressive. Fortunately for us, we looked where we were told to look and found not one but three nests of yellow jackets. We then make a wide detour around them, marked their location with a big arrow, and later wrote their location on the shelter logbook. Of course, many hikers will pass by this shelter and miss the message. We really cannot blame them for passing by this shelter. It is 0.3 miles downhill, a very steep downhill, and reported to be with a dry spring. Several southbound hikers had told us of a dry spring and no water so we carried a two-day supply of water giving us an additional weight of about seven pounds. That seven pounds may not seem to be much, but it is in addition to our backpacks maxed out. This was a short but strenuous day. We were more than a little peeved when we found not only a spring but a free flowing wonderful little spring. So much for the honesty of the other hikers!

We had been so concerned about the lack of water here that we had refilled to maximum about three miles back of the Trail. We had passed a nice spring and creek and stopped for water refilling, a much needed bath, and clothes washing. This place was right on the Trail and next to a gravel road, but none passed as we got cleaned up. We needed the bath more than we needed to maintain our modesty. Our Monday morning shower was getting kind of "used up", and our limited supply of clean clothes had reached the bottom. All in all, we felt better. Now, all that we have to do is get our clothes dried. That may take more than a day.

Rain was predicted for today, and it has been looking like rain for most of the day. This area really needs it. We do hope that it gets it but after 8:00 P.M. and before 7:00 A.M. Sounds kind of choosy, doesn't it?

We have been in full forest all of the time except when crossing roads. We rarely leave the sound of road traffic so we know that the roads are always near to us. In some other states, we are usually many miles from any roads; Maryland is a bit different. I suppose that they do not have that much wilderness.

There is an interesting item near to the shelter. It is a "rock river". Formed millions of years ago when a rocky plateau was disturbed by geological forces, the rocks form a path about 150 feet wide on average and extend downhill at least a quarter mile. The rocks range in size from small fist-size ones to refrigerator-size boulders. Some are even larger and are too heavy to lift. There is soil and forest on both sides of the river, but nothing but rocks in the river. We understand that rains and freezing conditions actually cause the rocks to gradually slide down a very small amount. This whole thing is strange to look at, interesting to behold, and a sight not to be forgotten.

This shelter appears to be even older than some that we have visited so far. It is well kept up, but the logs are really old and weathered. We feel certain that the roof and flooring have been replaced. However, it was a welcome sight, even if it is 0.3 miles of rocky downhill to get here. We are not looking forward to have to climb out of here tomorrow. That kind of start does not put smiles on hikers' faces.

We saw a couple of young deer a few days ago and five deer in a person's yard when we went into town yesterday. Today, we came across a four-foot black racer snake in the Trail. Unlike the copperhead, he did not want our company. Also, he did not like to have his tail petted. Some animals are just rather touchy.

Since we came into the shelter early, we treated ourselves to a bowl of hot soup. It was good, thick, and welcome. Energy bars are good, gorp is always welcome, but hot soup really takes preference.

All of the shelters now seem to come equipped with a privy. Back when David first started hiking the A.T., privies were a rarity.

At that time, everyone had to carry a small spade. We must admit that we prefer the local privies.

This shelter is named after another rock field that we had to climb. There were plenty of rocks and boulders and much "ups". Devils Racecourse is well named!

Sept. 20, 2001   Deer Run Shelter
Trail Distance: 9.6 miles

This was not an easy day. The morning got us to Pen-Mar County Park, a beautiful place almost on the border with Pennsylvania. As soon as we arrived, it started to rain. We had our lunch in a picnic shelter, was able to purchase a couple of cans of pop, and Mina was able to take a short nap. Leaving there after lunch, we had our rain suits on and really perspired. That really fatigued us! After about an hour of going uphill and sweating like pigs, exhaustion forced us to take the rain pants off. That did help. We were then able to continue as it had almost stopped raining. The Trail continued to be very rocky, though, and that slowed us down. By being in our little sweat chambers, we both got to feeling mighty weak.

There earlier was a thought of going an extra 2.4 miles to the next shelter. But fatigue and Mother Nature made the decision for us. We had started hearing thunder, and the sounds were getting closer. When we reached this shelter, we decided to stay. The spring near to the shelter was dry but there was another 0.25 miles down a blue-blazed trail. That spring was almost dry and was full of sediment. We were able to filter enough for supper and to fill our canteens for tomorrow. We had been hoping to make town tomorrow for food, supplies, and a motel. We believe, however, that the distance will prevent it. Surely, by the next day we can make it.

By the time that we finished filtering our water, the rains came again. It is now 7:45 P.M., getting very dark, and it is still raining. The area needs it but we do not!

High Rock was worth a short side trail today. The view was

nice although a bit cloudy. The site of a former pavilion, the Rock is now a little park but we were the only visitors.

The shelter tonight is actually two shelters a few feet apart, identical in structure, and each with room for six sleeping bags. Again, we are the only inhabitants. We suppose that is kind of normal for this time of year, but we do enjoy the company of others. We passed three south bounders today, but no north bounders have passed us for the past two days.

Unlike the summer months, we have about three less hours to hike in. It is dark until about 7:00 A.M. and it gets dark again about 7:00 P.M. Rain clouds shorten the day even more. We still see ruins of past homes, businesses, and habitation. Some of the trenches lined with stone strongly suggest Civil War sites.

The night sounds are few and the day sounds are not much more. We think that we hear some turkeys cackling and the pileated woodpecker makes itself heard frequently. We cannot identify the other few sounds that we hear.

This was a tiring day. Hopefully, tomorrow will be better. Sure hope that we can make the nearby town.

Sept. 21, 2001   Fayetteville, PA
Trail Distance: 13.2 miles

This was hoped to be a long day so that we could get to Fayetteville, Pennsylvania which would allow us some good restaurant food, a motel, supply store for groceries, and possibly a doctor for Mina. Her problem, though diminished, still exists. Early in a hike, lower pain on her left side starts up and continues for an hour or so. Mina keeps thinking that it is a residual of her earlier bout with a virus. Neither of us really knows for sure. We *do* know that it has lasted far longer than a virus should have lasted. Also, during the nights, the pain can make sleep impossible. We are seriously considering a visit to a doctor or a medical clinic.

Shortly in today's hike, we came to the Chimney Rocks, a great viewpoint near to the A.T. Of course, we just had to climb the rocks (optional, not required) and view the countryside. It was a fine view and surprisingly, the view was almost all of forests. We had expected farmlands, houses, and perhaps a small town, but all that we saw were trees. It was still very lovely, though.

Our trek today took us through the Old Forge Park where we were able to wash our dishes from the night before and fill our water canteens. There were several Trail shelters within a 3.5-mile range. We had need for none of them, but the midsummer months probably saw them all full. This is about the midpoint where the southbound and northbound hikers meet. Their meeting should make for some interesting story telling.

We were making good time today, but Mina *was* getting tired. When we came to the turnoff for the Rocky Mountain Shelter at about the ten-mile mark, we had a choice to make. The shelter was 0.3 miles off the A.T. and the reported spring was another 0.3 miles away. Rather than do an extra 1.2 miles off the Trail, we decided to continue three miles to the next town. David was really pushing for this as the shower and restaurant food were tempting. A long break was taken on the Trail and naps were attempted. Sleep could not come as bugs and flies did not cooperate. The three miles were billed as all down hill, and it looked to be a snap. It was just not to be!

Shortly into the last three miles, the A.T. crossed many boulder piles. If you can imagine a giant ice cream scoop of boulders, all sizes and shapes, piled in a great mound and each mound separated by about fifty yards of relatively smooth trail, you can begin to get the picture. Those rock piles were exhausting to cross. Care had to be taken to prevent injury and progress was slow. Expecting to make the three miles in one and a half hours, it took over one hour just to cover the mile-long rock piles. Fortunately, the last two miles were as expected and progress was better. By now however, Mina was thoroughly exhausted and frequent rest stops were necessary. David did not realize just how exhausted she really was until they got in a warm motel room and she could not get warm. A long, hot shower finally brought her to a semblance of normalcy.

The A.T. had crossed U.S. 30, and traffic was heavy. Fortunately for us, a former *and* current hiker picked us up and took us to a local motel where there was a restaurant across the street. Showered with a good meal, we felt, looked, and smelled better. To all three, we can attest.

There are decisions to be made tomorrow. This town is too small for either a doctor or a clinic so we would have to go to Chambersburg to visit either. We will decide tomorrow morning. In the meantime, a soft bed (even a hard one) sure looks inviting.

Sept. 22, 2001   Quarry Gap Shelter
                                      Trail Distance: 2.7 miles

After a good restaurant breakfast, we trekked about half a mile to the local Laundromat. It was supposed to be "just up the street", but that term has separate meanings for hiking and driving. However, we were in shape and did it fine.

Mina gave serious consideration to going to a doctor or clinic in Chambersburg about five miles further on. She was sure that they would order blood tests (they have to be certain) and these could take several days to get a result. As today is Saturday, it would really put a crimp in our plans. So, she decided to do nothing except get a good supply of Excedrin. Actually, yesterday's hike gave her a hip pain that bothered her more than the low body pains. However, each day, she insists that she is better!

The motel owner drove us to a grocery about half a mile from the A.T. There, we resupplied and got a good sandwich for lunch. Rather than trying to get a ride to the Trail, we hiked to it and began the hike to our shelter for the night. We wanted today's hike to be short in order to give Mina some more time to get back her strength. Although uphill, the hike was relatively easy.

This is a really neat shelter, different from any that we have seen so far. There are actually two shelters, about twenty feet apart, each having space for four sleeping bags, and all covered by a single roof. The open space between has a camp table and extra pegs for holding bags or whatever. In the back of the shelters, under the eaves, there is a clothesline complete with clothespins.

A scout troop is tenting out nearby with something like thirty-two boys. We are *so* glad that they did not take over the spare spaces in our shelter. That probably would have been rather noisy for most of the night.

The days continue to be nice and warm with the nights comfortably cool. We have not seen, heard, or found any evidence of mice. Did they go south for the winter?

When we hike through some of the oak forests, the falling acorns sound like miniature machine guns. They fall so frequently and make so much noise that a person would expect them to weigh a half pound apiece. We are lucky as there have not been any oak forests near to the shelters. We do not believe that the acorns would allow for much sleep.

We know that we are close to civilization here, but it seems like we are miles from anything. When night falls, the seclusion is complete.

Sept. 23, 2001   Birch Run Shelter
Trail Distance: 7.4 miles

This day was a snap! We had been informed that it would be rather rough and rocky. We found it to be mostly smooth and easy. Of course, some of the small hills encountered caused some rest stops, but they were easy compared to some that we have seen.

Leaving at 7:45 A.M., we arrived at our shelter by 12:15 P.M. Normally, we would not have quit so soon, but the next shelter is 6.3 miles away and the hostel planned for tomorrow is ten miles. It makes no sense busting ourselves on a thirteen-plus miler just to do a less than four miles the next day.

One of our fellow hikers informed us that heavy rain is forecast for tomorrow. Many things that we are told do not hold up, so we are hoping that this is another.

We cannot give sufficient thanks to the Potomac A.T. Club. They have really kept this part of the Trail in superb condition. We are sure that they do things that we do not even notice, but what we *do* notice is worth many thanks. The Trail, normally rather narrow, has been cut wide enough for two to walk abreast. Some of the flat, rocky portions of the Trail have been covered with a ground up filler. It *does* make for better hiking.

We meet and talk to various persons that we meet on the Trail. Yesterday was an especially fun encounter. We met about ten young girls in the nine to ten age range with two adult lady leaders. One of the leaders said that the girls could earn a special badge for interviewing a backpacker on the A.T. We had the time and it was fun for all. The girls were super nice, raised their hands for recognition to their questions, and were all attentive, interested, and curious. It was a real joy for David and Mina.

Our shelter for the night is one of two shelters. They were constructed side by side by the CCC in 1935. Each sleeps four, and there is nothing fancy about them. We have no table, sit on cut logs, and have two fire pits but no wood. There is no wood to burn at any shelter as earlier hikers have gleaned the forest. Today, we saw several day hikers and several runners. You couldn't get *us* to run these trails! However, take off the backpacks and take off forty years—nah, *still* wouldn't run it! We had thought that we could have a young couple joining us for the evening, but they just stopped by for a nap and have gone on their way. The girl was possibly from the military. She was in camouflage and wearing military boots. They may have been required in the military, but I do not think that they would be comfortable on the A.T.

Water is on every hikers mind. This part of the country has had a long dry spell and the springs and streams are mostly dry. We ask the southbounders about the supply further north and inform them where to find water in the south. This shelter has a spring (dry) and two streams coming together. One stream is dry while the other has sufficient water flow for us to replenish our needs.

It is now about 5:00 P.M. and time to change to warmer clothing and start our evening meal. Tonight, we have planned hot chocolate, doctored up soup, potatoes and gravy, beans and rice, and a pudding for dessert. It may not sound all that great but it is better than the staple macaroni and cheese that many hikers seem to favor. Actually, we eat rather well on the Trail, but never turn down a chance for a restaurant meal. Sure hope that tomorrow comes in warm and dry.

Sept. 24, 2001   Ironmasters Mansion Hostel
                       Trail Distance: 9.9 miles

Because we had heard that the day could be rainy, we got up and left an hour early. It was still fairly dark when we did leave. Not only was it dark, but it was foggy and grew *more* foggy as the day wore on. Light rain started after about two hours and intermittently continued all of the time that we were hiking. When we got to within about one hundred yards from our destination, the rain picked up heavy and continued until we arrived at the hostel.

Most of today's hike would be considered flat and easy. Going was fast, for us, and we did 9.9 miles in five hours. The last mile was a bit rough for David as he pulled his back and it is now in the "S" figure. Trying to keep a pack on and balanced with a crooked back is just no fun. Hopefully, a long evening's rest and a soft bed may amend things. David knows that he simply cannot hike with a back like it is.

Today, we passed the official half way mark for the A.T. It was 1,069 miles to the southern point and 1,069 miles to the northern point. We cannot claim to have hiked half of the Trail. We both skipped about 220 miles in southern Virginia, and Mina has not done about five hundred miles of the far southern portion. However, it was still interesting to see the mid-point of the Trail.

We arrived at the hostel about 12:15 and found it to be closed until 5:00 P.M. Having nothing better to do and nowhere to go, we simply waited. The manager came around about 2:00 P.M. with some volunteer workers and agreed to let us in early. Thankfully, we were able to get an early shower and get our laundry done. The hostel, itself, is an old mansion dating from the early 1800s. The home of a founder of an iron-producing plant, it has many rooms and was used as a safe haven on the old slave Underground Railroad. Now named as the Ironmasters Mansion Hostel, it is open to all and is directly on the A.T. Naturally, many hikers utilize the facilities.

The Trail today was kept in as good condition as we have seen. It really makes for some nice hiking. Scenery was rather sparse. It was mostly forests and the constant fog made for some good Halloween scenes.

Our last evening at the hostel was a memorable one. One of the hikers was also a career chef. He had been staying at the hostel for a couple of days waiting for new boots to arrive. Earlier, he had made arrangements with the manager to cook a dinner for all of the visitors at the hostel. Not knowing this, David had started for the kitchen about 5:00 P.M. with his meal preparations just to be interrupted by the manager saying, "Get that glop out of here. We're going to give you a *real* meal". About five minutes later, everyone was called in to a sit-down vegetarian dinner. It was superb! There was more corn-on-the-cob than we could eat, three kinds of squash, cabbage and potatoes, baked beans, and fresh baby tomatoes garnished with herbs. It was really enjoyed by all. Everyone, including Mina, had at least two ears of corn, and many had three.

After dinner, some of us were treated to some of the history of the mansion. Constructed in 1827-29, one part of the original basement was a secret hiding place for runaway slaves on the Underground Railroad. Not connected to the main large basement, it could be reached only by a secret floor panel in the closet underneath the grand staircase. Through a narrow hole in the floor, a ladder descended about six feet into a narrow center section that separated two side rooms that could probably hold twenty persons each if they didn't mind being crowded. Headroom was only about five feet at best, and there were no noticeable toilet facilities. A tunnel, now filled in, connected the special basement to an outlet in the nearby forest. With the exception of the tunnel, the rest remains much like it was when it was in use.

Sept. 25, 2001   Carlissle, PA—Motel 6
                        Trail Distance: 19.4 miles

This turned out to be a day that we will never forget and hope to never repeat. A person can take only so much excitement and drama and this day overflowed. But first things first!

Leaving the hostel with clean clothing, clean bodies, and full tummies, we hiked 7.3 miles to the first shelter. Arriving at 11:30, we remarked that it was an easy and fast hike. The next shelter was just 8.2 miles away, we were well rested, so we decided to continue on to it. That 8.2 miles was as brutal as the first 7.3 was easy. We again encountered those mounds of boulders and these were bigger and meaner than ever. We had to crawl, climb, and assist each other in getting through the various mazes. Thinking that we could finish the hike by 4:00 or 5:00 P.M. at the latest, at 5:40 Mina told David that she was exhausted and could not continue without more rest. We had no idea how far it was to the scheduled shelter as the rock piles really screwed up our calculations. David said he thought it was at least a half mile further and maybe more. A decision was made for David to go ahead to the shelter, drop his pack and come back to help Mina with her pack.

David left Mina at 5:40 and went as fast as he could to the shelter. He reached there at 6:05 and hurried back to meet Mina. The shelter was 0.3 miles off the A.T., and David retraced his steps back as far as the point where he had left Mina. Not finding her, he went even further back on the Trail, calling her name and getting no reply. Thinking that perhaps Mina has missed the turnoff to the shelter and retraced her steps to it, David then hurried back to the shelter. Still there was no Mina! She had disappeared! As David's water bottle was used up first in the day, he went to the nearby spring to refill his canteen. The spring was dry! It was probably just as well, as Mina was carrying the filter pump and David could not open the extra bottle containing the iodine tablets. It was fast getting dark, and there was no trace of Mina. Mina had both flashlights and was equipped to spend the night outside, *but* this was supposed to be a cold night, she was exhausted, and she had simply disappeared. David needed help to find her.

Taking his pack with him, as he may have to spend the night in the forest, David left the shelter a little after 7:00 P.M. Now almost dark, there was 3.9 miles of Trail before he could reach a

highway for help. At first, David could see the Trail fairly well and up
to about 8:00 P.M. he could follow it. After that, David had to sense
where the Trail was as it is continually rocky and free from debris.
This went on for about another thirty minutes. There were a few logs
that had David falling on his face, steps into drop-offs on the Trail,
and once he walked head-on into a tree when the Trail turned and
David didn't. He finally reached the point where he lost the Trail and
could not locate it again. Dropping his pack, he was able to light his
one remaining candle. With the wind blowing, it took many matches
getting the candle lit and keeping it lit. Finally, getting the hang of it,
he was able to keep the candle lit and continued slowly. Although
lights could be seen in the far distance on the sides, none were visible
ahead. After about another half hour, when the candle was down to a
nub, David saw a light about one hundred yards to his left. He headed
for it across the forest underbrush. He saw that it was a house with
lights on inside so he knocked and waited. When a man answered,
David (who must have looked like a dirty bum) told the man, "This
is an emergency, I need to call the police, my wife is missing from the
A.T." The man, later identified as Tom Stout, did not hesitate. He
asked David in and immediately phoned the police. Not caring for
the time that it took the police to respond, he phoned again a few
minutes later and gave them specific directions on just how to find
his home.

When the County Deputy Sheriff arrived, David gave specific
details of what had happened, where it happened, and the concern
that he had. More telephone calls were made, and within minutes
the Stout home became the headquarters for a massive search. Fire
sirens were sounded, volunteer firemen from three different towns
began arriving, the county search and rescue, volunteers, the state
police and coordinators arrived. Probably twenty-five to thirty
people in all, a search dog, a helicopter with heat sensing devices
and men with ATVs were lined up for the search. From about
9:30 until dawn the search continued. All parts of the Trail were
covered, side trails were searched, old trails were searched, and the
shelter was not only visited, but a volunteer was stationed there all
night in case Mina showed up.

David kept telling the search director that Mina could not have gone far as she was totally exhausted. Anyway, the searchers started at the point where David had left the Trail and crisscrossed back ten miles and side trails for many more miles. Nothing turned up, the dog had no better luck, and the helicopter could not peer through the heavy foliage. By 3:00 A.M., they had covered all trails and roads and were getting ready to place grids over the area and intensely search each grid.

The state trooper, a Cpl. Wilson, who was not super convinced that the whole thing was not a hoax, closely questioned David. He stated that the State of Florida had no record of a Mina Swan even having a driver's license. *That* made him hesitant. However, after questioning David for an extended period in his patrol car, having David show each night where they had been staying along with receipts from the motel and the hostel, and showing Mina's car insurance papers with her name just as it was on her driver's license. He finally stated, "I'm convinced".

The search parties had to let the Stouts have their home back, so at 3:00 A.M. they changed their command post to another location, and the state trooper drove David to a motel near to his headquarters. David got to bed about 4:00 A.M., was awakened at 5:00 by a call from Mina's daughter, Noel Brewer, where he explained what had happened and the fact that Mina still was not located. The state trooper was going to call Noel at about 10:00 P.M., but David asked him to wait until morning for surely Mina would be found. David was awakened again at 6:00 A.M. by the state police who informed him that a new trooper was now on duty, and at 7:00 David got up and showered as he expected Noel and Kevin to show up momentarily.

About 7:30 A.M., Mina appeared at the motel with a man who had first noticed her. He had found her near to the highway that David had been trying to reach. She had spent the night there wrapped in her sleeping bag and was getting her gear together to walk *back* down the Trail trying to locate David.

A driver passing by Mina's "campsite" noticed Mina and

mentioned it to two co-workers when he reached his job location. One of the two stated that she could be the one that the big search was for during the night. All three then drove back to Mina and asked her if she was the one that had been lost. She then stated that either she was or her husband was! A call was then made to the search teams that Mina had been found. All teams and groups involved were notified that the search had ended happily. All were notified *except* David. *He* didn't learn until he saw Mina coming in the motel entrance. It was *some* greeting!

Within minutes of Mina entering the motel, her daughter and son-in-law arrived. *More* greetings! Anyone could tell that Mina was loved. Ultimately, the decision was made that Mina and David would rest up this day and go back on the Trail on the 27th.

Sept. 26, 2001   Boiling Springs—Super 8 Motel
Trail Distance: 0.0 miles

Noel immediately checked us out of the motel and informed us that we would be going back with them. After we had a few days rest, they would be coming back this way on the 29th, and we could then go back to the Trail if we so desired.

Noel was very persistent, but we finally convinced her that we *had* to go back to the Trail or we might never. She finally relented.

After a good breakfast with Noel and Kevin, David and Mina checked back into the motel, had a well-needed shower, and took an even more well-needed nap. Later, we called up the young man who had first noticed Mina alongside the road and invited him and his wife to dinner. He accepted but later showed up with another of the three who had found her saying that his wife had to stay home and supervise the homework with their children. The four of us had a fine dinner, talked and acted as if we had known each other for years. Like others that we met in this town, they were really super people. Kraig and Harry will long be remembered.

Sept. 27, 2001   Darlington Shelter
Trail Distance: 14.3 miles

Kraig picked us up early in the morning and drove us to where he had first seen Mina the previous morning. We had remarked that it was a good thing that he had seen her and said something as she was preparing to go back down the Trail to try to locate David. As that part of the Trail had already been searched, who knows how long it would have been for her to be located. Luck does sometimes play a part in events.

To keep the hike "legal", we then hiked from Mina's prior resting spot into Boiling Springs to visit the mid-Atlantic office of the A.T.C. We tried to get a replacement map for the one used by the rescue teams. They had none to sell, but we were able to peruse one to see what the next couple of days would hold for us. There seemed to be nothing unusual that would require us to do anything special.

The Trail going north passed by many corn fields with some of the tallest corn that we had ever seen. Some had to be thirteen to fourteen feet tall, but the ears were few and small. Later, we asked a knowledgeable person about these, and he stated that the fields got water at the wrong time and in the wrong amounts. The result was tall stalks but a poor crop. I guess you cannot tell by just looking. Later, still going north, we passed under dozens of black walnut trees. There were thousands of nuts on the ground. I would have thought that the "locals" would have harvested them, but they appeared undisturbed. Also, as valuable as the wood is, we were thankful that someone had not "harvested" the trees.

Actually, the day's hike was fairly easy. All but the last two miles *were* easy. The last two miles required some upgrades, and these were rather tiring. Coming into the shelter, we had a man and his grown son for company. The son was on a short leave from his submarine duty and had looked forward to this hike. They both seemed to be enjoying themselves.

After dinner, we made arrangements to hit our sleeping bags early. It was cold and getting colder. The shelter, although relatively new, needed some improvements in design. Normally, the open side of a shelter is partially enclosed. This structure had three straight sides and the fourth completely open. It was drafty plus there were open spaces between the flooring and the walls. A bandanna on our heads gave some protection against the wind. As tired as we were, the wind and the limited shelter made for an uncomfortable night, and little sleep was had by either.

Sept. 28, 2001   Duncannon, PA—Doyle Hotel
Trail Distance: 11.4 miles

The strong wind died down during the night, but it still remained quite chilly. Both David and Mina wore double layers of clothing, long pants on each layer, and both wore gloves. As the day progressed the second layer of clothing was gradually removed. The gloves went on and off all during the day.

There were some fine views to be had of the countryside and of Susquehanna River. From a couple of thousand feet up, the views are super!

Our original plans were to stop by the Cove Mountain Shelter just to take the packs off and rest a bit. Somehow or other, we completely missed the shelter. It may have been removed or someone may have tampered with the sign but we missed it entirely. About the time that we thought that the shelter *had* to be close, we came to the town of Duncannan that was supposed to be 4.1 miles on the *other* side of the shelter. We could not see how we could have covered that distance in the time that we had spent. We were having too much of a problem on the Trail. It was rocks, rocks, and *more* rocks. Going was slow and care had to be taken to prevent injury. When we came to the town, it was hard to believe (but easy to accept). We made reservations at an old A.T. hikers-recommended hotel. Built probably at the turn of the century, the *last* century, we do not believe that there have been many improvements or upkeep done since. Everything is old! We are on the fourth floor, there are no elevators, there is one bathroom per floor, and it costs only $20 per night. Perhaps the cost is an attraction to hikers. Also, we did not see any other motel or hotel in town! We were told that a few decades ago, the owner gave *free* rooms to A.T. hikers. The place does have atmosphere, and everyone is really friendly. We recommend it!

We soon found that Mina's experience made the local newspapers. They were complimentary, though. However, both reporting newspapers just had to report both of our ages. After a super meal in the local pub, clean clothes again, and a visit to the local mini-market, we are ready to try for another, hopefully, good nights rest.

Sept. 29, 2001   Peters Mountain Shelter
                               Trail Distance: 13.3 miles

Today, we found out just why the prior day's distance seemed to be covered so quickly. We had come to the Doyle Hotel on *one* side of the town, and the Trail Distance had been measured to the *other* side of town. This was no problem, just a longer day's hike for *this* day.

The whole town seems to be hiker oriented. The Trail goes right through the town, and the townspeople will speak to you, ask which way you are hiking, and appear genuinely interested in you and your well being. A couple of persons got a good look at us and asked if we were the ones written up in the local newspapers. We had to admit that we were the guilty ones. The hotel wanted to know how we were doing on the Trail, and they had a hikers log for the tenants to sign. Even the local pub had a hikers' log for those lucky enough to sample their food. All in all, it was a most pleasant town for hikers to rest up. The hotel is not for everyone! Things *are* old but clean. A hiker used to staying in the Trail shelters would probably find it comfortable, but it would not be for the ordinary traveler.

The hike across town took us through "church row". For a couple of miles, there had to be a church on almost every block. If you could name your belief, there would be a church for you.

After crossing the town, we crossed two bridges over the Juniata and the Susquehanna Rivers. Both were obviously very shallow, and both were quite wide. They became even wider where they joined. As we continued to hike up into the hills, there were several spots that gave us super views of the rivers and the surrounding countryside.

We had heard that the water supply at our selected shelter for the night was rather low plus there was a difficult hike down to it and back. Accordingly, we stopped at the Clarks Ferry Shelter for lunch and to fill all of our water containers. It meant carrying a few pounds extra, but the water at Clarks Ferry was nearby and was easy to obtain.

On the way to our shelter, we passed Table Rock which gave a fine view of the Pennsylvania forests. David still finds it amazing that so much of the countryside is in forests. He had thought that Pennsylvania would be a combination of towns, villages, and farms. There *are* plenty of those but the forests seem to cover many square miles at each viewing point.

At almost every highway in Pennsylvania, there is an A.T. marker on the side of the road announcing the A.T. and pointing to the "North" and to the "South". The signs are about four feet wide and clearly visible to the cars going by.

This is a really super shelter. It has two floors and can easily sleep thirty hikers. Another lean-to shelter about 150 feet away can shelter another six sleeping bags but nothing else. Again, this is the first shelter of this design that we have seen. It is difficult to explain the construction; you just have to visit it!

Sept. 30, 2001   Raush Gap Shelter
Trail Distance: 17.5 miles

This was planned to be a long but not necessarily a difficult day. For Mina, it turned out to be *very* difficult. A southbound hiker had informed us that it was an easy hike. Other south bounders hedged a bit on the description. They said that *some* parts were easy but much was rocky. In addition, our data book indicated that the Trail followed an old coach road for seven miles on the crest.

Even though the Trail followed the crest much of the way, it was a rocky crest with many small ups and downs. The old coach road never materialized for any part of the seven miles. That seven miles were all rocks and boulders where no road of any kind could have ever existed. The three miles uphill to the crest *was* an old road, laboriously constructed, but very pitted and rutted. So the relatively easy seven miles that David promised to Mina never appeared and she suffered for it.

Starting the day out at 7:45 A.M., by 5:50 P.M. David said that he would go on to the shelter, drop his pack at the shelter trail entrance, and come back for Mina's pack. She was in agony and going on nerves only. David saw the shelter marker indicating 0.3 miles to the shelter, went 0.3 miles and could not locate the shelter. He then went back to Mina, got her pack and both then came to where he had left *his* pack. Leaving both packs, they then walked almost a half mile further on the Trail and neither could locate either the shelter or a blue-blazed trail to it. Retracing their steps, they picked up their packs and went back to the 0.3-mile marker. About fifty feet *prior* to the sign, a trail veered off without any blue markers, but it looked well traveled. Following it almost in the dark, they came to a very nice shelter. By now, it was past 7:00 P.M., rather dark, and Mina was aching and chilled. The first thing that we did was get her in her sleeping bag until she was able to get warm. However, the aches and pains continued even with Tylenol.

This shelter, like some others, was unique. We just wish that we could have gotten to it without wasting an hour *looking* for it. The builders had somehow diverted a spring through a pipe to a trough right outside of the shelter. We did not have to go for water; it was brought to us.

Without even trying to prepare a full meal, David made some soup with a main dish of rice and sauce. The hot food, although scanty, did help us both.

The next morning, breakfast consisted of hot chocolate, dry cereal with milk, and another hot soup. After this, the plans were to go to a nearby town to replenish supplies and to rest up.

October 1, 2001   Lick Dale, PA—Days Inn
                        Trail Distance: 6.0 miles

This was to be an easy day, and it was. Yesterday, we were supposed to hike through the ruins of Yellow Springs Village. We saw nothing except a mailbox announcing where the village used to be. There was absolutely nothing to indicate that anything had ever been built there.

Today, we were supposed to hike through the ruins of Rausch Gap Village. Again, there was nothing to indicate any prior habitation. We are thinking that our trail guide may be a bit out of date and just a bit inaccurate.

Our guidebook indicates 6.4 miles to PA. Rt 72. We covered the 6.4 miles over rocky and hilly trails in less than 2.5 hours. No way! At best, we did maybe 5 miles but not 6.4. In addition, our 2001 Data Book shows PA. 443 to be 1.4 miles *from* PA. 72. Actually, they were about fifty feet apart where we crossed. The trail guide does claim that there are a lot of relocations in this area. We suppose that some distances will be shorter than indicated and some longer. It's those "longer" one that hurt on an already long rugged day.

Once at the highway, we hitched a ride into Lick Dale where we were able to get a good meal, find a motel, a Laundromat and a grocery. Rested up, cleaned up, and resupplied, we will hit the Trail again tomorrow.

October 2, 2001   501 Shelter
                        Trail Distance: 11.4 miles

After a nice Days Inn breakfast (we sampled everything on the menu), we were able to hitch a ride back to the Trail. Getting there, we found out why the walk yesterday seemed so short. It really *was* short by about 1.5 miles. It seems that the highway was rebuilt a couple of years ago so that the Trail crossed it three times instead of just once. We had gotten off at the first crossing and should have waited until the third crossing. Yesterday was short by about 1.5 miles so we had to make it up today. It was *not* a welcome makeup.

For the first seven miles or so today, the Trail was very rocky and rough to hike on. We know that Pennsylvania is noted for its rocks, but those things can really get to be a pain. That "pain" is both figuratively and literally speaking. Mina's boots, although made by the same company and considered the top of the line, as are David's, just do not compare to David's. His soles are much thicker and can take the rocks better. Going over miles of rocks are obviously painful to her. Rest stops just to take the boots off are sometimes needed.

There were a few nice viewing spots on the Trail today. Now, the valleys have houses and farms on them. *This* viewing is more realistic.

The weather is still holding dry and surprisingly warm. All of the area seems very dry with little vegetation undergrowth. We simply do not see how the deer can survive. There appears to be nothing for them to eat. Squirrels can have a field day though. Acorns, hickory nuts, and black walnuts are in abundance.

This is now bow-and-arrow season on deer. We have passed several hunters in the past, but today is the first time that we have passed anyone dragging their kill out. Two hunters had bagged a beautiful doe and were dragging it out via the A.T. We know that hunting is necessary as many deer will starve for lack of food. We don't really object to their hunting; we just can't do it ourselves.

At the end of our hike today, we came to a rather unique, beautiful shelter. It is a building, completely enclosed, with a central skylight, twelve bunks, a long table and plenty of soft chairs. A volunteer who lives nearby with his wife and two dogs permanently maintains it. Running water is available by the side of his house, garbage cans are provided, a port-a-potty is nearby, and it is one cozy place. With our candles lit at night, it is homey and comfortable.

We were able to cook a good dinner and enjoyed it sitting at a table with a tablecloth. Now, *that* is unusual! Tomorrow's hike is supposed to be rather long for us, but not too difficult. With even less rocks predicted, we will wait and see.

It is now almost 8:00 P.M., way past our bedtime, and we need the sleep. That soft bed last night did *not* make for a restful sleep.

October 3, 2001   501 Shelter
                            Trail Distance: 0.0 miles

We opted to spend another day at this super shelter. Mina's feet and legs demanded another day of rest. Since we do not *have* to be in any given place at any given time, this is a very nice place to take it easy. Sleep last night was fitful; a nap this afternoon helped.

We have decided to end this portion of our hike in Eckville, Pennsylvania, and plan on getting there in four days. Time wise, we could go on for two more days, but there would be no feasible place for our shuttle driver to find us. Plus, we will be about sixty miles short of where we had hoped to end the hike. We sometimes have to remind ourselves that we are here to enjoy ourselves, not to forcefully meet some goals.

Late this morning, we started hiking into Pine Grove, Pennsylvania, in order to make arrangements with our shuttle driver. Fortunately, he was home and will meet us at the Hawk Mountain Visitors Center at 4:00 P.M. on October 8. While in town, we had a fine lunch at a nice restaurant. We find it hard to believe the prices in some of these small towns. For lunch, we had two meals of stuffed peppers with two vegetables, hot buns, two slices of pie, two iced teas, and all for $11.80 plus tax. We sure could not get that back home at anywhere near that price.

Although we had started hiking to town, without our packs, we passed a parked pickup on the side of the road, and the driver brought us directly to the restaurant. Later, as we were leaving town, a car had stopped to pick us up when the earlier driver stopped by. He had a bag of eight apples and two peaches (all great) that he was going to bring back to the shelter for us. Now, this place does have some super people!

Hopefully, with a good night's sleep (please), we can tackle the fifteen miles tomorrow.

October 4, 2001   Eagles Nest Shelter
Trail Distance: 15.1 miles

We rather hated to leave the 501 Shelter. It was so comfortable and cozy, water and privy were close, and the large octagon shaped skylight kept it as light inside as out. Another couple stopped for the night, but they chose to sleep outside under the stars. That was their choice as there was more than enough room inside. Even though we found the shelter clean, we left it cleaner and neater. With no fees charged, we *had* to do something to show our appreciation.

We are still on Blue Mountain where we have been for a couple of days and will remain for two more days. The trails are rocky and are no fun. These rocks are still especially hard on Mina's feet. Her boots just do not meet the minimum standards for A.T. hiking on Pennsylvania rocks. One would have to see the rocky trail to appreciate the hardships on hiking it. Getting off the Trail or taking a different route is no answer; *all* of the area is chockfull of rocks. Walking is treacherous, and the sharpness of many rocks is downright painful. Pennsylvania is noted for rocks on the A.T. We can add our attestation to that. In addition, Pennsylvania is noted for the place where boots "come to die". A hiker soon finds out just why.

This was originally scheduled to be a long but not especially difficult day. For us, it was long, difficult and had an unpleasant ending.

There were some beautiful views along the way. We tried not to pass any by. Most were quite close to the Trail and did not require much additional walking. Being on top of the foliage color change and seeing it from above rather than looking up into the trees makes it especially beautiful. With David's "color difficulty", he could not fully appreciate the colors, but Mina's appreciation made up for his lack thereof. The Shikellamy Overlook was worth mentioning. The view was worth the extra effort to reach it.

One of the places of interest that we passed was a marker to the Fort Dietrick site that was constructed in 1756 as one in a chain of forts to guard against the Indians. Mina and David had a little mishap here. The Trail that we were on kept going straight, and we followed it. After a few hundred yards, we noted that we did not see any A.T. markings. Retreating to the monument, we saw that the Trail took a left turn, and we followed *that* path for a couple of hundred yards. *Again* noting the lack of A.T. blazes, we again retreated to the monument. There, we saw that the A.T. blaze that we had taken as a northbound left turn was actually a *southbound* left turn. This was not only a slap at the ego, but was rather tiresome to boot.

Much of this portion of the Trail was billed as relatively easy hiking. Not so! It was rocky and really no fun.

Mina's feet were really bothering her. We went slower and took more breaks, but all it did was lengthen the hike and spread the misery. Also, after hiking an estimated two miles *past* a noted spot on the Trail indicating the shelter to be 4.5 miles away, we came to a sign indicating the shelter still to be 4.2 miles away. That was a real downer! Only later did we find out that the 4.5 miles was correct and the 4.2-mile sign was someone's mistake.

There was to be a walled spring 0.7 miles from the shelter. It was dry! A stream shortly before the shelter was also dry. This part of the Trail looked as if it had not been getting any rain. We were to learn the next day that this side of the mountain had been missing out on the rain. The *other* side of the mountain got it all.

Now, we had a problem! We had been carrying only enough water to reach this shelter, and we could not replenish. We still had about half a liter left, and this was not sufficient to prepare dinner. Looking at our data book, we saw that about 2 miles further on was a road that could take us to Shartlesville, Pennsylvania. We then decided to have a couple of energy bars, ration our water, and go to Shartlesville the next morning for water and a good breakfast. It was a thirsty night, albeit a rather warm one. Nevertheless, we were in our bags by 7:00 P.M.

Mina's feet were painful, and her legs continued to cramp. A massage may have helped; at least she did not have leg spasms during the night. This was a long, rocky, and painful day. We were both glad it was over.

October 5, 2001   Port Clinton Hotel
                                       Trail Distance: 8.6 miles

The Eagles Nest Shelter had a rather unusual privy. It was a compost privy, experimental we believe, and a "user" had to climb up to the seat. Apparently, the underside (the containment portion) was in a large sealable compartment that could be replaced with an empty one. We have no idea of how they could haul it away. There was nothing like a road anywhere around.

The privy had something else unusual. David had noticed it the night before, but it just did not register with him. The privy, small as it was, had gutters that ran down into a screened rain barrel. Surprisingly, the rain barrel contained about fifty gallons of nice pure rainwater. It did not take long to get the filter out and fill up the water containers. We also noted this fact in the shelter logbook. Hikers that we had met missed this fact also. Here there was plenty of water, and we did not have to rely on the spring.

With water, we were able to drink our fill, make some hot chocolate, and prepare a hot, nourishing soup. *This* day started all right.

Our trail guide indicated that the last six miles of our hike would be rocky, but the rest would be "surprisingly rock free". That "rock free" portion carried over from yesterday. This may have been someone's idea of a sick joke but it sure wasn't funny. Actually the six miles of promised rock turned out to be not so bad after all. It sure was no worse than the twenty miles preceding it.

We did not have the views today. That road to Shartlesville that we had planned on using to go for water turned out to be a dirt path that probably had not seen *any* type of vehicle in years. If someone had not thought to put gutters and a rain barrel at the privy, there would have been two very thirsty hikers out there. As far as we would tell, there was no more water to be had until we reached Port Clinton.

Port Clinton is another hiker's town. We stayed at the Port Clinton Hotel, and almost every room has a printed notice on the *outside* of the door giving specific instructions to hikers. When we went down to dinner, the dining room was full, and we had to wait a bit. Apparently this is a favorite restaurant for the locals. We soon discovered why. The food was superb, there was a lot of it, and the prices were most reasonable. David is amazed at how much Mina can eat when she has been hiking. A *full* slab of ribs, two vegetables, a small loaf of bread, iced tea, and a huge hunk of cake finished in record time finally took care of her appetite.

We had firmly decided early in the day to end our hike here. Accordingly, we phoned our shuttle driver, John Hess, and asked him to pick us up here rather than at Hawk Mountain. Hopefully, he will get here in the early afternoon tomorrow. So, for this section our hiking is over. If we can find some good, rock-resistant, water-resistant, comfortable boots for Mina, we will return. We had hoped to complete the Pennsylvania portion of the A.T., but we fell about seventy-seven miles short. Whatever, we are glad that we came, glad that we did the hiking, and glad to be going home.

David's total miles on A.T.: 968.8

Mina's total miles on A.T.: 472.0

CHAPTER EIGHT

April 19, 2002   Preliminary to Hike

When we left our hike last year, we had not driven more than about fifty miles before we decided to come back this year and try to finish our hike. It is odd how quickly a person can forget the misery of the hike and want to go back and do some more of it.

For this year, we left the car at home and went by bus to Christiansonburg, Virginia, where we were met by a shuttle driver who drove us to the start of the Trail. We had already finished getting our supplies and did not wish to spend any more time in town.

April 20, 2002   Rice Field Shelter
                                  Trail Distance: 7.3 miles

This was a rather rough day for us. It was only 7.3 miles to the shelter but was mostly uphill. We had purposely skipped this part of Virginia last year because it *was* rough, and we were correct in our thinking. Our bodies were super tired, and then we had to go a half mile downhill for water. It was a long hard climb back up. The supper dishes could wait, as neither of us wanted to make that climb again. It has often been said, and we can attest to the truthfulness of it, that it takes two to three weeks to get "broken in" to the A.T. We knew it but those two to three weeks can be rough, nevertheless.

We got here just at the start of springtime in the mountains. Most of the trees and shrubs are just putting out new buds, and the trees are still mostly bare from winter. It will be interesting watching the foliage grow. Now, we can look straight through the trees and see the hills and mountains beyond. Soon, we will see nothing but trees and more trees. The air is just right for hiking—cool and breezy. We know that there will be some cool and cold nights ahead of us. We just hope that our several layers of clothing will do for us. Our weight restrictions caused us to leave our really warm clothing behind. It is usual for a first day to be rough on us and this one proved us to be correct.

April 21, 2002   Pine Swamp Branch Shelter
                              Trail Distance: 12.3 miles

The last shelter was relatively new as it was not on our maps of two years ago. We had thought that we would have to tent out but were pleasantly surprised to see a shelter where there was none before.

This day was just brutal! The A.T. was not that bad but 12.3 miles on the second day of hiking was a bit much for us. I was exhausted by eight miles although Mina was in much better shape. Her exercise classes sure helped her out. I was at the point of having to rest every fifty to one hundred feet, but Mina held out until about a mile from the end. We keep asking ourselves why we do this kind of thing, but so far we cannot get a good, or at least, reasonable answer.

The forests are not really pretty yet. They have mostly bare branches but the new growth looks hopeful. We did pass some abandoned orchards on a hilltop and the trees were mostly in bloom. We have no idea of what kind of fruit was there. Possibly the September hikers will be able to tell us. Obviously, there were several kinds as the blossoms were of different kinds.

We had rain last night and it continued this morning. Three male hikers shared the shelter with us and they all took off early in the rain. We decided to wait. If it were going to rain all day, we would just stay put. As it was, it cleared off about 9:00 A.M. and we started out. Fortunately for us, the rain did not return.

Unlike last year, water is not plentiful in these hills. Sometimes, we have to go a bit for it. The first shelter had a spring a half mile down the mountain and that was a "haul". We made only one trip and the dirty dishes just had to wait until today. For this day, the shelter is by a very nice stream that has plenty of water. For other hikers, we hope the stream lasts through the summer.

We did not make the shelter until 7:00 P.M., and we still had dinner to prepare before it got dark. After getting in our sleeping bags it started to rain and it rained hard all night. We were planning on sleeping late, and the rain helped us to do it. The next day was due to be a short, easy one, so we were in no hurry. We were both exhausted and slept for ten hours.

April 22, 2002   Bailey Gap Shelter
                                     Trail Distance: 3.9 miles

This is one where we think that they got their distance screwed up. The last 1.1 miles as marked had to have been at least three miles. After hiking much more than 1.1 miles, we thought that we might have missed the shelter. We both dropped out packs and went up and down the Trail searching for the shelter. Finally, we turned on our little walkie-talkies with me going down the Trail and Mina going up it. After several hundred more yards, Mina saw the shelter and called back to me that it was found. At 11:30 A.M., we were supposedly 1.1 miles from the shelter, and we located it about 2 P.M. We are slow but not *that* slow. This could have been another case where the Trail had been changed and the guides have not caught up with it. Water is from a nearly spring that was dry last year. Now, the spring is like an open fire hydrant.

Our three male hikers that were with us two nights ago, spent last night here. They are up to doing sixteen miles in a day—we are not yet there. The last two miles today that felt like five was all "up". I really had a slow time of it. There is no question about it. Currently, Mina is in much better physical condition for the A.T. than me. I had been working out with weights but her aerobics puts her in much better condition.

Turkey season is now open so I will *not* try any of my turkey calls. They have gotten responses in the past, but now is not the time to try it again.

One of the prior hikers stated in the shelter logbook that these four miles felt like forty. I guess we are not alone in questioning the distances. We had the shelter to ourselves last night, and it looks like it will be the same tonight. Probably in four to six weeks, this place will be packed along with all of the tent sites. Hopefully, we will be able to stay ahead of the thru-hiker stampede. We sure hope so. We are expecting some really cool weather tonight.

April 23, 2002   War Spur Shelter
                           Trail Distance: 8.8 miles

This day turned out to be a pleasant surprise. The extra distance that we thought we did yesterday was made up by a seemingly short distance today. The first two miles today were very rocky, and we were not looking forward to rocks all day. Thankfully, the Trail leveled off and was relatively smooth. Trees and shrubs are really turning green. However, it is very quiet. There are no bird songs. I mean *none*! We see a few juncos, nuthatches, and an occasional sparrow, but there are no bird songs. For us, spring is just not here without the bird music.

Our shelter this evening is being shared by two thru-hikers who started at Springer Mountain, Georgia, on March 1 and March 5. Now *they* have had some cool Trail days. Last night was very cool, and tonight is due to be downright cold. In fact, I am now so cold that I can hardly write. By the time that we were ready for sleeping, we had a total of five other hikers, four in the shelter and one tenting out. All had started at Springer Mountain in early March.

Today, we hiked past Wind Rock, a beautiful rock formation that allowed us to look over dozens of square miles of Virginia valleys and mountains. It was surprisingly bare of human habitation. There were a few roads visible, but mostly forests covered the countryside. Unlike some viewing spots that we had to hike to, this was directly on the Trail and we considered that a treat.

We are still tired and beat after a few hours of hiking, but the bodies are getting more used to it, and we are both coping better.

We can almost watch the buds opening on the trees. Where there were just buds a few days ago, there are now tiny leaves, and each day they seem larger. Spring *is* coming!

This shelter is surrounded by mountain laurels that have to be spectacular in full bloom. Alas for us, that will be several weeks away. Hopefully, somewhere north of here, we will see some more. They are a beautiful sight when blooming.

April 24, 2002   Laurel Creek Shelter
                            Trail Distance: 5.8 miles

Last night was cold! Our sleeping bags did not quite do it, and it made for uncomfortable sleeping. This morning, it seemed a bit warmer and the day turned out to be bright and sunny. Our hike today was relatively short but rather strenuous. We were not only tired when we reached the shelter but really exhausted.

Our food supply is getting low and we are hoping that we can stretch it three days until we reach a town and grocery store. That will mean about thirty-four miles of hiking in three days. We should be up to it. If not, we just may get a bit hungry.

The forests are still quite bare but the leaves are coming. When the hikers who started in April come through, they probably will not even be able to see the hills and mountains through the trees. So far, we have seen little sign of any wildlife. We have neither seen any deer nor seen any signs of deer. Hopefully, they are still in the valleys where there may be some food. There are not many signs of any here yet. Possibly with more foliage growing, food will become more available. The only mammal wildlife to be seen are little red squirrels. They are quite numerous. We did hear a couple of bird songs today, but none that we recognized. They were quite distinctive but new to us.

This shelter had six hikers visit after we arrived but all went on. One other south bounder will spend the night. He is an older, retired man who has been great company. As he said, it's nice to be able to talk to someone in his age bracket rather than all these young hikers around. The young ones are super nice, but they *are* in a different age category.

It is supposed to rain again tonight. That will be OK with us, but we do not wish to hike in the rain tomorrow. For that, we will have no choice as we *must* get to a grocery, and that is three days away.

The sun has set and it is getting very cold again. As it was last evening, I can hardly write. This is enough for now!

April 25, 2002   Niday Shelter
Trail Distance: 12.4 mile

This was a long, rough day. We were not exhausted at the end but we were mighty tired. Today, we heard a few wild turkeys and heard a ruffed grouse beat his wings a couple of times. The grouse must have found a mate quickly or else he decided that it was too early in the season to advertise. At any rate, he quit early. We have heard them in Canada beating their wings all night. We saw our first trillium bud but no flowers yet. Dogwoods are in bloom and brighten the forests all over. We have seen many wild irises in bloom, and they are gorgeous. It is a bit upsetting to think that our eighteen irises at home, properly refrigerated before planting, produced eighteen plants but only one flower. And that one flower could not compare to any of the wild ones seen.

There was an eighteen-foot circumference oak tree on the A.T., and we missed it! I think that we passed it in the rain and simply did not notice it. Yes, we were in the rain most of the morning. It rained all night and continued lightly until almost noon. We have the wind also. It is strong and cold and continued all day.

We know that we can never remember all of the sights that we see. Cameras just cannot catch it all. We get views from both sides of the ridgeline, and they all are great. The A.T. follows the crest line of Sinking Creek Mountain, and it is a dilly. It is mostly rock at about a forty-five-degree angle, and the rock *is* the Trail. We do not think that OSHA would approve. But then, we do not think that anyone from there would have the nerve to check it out. Good rock boots are a must, but it probably would still be risky in the rain. There is no alternative to the Trail. You *must* go over the rocks, and there is something like a half mile of them. Once over, it was downhill to the shelter. As usual, it took us about three-fourths of an hour longer to reach it than we had expected. It was a long day, and we were tired but not exhausted on our first twelve miler.

We shared the shelter with one middle-aged married lady who had left her husband working. Also in the area, there were two Virginia Tech students who would be graduating in a couple of weeks. That couple decided to tent out as they wanted their privacy. There were only three of us in the shelter, but that other lady could snore as well as any man that we have heard. We are not looking forward to sharing the next shelter with her as she plans on going there also. Tomorrow is scheduled to be a shorter day and should be easier to take.

April 26, 2002   Pickle Branch Shelter
                              Trail Distance: 9.9 miles

Today we had shorter mileage, but I was really exhausted when we finally came in. I can handle the levels and the downhills OK, but the "ups" took all of my energy. We believe the main problem now is just a lack of calories. Our food supply is getting low, it is taking us two days longer to reach a store than planned, our dried milk supply was two days short, and we need more food just to maintain our status quo.

The views from the crest are beautiful but rather strange. To the west, you see farms and roads in the valleys. To the east, there is nothing but forests with absolutely no signs of human habitation.

Today was supposed to be shorter and easier, but I just ran out of steam. When reaching the shelter, I tried to take a nap in the sleeping bag but could not get warm. I was so exhausted that sleep and warmth could not come. Mina took the dirty dishes from last night down to the water source, got them cleaned, and got a good supply of water for dinner. With some hot tea, hot chocolate, two kinds of soup mixes, potatoes, grits and gravy and a helping of hot oatmeal in me, I finally revived. We have cereal for breakfast, but no more food at all. Tomorrow, a grocery store is a MUST!

We saw and heard our first scarlet tanager today. We also heard our first owl and saw our first deer. These places really cool off at night. Again, it is so cold that I cannot write any more.

April 27, 2002   North Mountain Trail
Trail Distance: 6.0 miles

This day did not quite turn out as expected. We were due to reach VA 624 and a store for lunch about noon. We just did not anticipate Dragons Teeth and the formidable array of stone teeth that we had to pass before we reached Dragons Teeth. Each "tooth" demanded a climb up and over a fifty- to one-hundred-foot-high hill of rocks and boulders, and these were on top of a very sharp ridge so that there was no way to go around the rocks. With the sharp ridge and the sharp hills of rocks, it does appear to be a giant nature production of a dragon's jaw. It may appear pretty from a distance, but it was a real bear to hike and climb. Each tooth required a climb, and each climb took its toll. We kept thinking that there could not be another tooth and there was! Was there twelve, fifteen, or twenty? We could not tell, but they were tough. Getting to the end of the teeth just started the problem. Getting down was another! Climbing down the rock face was downright dangerous, and the backpacks did not help the situation. Several times, Mina had to take her pack off in order to climb down some of the more critical areas. In places, a single slip could have meant either serious injury or death. That rock face was nothing to be careless about.

After coming down from the more "interesting" aspects of the climb, we noticed a man resting on his way up. He was big! We later found that he weighed 330 pounds and had lost his job as a policeman because of being so overweight. On top of his own weight, his pack must have weighed another eighty to ninety pounds. Pots and pans were hanging all over it. He was going to hike the A.T. in order to lose weight. We really felt for him as he had a most difficult climb and hike ahead of him. We honestly did not think that he could make the climb.

Our twelve-plus-mile day turned out to be six miles. Taking over six hours to go six miles took its toll on us. Knowing of a hostel only 0.3 miles away, we jumped at the chance. This was a rather crude hostel but was well worth the visit. Joe and Wanda made us feel right at home. Joe drove us to a nearby store for much needed supplies and a much awaited lunch. The hostel is in a six-car garage, which could easily fit twelve cars. With no cars inside, there are five cots set up and more promised, hot showers, a stove and refrigerator, towels, and good company. We loved it!

There were seven of us hikers that Joe drove to the Homeplace Restaurant, which is considered by many hikers to be the best on the A.T. Two other hikers came in by the time Joe was called to pick us up. Their takeout dinner for two consisted of eight pieces of chicken, eight biscuits, sufficient pinto beans, string beans, some kind of super salad, mashed potatoes and gravy, peach cobbler and ice cream. Six people could have had sufficient food for dinner, and the $12 *total* price did not seem possible. That is one super restaurant. It was said that they feed from 1,500-2,700 people a day, and they feed them fast and as many refills as desired. The lemonade and iced tea just kept on coming.

It is raining again and is due to rain tomorrow. If so, we will just stay a while. We really do not wish to start out in the rain. We can't help it if it starts after we do, but we *can* help it if we wait a bit. We now have food for about four days so we can afford to wait. The people here are super, and the hikers are equally nice. For all that we know, some will also wait out the rain. We do hope that some of this rain makes its way to Pennsylvania. That state surely needed it.

Last evening we heard two kinds of owls and coyotes calling. Bird songs are becoming more common, although there are parts of every day when it is silent. The nights are still quite cool, and the mornings are sometimes hard to face. It is usually about 1:00

P.M. before we can take our gloves off. We keep thinking that summer is getting closer and we would like for it to hurry. We will have to wait for three more days before we can get our laundry done. We need it now! We got our much needed showers but our clothes will just have to wait.

April 28, 2002   Catawba Mountain Shelter
Trail Distance: 7.9 miles

Joe and Wanda Mitchell at the Four Pines Hostel are just super people. When we were ready to leave this morning, *after* having our cold cereal breakfast, Joe came up to the hostel and asked if anyone was ready for breakfast. He and Wanda had prepared another feast for us. We all waited the half hour that he said it would take, and he went into his home for our meal. We had fried eggs, homemade biscuits, sausage gravy, grits, bagels and coffee in more than sufficient quantity for all. We really hated to leave, but it was a necessity. This was one day when we felt that we had enough fuel to last us for the day. As it was, our energy level stayed high all day.

Just about the time we were planning on stopping for a lunch break, we came to the exit for the town of Catauba. Awaiting us after coming down the trail were three coolers containing various kinds of cold pop, candy, fudge, cookies and other goodies left there by "Grizzly" for the thru-hikers and section hikers. We left him our thanks as the timing was perfect.

We had three shelters to choose from today, one at seven miles, one at eight miles, and one at ten miles. One of the most popular viewing points on the A.T. is McAfee Knob, a large anvil-shaped block of rock jutting into space. It is between the eight-mile and the ten-mile shelters, and we wanted to see it in good light. We had earlier decided to wait until we reached the eight-mile shelter to make a decision on going on to McAfee Knob. As the day turned out, we started hearing thunder and the sky started darkening just before we reached the eight-mile shelter. We were lucky! Shortly after we arrived, the rain started.

First it was gentle, and gradually it increased in intensity. Finally, it became a deluge along with marble-sized hail. Within a short time, the picnic table and the ground became almost solid white. It melted fast, but it *was* a sight. Right in the middle of the hailstorm, a young man dashed into the shelter, very wet, and trying to protect his head from the hail. He was so thoroughly wet that he got one-third of the shelter wet. He just stayed until the rain stopped and went back to the Trail on his way to his car. A young Virginia Tech student, he was just out for a nice hike. Fortunately, the shelter dried up by the time that Sarge, a section hiker, came to join us for the night.

A very nice spring is close by so water is near and plentiful. The welcome sun came out after the rain and is expected to be with us tomorrow. The next two days hiking are not expected to be long or too hard. We shall see!

April 29, 2002   Lamberts Meadow Shelter
                                     Trail Distance: 8.2 miles

This day was an experience not for the faint at heart. It started with a relatively easy uphill one-and-a-half-mile hike to McAfee Knob, one of the most impressive rock formations on the A.T. This day was windy, far more windy than any remembered in the past. When we finally arrived at the top of McAfee Knob, "Sarge" was there resting. We took pictures of each other and they should have been motion pictures. The wind made it difficult to stand upright, difficult to keep a cap on, and even difficult to even stand still. Trying to stand on a slab of rock jutting into space with nothing under you for hundreds of feet and the wind trying to blow you over was a little beyond the "fun" stage.

Finally getting our fill of pictures and views, we started the hike down. We followed the crest line as usual in a large arc curving to the north. Miles later, we could look back and see where we had been. Looking to McAfee Knob, we were both amazed and impressed at what we had done.

A picture of McAfee Knob is featured on the front cover of the *Appalachian Trail Guide to Central and SW Virginia*. The views from there are most impressive.

Following the crest of the Tinker Mountain as it arcs north, the A.T. comes to the Tinker cliffs. For several hundred yards, the Trail follows the cliff edge, sometimes within two to three feet of the edge and always within just a few feet. The Trail here is definitely not for little children or those with a fear of heights. While the view of the countryside was just magnificent, the continual high winds took some of the pleasure away. As we got down from the Tinker Cliffs, we lost the wind for a while as we went down on the far side of the mountain. This did not last long. The wind caught us again, followed us to the shelter, and stayed with us most of the night. As the shelter is rather old, it has many cracks, and the wind found every one. It was not a good night for sleep.

We had passed a small stream yesterday full of watercress. I love the stuff and normally would have made a feast of it. As it was, I had none! The stream is also frequented by cattle, and we have already been warned that several hikers in the area have gotten sick after drinking untreated water. So, we passed up the watercress. Perhaps we will find some more later at a more remote area. I did find a morel mushroom by the side of the Trail, picked it, but could not get the grit and dirt out of it. Hikers had really covered it with grit. I did find and harvest a supply of wild onions. I also found some wild ramp but did not take any. We have to finish the onions first.

A small bird had built its nest inside the shelter in the rafters. Apparently unconcerned with human visitors, she continued to sit on her eggs while we were there. We never did find out the species of bird. We have some younger hikers staying for the night, and they all have very light packs. Examining their gear makes it fairly plain that they do not eat very well nor do they sleep comfortably. They just do not carry much food, and their sleeping bags are very thin. They are sacrificing comfort for light hiking weight. Everyone has to compromise, but they seemed to have gone overboard.

April 30, 2002   US 11, Troutville, VA
Trail Distance: 10.7 miles

This was a most pleasant day knowing that a town, a shower, good food, good sleep, and clean cloths awaited us. All in all, it was rather uneventful as the sights consisted of forests and beautiful views form the crest line that we had been following. Most of the land to our right was uninhabited as we could see no signs of it being populated. We did get good views of the Carvin Cove Reservoir. In spite of all of the local heavy rains, the reservoir was very low. The lake edge was at least a hundred feet from the end of the boat piers. It seems not to have received any of the local heavy rains that we were able to witness.

Our main concerns today were getting to town, to a shower, to a Laundromat, to a good meal, to a good grocery store, and to a nice soft bed. We received these items with pleasure and with our thanks.

Checking in at a local motel, we made the desk clerk a bit nervous. We had located a tick just as we checked in. We didn't like the tick either, but the clerk acted as if he had never seen one before. Fortunately, we have not found many ticks on us.

I tried to outdo myself at the grocery. Trying to get seven days supply, I actually got anywhere from seven to ten days supply of certain items. The result is a very heavy pack and I really feel it.

May 1, 2002   Wilson Creek Shelter
Trail Distance: 9.7 miles

Leaving Troutville with a heavy pack, the morning offered some concern. Luckily, the A.T. north was uphill but gradual. We had thought that we could only go 3.5 miles to the first shelter. Arriving there in super time, we felt fine and continued on to the next shelter.

We now hear much bird life, and the forests are fast turning green. The flowers are blooming, and the berries are budding. Perhaps in three to four weeks, other hikers will be able to enjoy some of the harvest. Dogwoods in bloom are very frequent as are some that we cannot identify. We still have not seen any mountain laurel. We suppose that we will just have to wait some more for these.

It rained again last evening but stopped by daybreak. We have been lucky so far. There have been many rains but they have been mostly at night or after we have reached a shelter. We know that it is just a matter of time before we get caught in a good one.

May 2, 2002   Bobblets Gap Shelter
                                Trail Distance: 7.3 miles

This shelter was not our destination. We had planned on hiking another three miles or so to the highway and hitching five miles to a campsite. Approaching this shelter, the sky started turning dark, and we heard thunder. That did it! We stopped at the shelter, and it started raining almost immediately. The rain increased along with lightning and thunder. And our old "friend", the wind, returned. Again, it was strong although not quite as strong as when we were on McAfee Knob. Several other hikers have stopped for the night, and more may arrive later.

The rain has now stopped and it has warmed a bit. Everyone is cooking inside, so the aroma is really appealing. We had hot tea and soup when we arrived, and that warmed us up a bit. We will be trying to eat as much as possible just to reduce our pack weight.

Three days from now, the Trail is all uphill for about five miles, and we really do not look forward to it. We can probably eat off three to four pounds of supplies, and we are going to try for it. It is now dinnertime for us so our cook has to stop writing and get back to his duties.

May 3, 2002   Peaks of Otter Recreation Area
                                Trail Distance: 3.2 miles

This was purposely a short day. We had intended on arriving here yesterday but the rain put a damper on that. It is probably just as well. The tent sites do not open until May 10 (our handbook just says May), and we had to stay in the lodge. Actually, when we arrived, we *chose* to stay in the lodge. It is quite cool and the idea of tenting a mile from the restaurant was not appealing. We made good time to the highway, covering 3.2 miles in 1.5 hours. As can be seen, the Trail was relatively easy. So far, it stays very close to the Blue Ridge Parkway (BRP) so that traffic can usually be heard and often seen. However, tomorrow, the Trail makes a wide swing away from the BRP, and we will not see the parkway again for about two days.

For those hikers expecting to pay $12 for a tent site here and then having to pay $89 for a room could be a real shocker. This is another example of not being able to believe all you read.

We did find out today that the very overweight hiker that we met earlier had retraced his steps to the hostel where he stayed two nights and was then driven to a bus station to return home. We really felt for him but the A.T. was no place for him. Hopefully, the shock of seeing just how out of shape he was will give him motivation to return to normal living conditions.

We are still amazed at what hikers will do to decrease their pack weight. Most sleep in what they wear during the day, have only one change of clothing, and eat the bare essentials. We have met no one who carries milk, either real or powdered. None have puddings, and most eat only a one-item dinner. Candy bars seem to be in preference to energy bars and few filter or treat their water. Bandaged feet seem to be the norm, as really good boots seem scarce. For the most part, all hikers that we have met have been super friendly, and helpful with advice, trail conditions, and what to expect ahead.

Getting a ride here once we left the Trail was a bit of a problem. There are very few vehicles of any kind on the BRP this day (Friday). Hopefully, more will be available tomorrow to take us the five miles back to the Trail. It took us about an hour to get a ride this morning and we were passed by less than a half dozen vehicles. Finally, a fellow hiker stopped and gave us a ride to the Peaks of Otter Recreation Center. This is a beautiful spot with great views of Sharp Mountain. The lines of the mountain look unreal. They make two almost straight lines converging on the top which is capped with large boulders. We just know that the A.T. Conference would love to reroute the Trail so that it could go up, over, and through the rocks on top. Well, perhaps some day they will but not now.

We still feel more comfortable in the eight- to ten-mile-a-day range. Our stamina is not up to much more than that. Perhaps as we get more realistic with our food supply, we will be able to average more. Mina still has a continuing problem with her backpack, and it does not appear to be correctable. It seems that the waistband used to settle the pack on her hips is just as wide as all others. There seems to be no allowance for those persons with smaller body frames. The result is the waistband is so wide that it pushes into her ribs so that she cannot tighten it sufficiently to allow the weight to rest on her hips. She has a condition where much of the weight rests on her shoulders and this is not good. It is fatiguing and can get painful. Her boots also have started giving her problems, either after a long day or going downhill. She is not one to complain but the discomfort is obvious. Hopefully, the Trail will toughen her; we know of no other solution.

By having a good cafe lunch and a full restaurant dinner, we hope to have the energy to tackle tomorrow. It is expected to be cool with possible showers. We do want our luck with the rain to continue.

May 4, 2002   Bryant Ridge Shelter
                              Trail Distance: 10.1 miles

This turned out to be a relatively easy day for us. We had been a bit concerned about getting a ride back to the A.T. Traffic is slow on the BRP and especially so early in the morning. After a super restaurant breakfast, one of the first cars stopped for us. It was driven by an Australian man who was sightseeing in the United States. He had just stopped at the lodge for a potty stop and was on his way west. We had a very pleasant conversation with him and found that he was a Civil War buff and was touring some of the battle sites. We wished that we could have spent more time with him, but our Trailhead came up fast.

At this point on the A.T., the Trail bears away from the BRP and will not rejoin it for two hiking days. So far, the Trail has been relatively easy, and we were making some good times. The rain came back during the day, requiring a cover for the backpacks. Since the rain was slight, we elected to not put our rain gear on.

We had looked forward to visiting this shelter as it was billed as being one of the largest on the entire Trail. It *was* large but it had one bad draw back. It leaked like a sieve! We had to change sleeping bag positions twice to get out of the drippings. With wet spots in our bags, we had to be careful to find dry areas in the shelter.

This shelter was also host to eight young men from Buchanan, Virginia. They had been here one day and were staying for two more. They partied all night with loud music all night. By the next morning, they had all fallen asleep, but the music carried on. These young men were the loudest, most profane, and most vulgar of any encountered. They apologized profusely for their language, but they did not stop. When I tried to get them to at least respect Mina by requesting them to use language that they would use around their mothers, they replied that their language *was* used at home. *Everybody* spoke that way! *All* their friends spoke that way. That was one profane bunch that we hope to never see again.

May 5, 2002   Thunder Hill Shelter
Trail Distance: 10.3 miles

We had not looked forward to this day. It meant an almost constant climb for seven of the ten miles that we were to hike. We were to go from 1,300 feet to over 4,400 feet, and we felt the drain. The Trail crossed the peak of Apple Orchard Mountain, at 4,425 feet, the highest peak that we will pass until we reach New Hampshire.

When we started hiking, we noticed a large radar facility on top of one of the distant mountains. We did not realize that ten miles later, we would be on top of that mountain and passing right in front of the facility. Shortly after passing the peak, we passed under the "Guillotine Rock" a large stone wedged between the stone bluffs. Naturally, the Trail passed under the guillotine. Actually, the "blade" did not seem that sharp, but it probably would not make any difference with a ton or more of stone coming down.

This was a nice shelter with a small stoned in spring for water. We are glad that we have it, but cannot believe that the spring will last through a dry summer.

After being almost sleepless the night before from the partying, we both slept very well this night. As this area is much higher than where we have previously hiked, the foliage on the trees is much more sparse. However, the birds are here. Our alarm clock in the morning is the singing of the birds. Now, *that* is our idea of a wake up call.

May 6, 2002   Matts Creek Shelter
                                 Trail Distance: 12.4 miles

Sometimes, a person just cannot believe all that he may read. This was thought to be an easy day. It was twelve miles, but was mostly thought to be downhill. As it turned out, the downhills and the uphills were often straight up or straight down. We had thought that we were making good time, but the markers that we encountered indicated that we were much slower than thought. Expecting to arrive at the shelter about 2:00 P.M., we did not arrive until 4:30 P.M. We both thought that we had covered much more than 12.4 miles. It felt more like fifteen or sixteen.

We are lower in altitude so we expect the temperatures to be more acceptable to us and the vegetation is definitely denser. We have seen many lady slippers, a few jack-in-the-pulpits, and acres of trilliums in full bloom. The flowers are many and profuse. It is too early for berries. Again, we have found morel mushrooms and *all* have been right by the Trail or directly in the Trail.

In two more days, we will go in for supplies and our restaurant and motel "fix". Our supplies are getting low and it will be time to restock and get cleaned up.

May 7, 2002	Punchbowl Shelter
	Trail Distance: 12.6 miles

Our views yesterday of the James River were spectacular. From far above, it seemed to be a tiny stream. We reached the river today and crossed it on a six-hundred-foot footbridge that had been endorsed by Bill Foot, a 1987 thru-hiker. This was no inexpensive undertaking but a well-funded engineering feat. This was a beautiful, permanent, steel and wood constructed bridge that should last for many, many years.

We both found the "ups" this morning to be surprisingly strenuous. By midmorning, we were "bushed". Reading about this section later, we were informed that it really *was* strenuous, rising one thousand feet in just one mile. By the time that we reached the top of big Rocky Row, we did not have much energy left.

As is becoming rather typical in late afternoon, we saw the skies darken and began to hear thunder in the distance. We debated whether to put our rain gear on and to change from boots to our Tevas. We decided not to change as the rains had been slow to start and were not usually heavy. Wrong decision! After one especially loud blast of thunder, the rain started in earnest and grew in intensity along with heavy winds. Within minutes we both were soaked along with sodden boots. Fortunately for us, the weather was relatively mild. With us moving fast, we did not feel the chill.

The Trail was very good and allowed us to move a bit faster than we normally would have. We still had to cross the crest of Bluff Mountain and the thunder and lightning was getting uncomfortably close. Just as we crested the mountain, one blast and accompanying lightning had to be *very* close to us. The sound and lightning were simultaneous. Needless to say, we raced as fast as we could down from the mountaintop.

The A.T. path was now a small stream cascading down the

mountainside. Even if our boots had not been soaked before, we could not have kept them dry. With the Trail narrowly hemmed in by foliage on both sides, we *had* to walk *in* the stream. The rain continued very heavy for many long minutes. By the time that we reached the shelter, it had slowed down to a drizzle. However, by that time, we were sodden and anxious to change into dry clothes.

Shortly after we arrived at the shelter and before we could change clothes, a single man and a husband and wife couple came in. I had the men wait outside to allow Mina to change. I just said, "I'm changing", and allowed the woman to turn her back, which she did. Without the energy expended on hiking, the wet clothes were beginning to feel downright cool.

It was a small but comfortable shelter, and we all got along very well. The others were hiking south, and the single man opted to sleep in his tent as many hikers choose to do.

With a small pond nearby, we were serenaded by various sounds throughout the night. The *other* night sounds were so noisy that you could hardly hear the bullfrogs. Sleep came easily and lasted all night. In our bags by 8:30 P.M., we did not arise until after 6:00 the next morning.

May 8, 2002   Buena Vista, VA
                               Trail Distance: 10.4 miles

On some days, we really hit it right. This was an easy day and a very nice one. Most of the Trail was well maintained with no steep "ups" or "downs". We had been informed that a past thru-hiker was at a point on the Trail about five miles up serving pancakes and bacon to the hikers. Only donations were accepted. For this, we eagerly awaited the treats. When we reached the designated spot, he was gone, but his camp and supplies remained. There were pancakes, sausage, and bacon that we heated up along with hot chocolate and apples for dessert. Tables and chairs were set with the morning newspaper (two days old). All of the fixings were there except for our host. We stayed for about an hour and got thoroughly relaxed. We did leave something in the donation box along with a note telling him who we were. However, he did not get a picture taken of us as we were told that he normally took a photo of his guests. It was probably just as well. I am looking kind of grizzly, and Mina would not wish to go to church looking as she does. This was just another pleasant experience from a stranger on the Trail. Hikers call it, "Trail Magic"!

Later on our hike, we passed a southbound-hiking couple who were out just for a day hike. For whatever reason, they insisted that we take two of their cold cokes. Actually, they did not have to insist very hard. Those cold cokes really felt good.

A few days back, a "Trail Angel" had left a case of orange pop in one of the shelters. We had stopped there for lunch and partaken of two of the cans. As firm believers of the slogan, "You pack it in, you pack it out", our Trail garbage now included four crushed pop cans. It weighs very little and is easily disposed of when we reach a trash container. Most of the hikers do the same. Only when the Trail crosses a road or when a shelter is very near to a road do we find any trash. A.T. hikers are a breed apart as they are super neat.

Shortly after partaking of our pancake lunch, we reached the Pedlar Dam, holding back a lake containing the drinking water for Lynchburg, Virginia. The dam was overflowing sharply in contrast to the drastically low level of the Carvin Cove Reservoir that we had seen earlier in our hike. The dam was not that wide but was relatively high. Only when we had climbed the hills beside of the lake were we able to appreciate the size of the lake. No fishing or swimming is permitted in the lake. We can appreciate the no swimming part, but the no fishing seems such a waste. Lakes, like fields, simply need to be cultivated and harvested.

Later in the day, we passed by the remnants of the Brown Community, a community founded by freed slaves after the Civil War. We saw traces of old chimneys and stone fences that were still in fairly good condition. Even though the community disbanded early in the twentieth century, the well-constructed fences have lasted. It had to have been a difficult life with share cropping the less than fertile and very rocky soil. We understand that tobacco, corn and wheat were the main crops in the little valley.

Hiking to U.S. 60, we then hitched a ride to Buena Vista, Virginia, a small town about nine miles from the A.T. Since our boots were still very wet, we wore our Tevas, which worked very well indeed. In fact, it was about the first day that Mina had no complaints about her feet. We wouldn't mind continuing hiking in the Tevas *except* that carrying the boots on our backpacks added several pounds to the pack. Believe me, we did not appreciate the added weight.

May 9, 2002   Buena Vista, VA
                              Trail Distance: 0.0 miles

This was planned to be a "zero" day as we needed to restock, refuel ourselves, shower, clean our clothes, and get a few special items that we needed. Our water filter broke, and I had hoped to repair it. Tomorrow, we shall see if I succeeded. Otherwise, our chlorine drops will have to work for us.

Buena Vista is a friendly place but rather spread out. We had to take a cab to the grocery as the nearest is about two miles away. Tomorrow, a local resident has agreed to drive us back to the A.T. It is too far to walk and this location is not a good place to get a ride. Mr. Mitchell will be picking us up at 7:30 A.M.

Tomorrow will probably be a long day for us. It will be twelve miles before we will have a tenting site and another two miles to the shelter. However, the first three miles will be continually "up". Down in the lower levels, the weather has been mild. Tomorrow, we will go back to the four-thousand-foot elevations, and it should be much cooler.

It rained heavy again today. It was not predicted, but now the weather channel claims that we can expect more and some may be rather severe. We *are* quite amazed at the hail reports that we have been receiving. Golf ball sized and grapefruit sized hail is nothing to just brush off. Our marble-sized hail was bad enough; we do not want anything larger.

Yesterday, we passed a recent casualty of our high winds. A tree perhaps two and a half feet in diameter blew down and took the Trail with it. At that spot, the Trail was cut into the side of a steep hill. When the tree went, its roots completely removed the Trail. All that was left was a large hole about four feet deep, full of mud, that we had to slither down into and then climb out the other side using the tree roots as a ladder. It was *not* a clean operation. There was no way to go around the hole; we *had* to go through it.

We carefully measured our food requirements and purchased absolutely no more than we will use in five days. I had just estimated at our last resupply stop and we *still* have a five-day supply of some of the things purchased then. No wonder my pack was so heavy.

Tomorrow's weather is supposed to be mild and sunny. Hopefully, this will hold true. With a renewed full pack and a long climb, we really would like for Mother Nature to cooperate. However, with an extra days' rest and full tummies, we think that we are up to it. We know that our bad habit acquired of eating everything in sight *plus* a calorie-dripping dessert is something that can be only temporary. But it does feel good while it lasts.

May 10, 2002   North Fork Piney River
                         Trail Distance: 12.1 miles

Today was my daughter Janet's birth date, but there was no way that I could call her to wish her a happy birthday. Hopefully, she will know that I remembered. We didn't know if we could make the next shelter today. Depending on what you read, it was 14.0, 13.6, or 13.1 miles. However, by the time that we covered ten miles, we knew that we couldn't make any of them. Surprisingly, Mina was the more tired today. She sounded as if all body parts were aching. Rather than making us both more miserable, we opted to tent out by a stream with some good tent sites available. We thought that others would be joining us, but they chose to go on to the next shelter.

Today, we crossed Bald Knob, which wasn't bald at all. It may have been at one time but it is covered in trees now. Two miles further on, we crossed Cold Mountain which was as bald as it gets. Not only does it not have any trees or bushes, but the government keeps it mowed so that it will stay bald. There were beautiful views from the top that were enjoyed as we had our lunch there.

This was the first night of this trip that we used our tent. It had been used frequently on non-hiking trips so that it was no big deal setting it up. It does offer certain advantages to us. Not only does it offer privacy, but also it is warmer, and it protects us from the wind. Even setting it up and taking it down requires little time.

Even though bears are not common in this area, we do have to act as if they are here. Accordingly, our food supply was sacked and hung over a tree branch about ten feet off the ground. Our backpacks were covered with their rain covers just in case it might rain. The morning found all in good condition. We had no bears and no rain *plus* we got a good night's sleep.

May 11, 2002   The Priest Shelter
Trail Distance: 8.8 miles

This was another short day for us as we reached the shelter at 2:20 P.M. We had been passed by many hikers today, but only one stayed for the night. (We just this minute saw a beautiful doe stroll by the edge of the clearing). Water is from a nearby stream that we doubt will last for the summer. It is flowing very well now, but it *and* the shelter is near to the crest of the mountain. Reason claims that there is very little upper ground for the water supply to be continued for very long.

We have had some warm days, but this was a cool one. Right now, we have layered our clothing and jackets to the point where we are wearing all that we can. I am still shivering!

Although rarely seen by us in the past, we are seeing dozens of jack-in-the-pulpits. As they are rather hard to spot, there are probably many more that we do *not* see. Passing old, abandoned orchards on some of the hilltops, we can expect the September-October hikers to be able to harvest some of the different kinds of fruit. Passing strawberry, blueberry, and blackberry vines, we know that it will be just a short time before some of these berries will be ready for picking.

Once again, the chill is getting to me and affecting my writing. I can hardly read what I have written.

May 12, 2002   Maupin Field Shelter
Trail Distance: 14.6 miles

We knew that this would be a long, strenuous day, and it turned out to be all that and more. Leaving at 7:30 A.M., we did not reach the shelter until 7:00 P.M. The first five miles was steadily downhill and then we had about six miles of uphills. The first part of the uphills was relatively nice, but the going kept getting harder and steeper. We were not hiking anymore; we were climbing up and over rocks, rock steps and steep inclines. Mina became physically spent. Once at the top of Three Ridges, it was three miles downhill to the shelter. We were both spent by the time that we reached it. There were absolutely no tent or water sites within six miles of the shelter, plus our limited food supply forced us to continue even though the bodies demanded rest.

There were three others in the shelter and possibly six others tenting out. It was a good tenting area, and we chose to tent also. By the time that we got the tent up and got dinner cooked, we ate in the dark.

Sleep did not come easy for Mina. She ached all over! The next morning, we had a slow start. Mina was still sore all over, we both were slow, and it was almost 8:30 A.M. before we were able to start out.

May 13, 2002   Dripping Rock Parking Area
Trail Distance: 6.5 miles

This area gets its name because of a natural spring right beside the highway that seems to come out of a pile of rocks. Actually, the water is coming from under the rocks, but the appearance is striking. Besides, a place called Dripping Rocks is catchier that Spring Under Rocks.

Mina was still sore and tired from the previous day, so we were rather slow on the Trail. Actually, the Trail was relatively easy. However, when you are bone tired, everything is difficult.

We had been planning on camping out near a spring at about the eleven- or twelve-mile mark. Mother Nature changed that! It started to rain lightly and looked as if it would continue. Rather than putting a tent up in the rain and cooking in the rain, we decided to hitch a ride into town where the Trail crossed the BRP. About the second vehicle to pass was a small motor home that we just waved to as we did not think that they would stop. We guess that that intrigued them. The motor home continued on, turned around when it could, and came back to see if we needed help. A super couple from Florida, they not only took us to Waynesboro, but also stopped at the outfitters while we shopped, and then drove us to a motel. They were really fine people as are many that we meet while hiking.

After a shower and clean clothes, we "pigged out" at an "all you can eat" family restaurant. We had a ball! Later, we were able to do our laundry and completed a limited grocery shopping before sleeping a most restful night.

May 14, 2002   Rockfish Gap, VA
                                   Trail Distance: 14.6 miles

A local shuttle drive took us back to the Dripping Rock parking area early in the morning. We then limited our packs to only what we would need if we had to stay on the Trail for one night. We took no tent, no extra clothing, and only one day's food supply. With the super light packs, we thought that we may be able to cover the fourteen miles from Dripping Rocks to Rockfish Gap. As it was, we did! We were able to move much faster and with much more ease than we had been used to. Probably, our packs now weighed somewhere in the neighborhood of what the younger hikers carried. At any rate, we were able to really move!

The day was clear but extremely windy and downright cold. We were stuck wearing our shorts as we took nothing extra. We did have a jacket to cover our short sleeved shirts, but we were continually cold until past noon. It then warmed up a little and then got cold again. So much for the seventy-two degrees the weather channel promised us!

We moved fast to try to stay warm. Most of the Trail was very nice indeed so we were able to cover distance at a better rate than we were used to. Of course, anytime the Trail came close to a lookout point, we had to view the countryside. Here, the views were of homes and farms in the valley. It is quite a bit different from previous mountain views where all you could see were forests covering everything.

Now that we had completed hiking this section, our plans were to take a bus the next day to Port Clinton, Pennsylvania, where we left off last year. The bus was supposed to leave at 8:15 A.M., but we had some misgivings. Greyhound did not have the correct phone number for the bus stop. It is not a bus terminal, and the name given for the bus stop changed eight months ago. We could only hope that the time was correct. When we finished our hike this day, it was no problem getting a ride back to our motel. When you are close to the Trail, most residents know that you are not just bums and most willingly give rides. Of course, it helps to have a lady hiker along. They *do* come in handy!

We now came up to the point where we had begun our hike into Shenandoah National Park last year. Accordingly, we must now get a bus to Port Clinton, Pennsylvania, were we had left off last year.

David's total miles on A.T.: 1,194

Mina's total miles on A.T.: 697.8

CHAPTER NINE

May 15, 2002   Port Clinton, PA
                      Trail Distance: 0.0 miles

By hiking into Rockfish Gap the day before, we had made connections with the start of our prior years hike. Our plan was to take a bus to Port Clinton and continue north on our A.T. hike. We did have some initial concerns about getting a bus ride. There is no bus station in Waynesboro, only a pickup and drop-off point. The Greyhound Bus "800" number left something to be desired. After going through a long, detailed menu that told us nothing, we were finally able to talk to a person who could barely speak English. Much of her information was either incorrect or out of date. The name of the business where the bus was supposed to stop had gone out of business about eight months before. The local phone number given was for an Exxon station that knew nothing about a bus stop. The only other things that we had were the time the bus was to stop, the address, and the fare. Fortunately, these were correct. We must say that the Greyhound buses were on time. They have always been within minutes of arriving or leaving on time.

After breakfast at our Comfort Inn, we walked the quarter mile to the bus stop and waited. Our concerns were for naught as the bus came by right on time.

We had to go to Washington, D.C., and transfer to another bus. In Washington, we noticed that about 75 percent of the U.S. flags were flying at half mast, and no one could explain why. In some locations, some of the flags were at half mast and others at full mast, including all the flags at the airport. It was puzzling, and we never did get an answer. Either all should have been at half mast or none.

Later, we had a two-hour layover in Reading, Pennsylvania, and were able to enjoy our third anniversary dinner in a very nice little Lebanese restaurant. As we were the only customers for at least a half hour, the young waiter stayed and chatted with us. It was a most enjoyable dinner eating foods that I was not used to. Mina had grown up on similar foods so did not find them too unfamiliar.

Leaving Waynesboro at 8:15 A.M., we arrived in Port Clinton at 10:30 P.M. At that time of night, everything, including the local hotel, was closed. Fortunately, we knew of a pavilion where hikers were welcome. Taking our packs there, we joined six other hikers who were fast asleep. For us, sleep was not easy as the highway traffic was heavy and continued all night. However, we were back in Port Clinton where we had left off the previous year, and we were ready to continue our hike north.

May 16, 2002	Windsor Furnace Shelter Trail Distance: 6.1 miles

There were several items on our agenda today, so we took them in order. First, a short hike to a nice restaurant that we remembered from the year before got us a super breakfast, one that we normally would not allow ourselves to eat. Then we visited the local post office where we picked up our general delivery package that we had mailed to ourselves. We had not listed just what we had included in the package and found ourselves with too much of certain items of food. Rather then be overweight with our packs, we mailed the excess to our next general delivery pickup point. Also, we mailed back home several pounds of clothing that we felt we did not need anymore.

After the above, we visited the local outfitters and purchased a new, lighter weight stove. The old stove was in excellent condition, but it just weighed too much. Probably, at least a pound was saved with the new purchase. The old stove got donated to the "hiker's box" for anyone else who might find a use for it.

After getting our chores done, we started the relatively short hike to the shelter. Oh yes, those Pennsylvania rocks were back.

We had not forgotten them; we just wished that they had forgotten us. They had not! Actually, the last half of the day was relatively easy to take.

We passed by Pocahontas Springs, which is stated to be reliable in even dry weather. There were actually three springs about ten feet apart that were really putting out the water. Volunteers had built rock mounds around each spring to protect them from debris and leaves. We were really impressed with the work that had been done.

Although most of our hiking was in the forests, we did get a few fine views of the surrounding countryside. Even with all of the fine views that we have seen, we still look forward to the next view.

Pennsylvania has had some rain since last year as we were happy to find out. We hope that it will continue through New York. We will have company at our shelter this evening as at least three hikers will join us. As usual, they are nice company and we looked forward to conversations with others.

May 17, 2002   Eckville Shelter
                              Trail Distance: 9.1 miles

Today, we hiked a section that we had hiked last fall without a backpack. Wearing the pack sure makes a difference. Leaving our shelter at 7:15 A.M., we easily reached Pulpit Rock and the Pinnacle before noon. Both were great viewing spots with the Pinnacle rated as one of the best on the A.T. The weather held good, and the viewing was great. It is really worth the hike up for the view. However, if a person had a choice, it should be done without a full pack. The rocks, the ever present rocks, do make for some troublesome hiking.

Nearing the end of our hike today, we both missed the A.T. markers indicating that the Trail had turned. The result was about a quarter-mile, out-of-the-way hike to a parking lot. We had been making good time on a good trail and simply did not pay attention to the lack of A.T. markers. Later, we did another quarter mile out of the way when I did not carefully read the directions to find the shelter. The written directions were good; they were simply not read!

This is another neat shelter. It is an enclosed structure behind a caretaker's home. Room for only six, each hiker has his or her own bunk. Water is from a faucet and solar showers are available although with our cool weather, we doubt that many will make use of it. A refrigerator is full of pop and will accept donations only. Complete with a flush toilet (we miss them) and plenty of reading material, it will be comfortable tonight which is scheduled to be wet and cold. So far, we have no company. The two men and dog that stayed with us last night went on to the next shelter. Perhaps if I had not fouled up so, we may have decided to go on. Oh well, it is too late for that now and useless to fret over it.

We did see a beautiful diamond back rattlesnake today. It was on the side of the Trail and started rattling just as I saw it. Coiled up, it was difficult to estimate its size, but was probably in the four- to five-foot range. Its body was as large as my forearm. We took a couple of pictures for the record and warned other hikers of its existence so that they would be on the lookout for it. This shelter has a large listing of snakes of Pennsylvania. The diamond back is not among them and only a timber rattlesnake is listed. Perhaps some expert can tell us exactly what we did see.

We easily can see that Pennsylvania has been receiving some rain. Many springs are in places that our maps do not show and the streams are running with a good supply of water.

We are hoping to be able call Mina's daughter and son-in-law tomorrow. So far, we have not been able to call them and may not be able to even call tomorrow. Pay phones are scarce even in towns. They may not even be able to see us, but we would like to make the offer. If not tomorrow, perhaps later!

Foliage is full now, but there are no berries yet and very little mountain laurel is seen. We *did* see our first pileated woodpecker today but still have not heard a single veery. Where are they?

May 18, 2002   PA 309, Blue Mountain Summit
Trail Distance: 11.5 miles

It rained last night, rained some more, and continued raining. Rain actually began about 6:00 P.M. and continued until 9:00 A.M. today. The rain gauge kept by the shelter attendant registered one and a half inches. That is wet enough! We all awoke about 6:00 A.M. to the rain, but no one chose to leave their bags until about 7:00 A.M. Accompanying the rain was some cool weather. It was only fifty degrees in the shelter and the day's high was supposed to be only fifty-two. Actually, we think it hit the high early as the day seemed to cool as it progressed. I kept two jackets and my gloves on for most of the day. Mina never took off her gloves.

We debated whether to stay in the shelter for another day to let the rain pass or start hiking in the cold rain. Finally, the rain slackened, and we decided to try for the next shelter. It was 7.4 miles away. If we arrived there dry and feeling well, we could always decide whether to go another 4.1 miles to a bed and breakfast and restaurant.

The initial couple of miles were rather interesting. The rainfall had caused the main stream to overflow its banks, caused many new streams to flow into the Trail, and caused the Trail to *become* a creek in many places. There were numerous places where we had to find our way around flooded trails. Gradually, we climbed in elevation leaving most of the streams behind us. As we went higher, the Trail remained wet, but the water content became replaced with rocks.

We early got our fill once more of Pennsylvania rocks and boulders. These things are difficult to navigate when dry. When wet, they are downright dangerous. Fortunately, we had no serious slips or falls. Going through one hundred yards of boulders is no fun. Then having to repeat it several times is even less fun. However, we did it! That is where the Trail was and we had to maneuver through the piles.

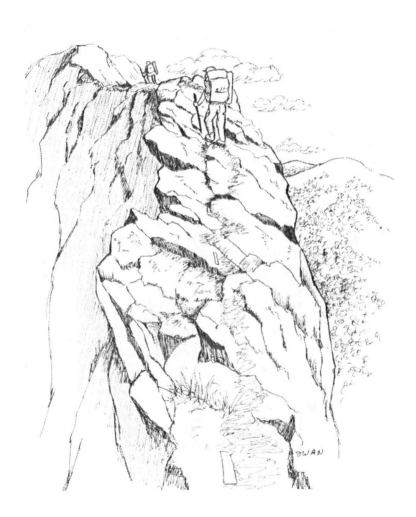

Over the past few days, we have seen several old stone fences
that had been constructed probably more than one hundred years
ago. Most are still in fine condition. Today, we saw something
similar but on a much larger scale. Mother Nature had constructed
a stone fence using much larger stones to a height from twenty-
five to thirty feet. It was in a virtual straight line and continued for
hundreds of yards. We were concerned that the A.T. would decide
to climb up to the crest. We actually expected it! However, it just
stayed below the wall on a rock path of its own and paralleled it for
a short distance.

Once up to elevation, the Trail stayed fairly even but was
extremely rocky and traversed many boulder fields. When we did
arrive at the Allentown Hiking Club shelter, it was fairly early; we
were not tired, so we decided to go to the bed and breakfast.

The Allentown Hiking Club has done some serious work,
making the Trail more manageable and easier to take. The shelter
is relatively new, rather modern in appearance, and well kept up.
The club is really making its presence felt.

Our stay in the B & B has been very comfortable. There are
only three bedrooms, although the restaurant serves a much larger
crowd. After a nice shower (much needed), we enjoyed a rather
large dinner to which we did honor.

The Trail from the Allentown shelter to the B & B was a "piece
of cake". It was level with no rocks and we covered it in one and
two-thirds of an hour. For us, that is fast. We have no idea what
tomorrow will bring. Our TV in the room has no weather channel,
and no one knows what the weather is expected to be. We guess
that we will just have to wait and see.

May 19, 2002   Slatington, PA
                          Trail Distance: 13.3 miles

Today was another experience! We had told you yesterday of
the rock ridges that we had seen and thankfully did not have to

cross. Today, we encountered an even larger one and not only crossed it but had to walk the peak for about one hundred yards. Now, that doesn't sound like too much, does it? Try and picture a boulder ridge with slopes of about sixty degrees with a one-hundred-foot drop to the ground on one side and a seventy-five-foot drop to the ground on the other. The A.T. follows the very crest! A person is either climbing up to or down from or trying to balance on the edges. It is no place for the faint of heart, for trail dogs, for those unsure of their footing, or for those afraid of heights. The views were great, however! It is locally known as "The Cliffs", but we call it the "Knife Edge". In addition to the rock ridges, we had our usual day of rocky paths and boulder fields to cross. We are sure getting tired of the Pennsylvania rocks.

We passed two shelters in order to come to Slatington. Here, we will have a room inside and availability for supplies, a shower, good food, and phone calls. Normally, an inside room would not appeal too much to a hiker but we have seen some record setting low temperatures in the area. When we are dressed and expecting cool days and nights, temperatures in the high 30s are rather uncomfortable. This lodging is far from being fancy or even reasonably acceptable, but the owner is nice, considerate, and graciously picks us up from the Trail and drops us back on it.

Our host also suggested that we may wish to "slack pack" the next portion of the Trail as it is unusually difficult. Between getting food supplies tomorrow and trying to get me a haircut and beard trim, we will have a shorter time to hike so "slack packing" a short distance sounds reasonable.

Normally, we could have phoned the lodge facility from a car dealership when we had come off the Trail. However, Sunday found the business closed so we had to "thumb it". A young lady finally stopped for us and took us directly to our destination.

With a fine meal after a fine shower, we were ready to sleep the sleep of the innocent. Tomorrow is supposed to be just as cold as today but we can only wait and see.

May 20, 2002   Little Gap
                               Trail Distance: 5.3 miles

Taking our host's suggestion, he drove us to Little Gap where we hiked back to the lodge. This was a short but very strenuous hike that we would strongly recommend to any person opposed to the actions of the EPA. We hiked over a mountain that had been nearly killed by the operations of a former zinc-smelting plant before it was shut down by the EPA. Try to imagine a mountain almost devoid of plant life and bird life in an area where other mountains are lush and green. Picture a place where there is little soil as it had been blown away because there was no plant life to hold it. Picture hundreds of acres of bleached, light gray rocks covering the mountain side and top it with dead trunks of trees dotting the scene. Like a scene from *Dante's Inferno*, it is both sickening and maddening. Some people's greed would destroy a mountain for profit. Slowly, plants are just beginning to grow again, but it will take many generations for the area to be acceptable again.

The views from the top were just fantastic. With no trees in the way, we could see to the horizon in at least a 180-degree arc. The day was super clear so we could easily see the river going through Lehigh Gap and the various major highways converging on the area.

Our restocked food supply should take us to Saturday where we may be able to meet Mina's daughter and son-in-law. It would be a pleasure for us and we are looking forward to it. Again, with a full meal under our belts, we think that we can take the Trail tomorrow with full "fuel" tanks.

May 21, 2002   Leroy Smith Shelter
                               Trail Distance: 10.8 miles

The mountain north of Little Gap was far different from the southern part. Whereas the southern portion is barren, the northern part is lush with vegetation. Fortunately, the effects of the zinc smelting carried for only about five miles.

It was a bit rocky getting up to the top of the mountain, but the distance wasn't too far or too rough. Once on top, it was the old story of rocky paths. All in all, we made reasonable time and reached the shelter by 3:30 P.M. I suppose we could have made it sooner, but our 8:00 A.M. ride did not materialize until 9:00 A.M.

Views were really limited today, and we saw no signs of any water. We have heard virtually no birds for the past few days and seen very few. We had become accustomed to seeing many flowers and now see very few. Put all of that on top of extremely cool weather and it seems that we are having an early winter. Hopefully, this cool spell will be gone in another couple of days.

When considering everything, we are not having too much fun. The nights are downright cold, the days are cool, views are scarce, and the Trail is very rocky. A person has to watch virtually every step. If he doesn't, he will be sure to trip or stumble. This is not hiking; it is more like rock walking. We will sure be glad to put Pennsylvania rocks behind us. For all that we know, we could be passing much large wildlife and never see them because of having to constantly watch each step.

May 22, 2002   Kirkridge Shelter
Trail Distance: 13.8 miles

If most of the A.T. was like today, we would quit real soon. Today was not hiking! It was more of trying to finish an obstacle course. There is such a thing as rocky trails and Pennsylvania has its share of them. Today, the Trail *was* rock. All but about the last two miles were rocks and boulders. Going was slow and treacherous. I tripped twice. The first time, my Chattahoochee cane broke my fall, but it broke. The cane (hiking stick) had been with me since the first day on the Trail, so it will be missed. My second fall could have been somewhat more serious. My foot got jammed between two rocks, and I fell rather than taking a chance of trying to free the foot and spraining it in the process. Mina got some practice in trail first aid as I did cut my elbow slightly.

Later in the day while going "over" Wolf Rocks, Mina took a nose dive on the rocks. There was concern on both parties as *these* rocks were more dangerous to navigate. There was usually some distance between the rocks, and the drop was normally more than just a few feet. Fortunately for her, her fall was onto a large flat rock that tilted a bit. She caught herself before she went over the edge. She got a few scrapes and bruises but no major damage. These rocks represent the southern glacial limit from the last ice age. The views are great from the top. We just wish that we had a choice of coming up to them for the view rather than being required to "walk the crest". Others have done it, the A.T. goes that way, so we must do it also. However, we do *not* plan on volunteering to do it again. Fortunately for us, most of the treacherous parts of the Trail that we have gone over have been in dry weather. Wet weather would have made some stretches downright hazardous.

This was a long day. While there were no great "ups" or "downs", the continuous rocks and boulders made it mighty tedious. We do not think that there were many views. Even if wildlife had crossed our paths a short distance away, we would have missed them. Watching your step, *every* step, does not make for fun hiking. We are hopeful that the Pennsylvania rocks will soon be behind us for good. Our trail guide states that most of the misery should stop at the shelter.

Crossing the Delaware River at the Delaware Water Gap, we are now officially in New Jersey. Our guides promise us that we may still see a few more of the Pennsylvania rocks and they will be with us all the way to Maine, *but* most of them will be behind us. We accept any blessings, small as they are, that may come our way. We are really sick of Pennsylvania rocks. Perhaps some day we may be able to joke about them but we are not in a joking mood now.

We have some hikers with us at this shelter that we have met before. They and their dog are good company. Today was especially rough on Mina. Last night, she was so cold that she got very little sleep. Still cold this morning, she had to hike thirteen miles with little rest. This was a rough thirteen miles!

May 23, 2002   Backpacker Site
                               Trail Distance: 11.2 miles

Shelters are non-existent on this section of the Trail. This site is the only one open to campers. All others are closed to camping as are open fires. We had not expected one, but a privy is provided. The ground is still rocky, but there is *some* soil around. By doing some searching, we found a spot reasonably free of rocks for us to put up our tent.

Coming into Delaware Water Gap, we had some fine views of the Delaware River and surrounding countryside from atop the ridge that we were hiking. It is beautiful country looking at it from one thousand feet up.

There was a hostel at Delaware Water Gap that we could have stayed. However, we are planning on meeting with Mina's daughter and son-in-law day after tomorrow, and our hiking budget required us to put in a few more miles today.

The weather is warming up a bit, and this day was sunny and clear all day. No rain is expected for the next couple of days, and we took kindly to this report. We are now back in bear country, some have been spotted nearby, so we must either hang our food supply out of their reach or put it in a "bear box" during the night. This campsite came equipped with a bear box so our food will be safe. We *think* we will be, also. A bear box is a metal chest about the size of a large cedar chest that can be latched so that animals cannot get inside.

Compared to yesterday, today was a snap. We covered the eleven miles by 3:15 P.M., and not once did Mina have a problem with her feet or her shoulders. Again, there were no large "ups" or "downs" and that may have something to do with it. We saw a young deer stroll by at a distance. Hopefully, we may be able to see some bears.

May 24, 2002   Blue Mountain Lakes Road
                              Trail Distance: 13.0 miles

Happily for us, this turned out to be a fairly easy day of hiking. In fact, some was very easy. Since the distance was relatively long for us, we really welcomed the easy hiking.

Soon after leaving our tent site, we passed by Sunfish Pond, a small lake left behind after the last glacier retreated. We have no idea how they can tell that. Since the lake has a high mineral content, only a few species of fish and frogs can live in the water. We drank the water, and it had no noticeable taste to us.

A little further on our hike, we came to the abandoned Catfish Fire Tower. Naturally, we had to climb the sixty feet to the top for a splendid 360-degree view. The tower looked and felt higher than sixty feet, but that was the stated height. At any rate, the views were worth the climb.

As is usual for us, we spent most of the day hiking the crest and got some beautiful views of the countryside. We also got a fine view of a hognose snake that was beside the Trail. For those not familiar with this kind of snake, it puffs its throat out like a cobra when it is excited. It didn't fool us, but we left it alone nevertheless. After all, we were invading *its* home territory. We are still amazed at how much of the land is in forests. It is almost as if all of the surrounding land is sparsely populated. This is a strange concept to me as I had always thought of Pennsylvania as being very densely settled all over.

Both of our guide books claim that there is tenting available right at Blue Mountain Lake road. However, once we arrived, we saw several signs warning that there was no camping allowed a half mile south of the road or 3.5 miles north of it. Being rather tired, there was no way that we could go another 3.5 miles, and we sure were not going to back up. Finally, we saw another sign that indicated that thru-hikers (that's us) could camp near the Trail. Some signs said we could not camp and one said that we could. We really had no choice so we set up camp deep in the forest. Before we got in our tent for the night, we took the bear reporting to heart and put all of our food and dirty dishes in a sleeping bag container and strung it about ten feet off the ground. As far as we could tell in the morning, we had no visitors. All alone in a pine forest, we slept like babies.

May 25, 2002   Culvers Gap
                                Trail Distance: 10.6 miles

This day was planned five days ago to come into town and visit with Mina's daughter and son-in-law who would drive up to visit with us. Hiking was fairly easy, and we arrived at the end of the Trail in early afternoon. Worthington's Bakery, famous on the Trail, greeted us so we bought a half dozen cinnamon rolls, ate four, and then called the local motel for a pickup.

After showering and getting cleaned up, we were greeted not only by Noel and Kevin but also by Bill and Lori, Mina's son and *his* wife. We had a really fine visit. With their car, they were able to help us with our grocery shopping and laundry. After taking care of our necessities, we all enjoyed a truly great meal. Mina really impressed her children with the amount of food that she was able to consume. Of course, I did my share, and all left satisfied.

May 26, 2002   Rutherford Shelter
                                Trail Distance: 11.8 miles

There may have been some good views today, but we could not see anything. In solid clouds for most of the day, it continued foggy and very cool. By late afternoon, the sun peeked through a bit and it did warm up some. All in all, the hiking was easy and fast. We had few of our ups and downs and that made for pleasant hiking.

Our shelter is 0.4 miles off the A.T., and it was a very pleasant surprise. Expecting an old unattractive structure, it *was* old but very nicely maintained. Complete with benches to sit on, a picnic, table, and a bear-proof container for food, it lacks only a privy. I suppose we should not expect everything.

May 27, 2002   Jim Murray "Secret Shelter"
Trail Distance: 9.6 miles

It is funny how a chance encounter can completely change a person's plans. We had planned several days ago to go into Unionville, New York, to make use of their hostel and get stove fuel. Last evening, a park ranger stopped by to see if anyone was using the shelter and to see how they were doing in their hiking. Probably, the real reason that he stopped by was to see if everything was legal. Fires are strictly prohibited with warning signs all over. However, camp stoves *are* permitted. In talking with the ranger, we had mentioned that we were planning on staying in the hostel this evening. He strongly recommended against it as it was over a bar and we would not be able to get much sleep for the noise. Instead, he recommended Jim Murray's "secret shelter" a couple of miles short of Unionville. We made a good choice in following his recommendation.

Jim Murray was a thru-hiker in 1989 and has a farm here. One of the small buildings on his farm has sleeping room for about five sleeping bags on the small second floor. The first floor contains a shower with hot water, a large sink, and a clothes' dryer. There is not room for anything else. All is privately owned, he charges no fee, will accept no donations, and claims that hikers keep it maintained so that he has to do nothing to it. It is most appreciated by us and by all who have benefited from staying here.

Today started out a bit on the rough side. It was foggy, and we had more rocks for the first two miles or so. Gradually, the Trail improved so that we arrived here at 2:10 P.M. It *was* a short day!

One of the points of interest today was the High Point Monument, a Washington Monument-type structure standing on the highest point in New Jersey. There was also an observation deck for viewers, but it was useless for us. The low-lying cloud structure made all views nil. All of the views today were, for the most part, shrouded in clouds. At least, we could look up periodically to see around us. Those Pennsylvania rocks required us to watch every step as every step could trip us up.

This place is really serene. The owner has two burros grazing nearby that let us hear some really weird braying. We have heard burros before but nothing like the sounds coming out of these two. Mina is having a ball with the bird life. Today, she saw her first indigo bunting and she has seen several scarlet tanagers that she has never seen before. However, most of what we see and hear, we simply cannot identity. So far, we have seen no bears but we still put our food and trash either in a bear box or hang it at least ten feet up a tree. Mice have not been bothering us either.

We have found several of the shelters with bird nests either in the rafters or under the overhang by the gutter. We are not sure what species of bird is doing this, but all are the same species. We are assuming that most of the nests have young in them as the parents are constantly flying in and out. They are most uncomfortable with the human presence. These little birds had better grow up fast as the main swarm of hikers will soon be upon them.

We have seen stone walls in the past but never as many as we saw today. There had to have been dozens of them. Most were rather crudely built as stones were just piled on top of one another to make a barrier four to five feet tall. A few were built by experts who took pride in their work. These had straight, vertical sides that appeared to have been built using a plumb line. Probably a couple of hundred years old, they looked as if they could stand just as straight for another couple of hundred years.

May 28, 2002   Vernon, NJ
Trail Distance: 14.4 miles

We started out today not knowing just where we expected to stop. We could have gone either ten miles to Glenwood, New Jersey, or fourteen miles into Vernon, New Jersey. After hiking the ten miles in good time, we decided to go on to Vernon. We were hoping to stop at the hostel in St. Thomas Episcopal Church, but a notice posted where we came to the highway stated that no hikers would be welcome until June 1. We later found out that the hostel facilities were being used to shelter some homeless persons.

As is fairly normal for us, we had no problem in getting a ride into town. A lady drove us to a motel and stated that the grocery store was only 0.1 mile further on with a restaurant nearby. After walking the 0.1 mile, we estimated that it was more like a full mile, and the restaurant turned out to be a small deli. We had our dinner at the deli, but were really looking forward to a full-sized restaurant meal. Oh well, it was still better than what we normally ate. At the grocery, we restocked as long as we were in a town where we could get everything that we needed except Coleman fuel. Now that is a *must*! We simply cannot leave town without it. We are "out" and cannot cook without a resupply. Tomorrow morning, we will have a try at getting some.

We forgot to tell you about an incident yesterday. At the shelter, Bluewater and girlfriend, Melé, were tenting along with their two dogs. The burros would bray periodically, and that would get the dogs to barking. The burros would then run to the far end of the field. They would then wait until everyone's attention was on something else and sneak back to the fence nearest to the dogs. Then they would bray furiously for a few seconds and then run back to the far end of the field. Of course, the dogs would start again. After a few minutes, the burros would repeat their stunt. This was repeated several times during the evening. We think the burros are still laughing at the fun that they had with the dogs.

As we entered the supermarket for our groceries, we were stopped by a young lady who asked if we were hikers. If we did not look it, we surely smelled it. Assuring her that we were, she responded that St. Thomas's hostel *was* open because of the rain that we had and were still having. She said that it was not meant to be open until June 1, but they opened it today because of the bad weather. We told her that we were already booked at a motel but would accept her invitation for tomorrow night if the foul weather continued.

Our next day's hike is scheduled to be a short one. It is only 5.4 miles away, and the next is another twelve miles. We know that we cannot do seventeen miles so we will make two days out of it. Shelters are few in New Jersey, camping sites are fewer, and hikers must stay only at designated sites. Many of the available shelters have no water nearby so that has to be obtained prior to staying. The younger hikers have no problem as they can cover seventeen miles, twenty miles, or whatever it takes. Mina's feet limit us to about ten to twelve miles, or she is in quite a bit of pain.

We did purchase two different types of insoles for her boots to see if that relieves the pain. If it does not, we may discontinue our hike. We just cannot be limited to ten miles a day without severe foot pain. The hike is not worth it, and I will not wish for her to continue. Either the feet get relief or we will terminate the trip. The next few days should tell.

Today was an easy hike, and Mina's feet gave her a problem even on level ground. Actually, today was mostly level. We had probably more than a mile, maybe two miles, where the Trail was over boardwalks. The ground was so marshy (it's called a swamp in Louisiana) that wooden boardwalks were constructed over them. Some of the walk ways were relatively simple, some were more elaborately constructed, and some were works of art that allowed the public to have access to open marshland. This land was home to many types of birds and to at least one beaver that we saw.

At any motel, one of the first things that a hiker does is turn on the TV and check the weather. It is also the last thing that he does before leaving in the morning. We are no exceptions to this.

May 29, 2002 Wawayanda Shelter
Trail Distance: 5.4 miles

As today was scheduled to be a short one, we were in no hurry to start. After the breakfast that we purchased at the grocery yesterday and microwaved this morning, we called a cab to take us to a hardware store in a nearby down. We only needed a quart of Coleman fuel but had to purchase a gallon of it. Our quart cost us $19.96! The cab fare added a bit to it. However, it was a must for us. We then visited St. Thomas and left the remaining three quarts of fuel for other hikers who may need refills. The church would have been nice, but we had already booked at the motel. In addition to offering a place to sleep, the church had restrooms, showers, laundry facilities, and kitchen privileges. Pretty nice, huh? And we would have been the only ones and the first to use it this year. No other hikers came in.

After a second breakfast at Burger King, we easily got a ride back to the Trail. The first mile of the Trail got us breathing hard as it climbs over one thousand feet in about a half mile. Most of that was not hiking but was climbing over rocks. Actually, we find that climbing steep rocks to be less tiring than hiking steep inclines. We do not know why but that is just the way that it is.

There is no water at this shelter so we have to go 0.3 miles to the ranger station to get our supply. Of course, we have to stop and "visit" with them a while. They are all helpful and courteous.

This is another shelter that has need of a real privy. This one is nothing more than a toilet seat on top of a block out in a "not-so-private" area of the forest. In fact, while writing this, the privy is in full view. Now, I would think that most people would like a bit of privacy now and then.

Today started out very foggy with 100 percent humidity but cleared and warmed. The birds are singing, and it really looks great in the forest. The gnats and flies are being pests, though. They really like to "bug" a person.

May 30, 2002   Wildcat Shelter
Trail Distance: 12.0 miles

This was another non-fun day. It was not hiking; it was a day of climbing up and over large boulders on the crest line. Our overall speed over the boulders was something like one mile per hour. A trail around the boulders would have been much better hiking and would *still* qualify as being moderately rough. Over the tops of the boulders is nothing less than being difficult for the sake of being difficult.

Of course, we had some fine views from on top, but a side trail could have worked just as fine. The Eastern Pinnacle and the Cat Rocks had great views but were downright difficult to ascend.

It was a most strenuous day so by about 4:00 P.M., we decided to go into town for a good dinner. Getting a ride to Greenwood Lake was easy and the resulting dinner gave us some additional strength to carry on to the shelter. Again, getting a ride back to the Trail was easy. However, the two young men who gave us a ride back to the Trail promptly rolled all of their windows down. We knew that we were kind of ripe, but we did not think it was that obvious. Obviously, it was!

We met up with Bluewater, his girlfriend, and their two dogs at the shelter. Since we did not arrive there until about 6:30 P.M., we thought that it would be just the four of us. However, six more hikers started showing up. Bluewater put up his tent, and one of the other hikers did also. Seven of us shared the shelter. It was cozy but comfortable.

This day, as with many, started out foggy and cool but warmed and turned sunny quickly. Crossing into New York today was marked only by a white line on a rock indicating New York on one side and New Jersey on the other. The Trail did not change; the boulders still looked the same.

May 31, 2002   Tuxedo Motel
                            Trail Distance: 9.9 miles

This was another rough hiking day. It seemed to be a day filled with climbing up rock faces just to climb down the other side. Some of these "faces" were something like seventy-five feet tall, so it took more than a little effort and extreme care had to be taken. Sometimes a person could not climb with the backpack on so it had to be handed up (or down) to a partner. A hiker alone could really have a rough time. Again, we had some fine views of the countryside but the views were not worth the roller coaster climbing up and down. We do not know if the Trail could have been made more hikeable. This is just some mighty rough terrain.

When passing a small road this morning, we noticed a sign saying "Deli—1/2 mile". Not only us, but every hiker that we met made the visit. All ten from the previous night's shelter made the visit. Back in the real world, we would not think of walking a mile to go to a deli just for a sandwich. Here, we could hardly wait to go.

We earlier had thoughts of going fourteen miles to the next shelter, but the difficulty of the hiking had us get a ride into Tuxedo, New York. The physical exertions required today really drained us both.

Showers and good food made us feel somewhat better, but we are still very tired. On top of it all, severe thunderstorms are predicted for this evening. It's a good night to be inside.

June 1, 2002   William Brian Memorial Shelter
                       Trail Distance: 9.7 miles

Normally, this would have been an easy day for us. The distance was not that far, and the Trail was mostly very nice. It would seem that whoever designed the trails in the Harriman State Park were more civilized and used far more common sense than we had seen in the past two days. The Trail was easy, but we were still tired from the past several days. We were tired, stayed tired, and stopped at a shelter 3.2 miles from our planned stop. We will have to hike a little further tomorrow so we are hoping that we will be more refreshed than we were today. Last evening, we had a great restaurant meal with all of the trimmings. We had thought that with full "fuel" tanks, we would have an easy day. It was not long but it *was* rough for us.

Harriman State Park is one large park. Its 46,000 acres are truly beautiful. It has rolling hills, rocky hills, with many areas covered by trees, bare rocks, and grass. The contour is about the same as what we have been experiencing, but it is just more "civilized". There is less undergrowth and more of the park to see. With its seventy square miles, we cannot possibly see it all, but we have enjoyed seeing what we have.

We still have not seen any bears, very few deer, a few squirrels, and one rabbit. Yesterday, Mina stepped over an eighteen-inch garter snake, pointed out an eight-inch ring-necked snake today, and saw a four-foot king snake today. The king snake was the one that is similar to a coral snake. We followed the old rhyme "red on black, friend of Jack, red on yellow, dangerous fellow". His stripes were red on black, so we enjoyed his visit. By the way, I did *not* try to pet him.

A group of New York City men had gotten to this shelter before us and literally took it over. It would easily sleep nine persons (four bunks and places for five sleeping bags on the floor), but the four of them had supplies over all of the bunks and spread over the floor. They said that there were three more of their friends coming up and they had permission on a "first-come, first-served basis" to kind of take over the shelter. It got a bit tense as we stated that thru-hikers had priority, that we were thru-hikers, and we were staying. After we showed them literature from the park that agreed with our assertions, we got that established, and things cooled off some. After a few minutes, we got friendly with all four of them. The other friends never showed up and never contacted them to tell them that they cancelled. At any rate, they offered to share their coffee and their food. We took their offer of coffee and later shared some of the huge steak that they had grilled. They turned out to be a friendly group, and Mina had a ready audience for her conversations.

One part of the Trail that we went through today is known as the "lemon squeeze". A hiker *has* to go through it, but it cannot be done wearing a backpack. The stone walls are something like eight feet tall on one side and twenty feet tall on the other. There is only about a foot of space between them. I got my pack through by pulling on one side with Mina pushing on the other. The pack got some scratches and scrapes in the process. Mina's pack was somewhat lighter and smaller, and we got it through with no problem. A lone hiker with a heavy pack would really have had a problem.

All in all, it was a beautiful day, and we were hopeful that we could get our body rested. We are talking about taking a "zero" day whenever we can just to be able to rest up. We are tired, our bodies are tired, and we look it. When we look in a mirror, a stranger is looking back at us.

One of the New Yorkers had his cell phone with him and offered it to anyone to make a call. He said that he had unlimited

weekend usage and any of us could use it. As we were in mountains, he had to climb on top of the shelter to make his calls. I took him up on his offer and called my daughter in Portland, Oregon. As with him, I had to climb to the top of the shelter to make my call. However, we did have a nice conversation, and I was able to see the planet and moon conjunction that she was able to tell me about. I had a pleasant view and a pleasant talk.

June 2, 2002   Hemlock Springs Campsite
Trail Distance: 11.2 miles

We felt a bit more fit today and were able to do justice to the hills that we climbed. We were able to enjoy many fine views today, but the best had to be from the top of Bear Mountain. It was not an easy hike up nor was it an easy hike down. Many people had come to the top but they took the easy way up. There were many cars, several dozen motorcycles, and about a dozen bicycles. The bicycles had a hard ride up but would enjoy the coasting down. Several people were hiking without packs, but we were the only A.T. hikers that we saw.

Bear Mountain is a part of the Bear Mountain State Park on land donated by the Harriman family. An interesting aspect is the first sections of the footpath specifically built for the A.T. project was constructed in the park in 1922-23. Much of the original route has been rerouted over the years, but a hiker will still be walking over a portion of the "original" built Trail.

Coming off Bear Mountain, the Trail actually goes *through* the Trailside Museum and Wildlife Center. Featuring many animals and plant life, the very lowest point on all of the A.T. is in front of the bear exhibit. At 124 feet above sea level, everything is "up" from here. At last, we saw our first bear of this trip, and he was in a zoo.

After crossing the Bear Mountain Bridge over the Hudson River, it was still a few miles to our campsite. We were expecting a few more hikers to join us; none did, and we had the site to ourselves.

It was another breezy day. We put the rain cover on our tent just to get some stable air. Shelters are either few or do not exist tomorrow so we expect to tent out again about twelve miles north of here.

June 3, 2002   Graymoor Spiritual Life Center
Trail Distance: 4.2 miles

This day did not quite turn out the way that we had planned. We knew that we had to get grocery supplies and thought that it would be a simple matter. We should have known better! Expecting a supermarket at 1.8 miles from the Trail, we easily got a ride there only to find that it was a small convenience store and would not begin to have the items that we needed. Our driver courteously continued on until we came to a "real" grocery. That was many miles and three highways later. Getting a ride back to the A.T. was not easy. Leaving the Trail prior to 10:00 A.M., we did not get back until after 1:00 P.M. That fouled up our plans royally. There was no way that we could do the almost nine miles before dark. Luckily, we had an alternative. Less than a mile from the point where we would get back on the Trail is the Graymoor Spiritual Life Center that offers hikers shelter in the soccer ball field picnic pavilion. In July and August, the first fourteen hikers each day are treated to dinner and breakfast. Since this was June we were not able to utilize the hospitality. However, we *were* able to have a shower (*cold* water) and get our clothes washed. Also, we will be under cover so we will not have to set up our tent. That will come tomorrow.

We expect other hikers to show up as some are already doing. As they each take their shower, we can tell when each hits the cold water. None can keep quiet! We had really looked forward to a "friar"-prepared meal but, obviously, that will not be. By late afternoon, we had a total of ten hikers staying in the shelter or tenting nearby. Almost everyone had their laundry spread out on the lawn or picnic tables to dry in the sun. Only one besides Mina was a female, an attractive 25-year-old who was celebrating her birthday.

June 4, 2002   Dennytown Road Camp Site
Trail Distance: 8.1 miles

This was an easy day or should have been. There were not that many miles, but we were both still tired. We are thinking that perhaps we have used up most of our body fat and we are eating into the muscle. The Trail is really not that tough but we are finding it *very* tough.

We have promised ourselves a "zero" day as soon as we can find a place to have one. At present, Pawling, New York, is our goal to "take a day off the Trail" to try to get our strength back. Today was another day when views were nil. Fog and low clouds can really spoil the views.

There is no shelter nearby but plenty of tent sites. We thought that others would be tenting near to us but no one showed up. The younger hikers can make the eighteen to twenty miles between shelters; the older ones have no choice except to tent out. Oh well, the forest is friendly.

June 5, 2002   Ralph's Peak Hikers Cabin
Trail Distance: 10.7 miles

We were awakened about 5:30 A.M. by thunder, and we really did not want to hear that. As fast as we could, we tried to break camp but did not quite do it in time. The rain started just as we had taken the rain cover off the tent. Quickly, we got the cover back on and dove into the tent with wet boots and fast-becoming-wet clothes. There we stayed for about an hour waiting for the rain, thunder and lightning to abate. When it got to the point of light drizzle, we reluctantly left the dry tent and again continued to break camp. All parts of the tent were wet by this time, and some of our clothes were also wet. By 7:30 A.M., we had gotten everything in order and were able to leave the tent site.

This was another day of poor visibility. The fog and clouds continued until midafternoon. Normally, there would have been some good views to observe, but we could not enjoy them.

Again, we were tired by the time that we reached the shelter. I am getting concerned about Mina as she complains about being tired after only about five miles of hiking. Normally, she is not one to complain so I know that she is serious. Unless we can find some thing or do something to increase her stamina, we will never be able to make Maine. We *must* be able to average about ten miles per day in order for us to complete this hike to Maine. That is just an average! To average that, we should be maintaining about twelve miles per day.

This is really a super shelter. Formerly a house, it was converted to a shelter that has six bunks and space on the floor for at least ten sleeping bags. With writing tables and good enclosure, it is a very neat place. We were able to get our clothes and our gear dried so we will start out tomorrow at least dry. The clothes lines here really helped. From the latest weather report, the dry weather may not last long. However, if we start out dry, we can usually keep our gear dry. It is a bit different from taking down a wet tent.

We hope to meet the caretaker of this shelter later this evening. There are three of us here now and we all hope someone shows up with a cell phone so we can all order pizza. A local pizza house will deliver, but it is too far to walk to

June 6, 2002   Morgan Stewart Shelter
Trail Distance: 9.0 miles

The caretaker never showed up so we were not able to thank him for the beautifully kept shelter. We were also not able to order our pizza. When we started out today, it looked as if it would be a great day. That was not to be! It turned increasingly cloudy and started to rain again. We finally had to put on our rain gear. The rain was not that bad but the gear was uncomfortable and slowed us up. Of course, the rocks were wet, slippery, and made us more cautious. It just was not a good day for hiking. Actually, we did reach the shelter before the heaviest rain started. Three other hikers who joined us were not so lucky and were really wet when they came in.

The rain continued all night without slackening and continued until about 7:00 the next morning. We did not even bother to leave our bags until it had slowed raining. With views limited and hiking slowed, it was not a fun day

June 7, 2002

Pawling, NY
Trail Distance: 8.3 miles

For most of this day, it was generally miserable. We had received something like three to three and a half inches of rain last night, and it made hiking very difficult. The Trails were frequently flooded, the surrounding areas turned into lakes and ponds, and the normal streams into torrents of rapid cascades. We were constantly having to take detours and many times had to improvise in crossing streams. The normal rock crossings were frequently flooded, and we had to look for fallen trees to scoot over. A person could not walk the trees as they were wet and dangerous. As the Trail is often just rocks, we had to be very careful in crossing them. The one bright aspect was the distance was not far, and we expected the next day to be a "zero" day.

We quickly got a ride when we had reached the highway and took pictures of the Dover Tree, reported to be the largest oak to be seen on the Trail. We could easily believe it as we guessed its circumference at twenty-two feet. It was one giant of a tree.

Our driver did not know where the pavilion was where we were going to spend the night. He had lived in town for fifteen years and had never heard of it. When he had dropped us off in the center of town, we asked around and got the directions to it. We then started walking and continued walking for about a mile. Finally getting exasperated, we decided to go back to the center of town to try to find accommodations for the night. As we were deciding what to do, a lady stopped and asked us if we were looking for a ride back to the Trail. Telling her no and that we were looking for a motel in town, she stated that there were not any but that she could put us up for the night in her guest cottage. That started a beautiful experience!

Betty and her husband, Joe, "put us up" in their old thirteen-bedroom home. It will probably take them a lifetime to fix up their home, but they should have fun doing it. We thoroughly enjoyed visiting with them and sharing their company. Taking *them* out to dinner was a treat for *us*. In the afternoon, Joe took us out in their boat and showed us the lovely lake that their home is situated on. We fell in love with the place and the surroundings. They are truly great hosts. We were the fourth A.T. hikers that they had hosted, and they enjoyed it as well.

Having a much needed shower, clean clothes, and a warm bed, we slept the sleep of the innocent.

June 8, 2002   Betty and Joe Marotta
                            Trail Distance: 0.0 miles

This was our "zero" day and Betty and Joe continued their hospitality. As soon as the post office opened, Betty drove us to Wingdale, New York, to pick up our package from the post office that we had mailed to us. We then went to the supermarket to complete our grocery needs. Now, we are fully supplied for the next five days and can safely get back on the Trail tomorrow. We will really hate to leave these super people. Hopefully, we will have a chance someday to host *them* in Florida.

Last night, we were awakened by something making noise on the front porch just outside our window. Checking it out, we found a skunk nosing through some debris there. Not really wanting to make a "big stink" about the noise, we just left the skunk alone and went back to bed. It was the strangest-looking skunk that we had ever seen. It was all white except for some black streaks around its face and chest, *plus* it was the largest skunk that we had ever seen.

Sitting by the lake writing this, I feel that the breeze off the lake is cool, but the scenery is great. We both hope that Betty and Joe continue to enjoy and utilize their home here.

June 9, 2002   Ten Mile River Lean-to
                         Trail Distance: 12.3 miles

After making a super breakfast, Betty drove us to the Trail bringing her two dogs with her. Then she and the dogs joined us for about the first half mile of our hike. We really hated to part but found it necessary. We had known Betty and Joe for such a short time but firmly felt that we had made lifelong friends. Hopefully, they will be able to visit us sometime in the future. We know that we would love to visit them again.

Yesterday, we had taken another boat ride and saw the localized destruction done by a tornado only a few days before. No one was hurt, but some massive trees got uprooted. It is sometimes amazing what just wind can do.

Interestingly, we passed an A.T. train stop that will actually pick up hikers at selected times on the weekend and take them to New York City. We did not feel the urge and passed it by.

Even though our heavy rainfall was two days ago, the trail was sill quite muddy and soggy. Fortunately, the rocks were dry, and that make things a bit easier.

We were able to go past the road that we would have had to take to visit the post office in Wingdale, New York. Since Betty had graciously taken us there yesterday, we did not have to take the time and effort to go there today.

We are now in Connecticut! There was no big celebration at the border but we were able to put New York behind us. Now, we have only five more states to cross. We both know that it is no "done deal". We both want to finish but the really rough going is still ahead of us. With our rest and several full meals, we felt better, hiked better, and came to the end of the day more rested.

David's total miles on A.T: 1,434.4

Mina's total miles on A.T.: 937.6

CHAPTER TEN

June 10, 2002   Mt. Algo Lean-to
                                       Trail Distance: 8.4 miles

This was not a particularly difficult hike, but both of us came in very tired. In fact, Mina was super tired two miles back on the trail. Again, we are giving serious consideration to curtailing our little adventure. If we are having difficulty now, we can just imagine what it will be when it really becomes rough.

I had expected New Jersey, New York, and Connecticut to be flatter and easier to hike. Was I surprised? Even though the hills and mountains are not as high as further south, the hiking is just as tough. We cannot see where our "zero" day helped us at all. We are just as tired and the body feels just as weak. Both of us feel much "older" than we did just a year ago.

There was a three-and-a-half-foot timber rattler on the Trail today that crawled away as soon as he saw us. He wanted to be left alone, and we were more than happy to oblige.

With clear skies and no rain, we actually got some good views today of the surrounding area. On Indian Rocks, so named as it is a part of the Schaghticoke Indian Reservation, there were some fine views of the Housatonic Valley. Even though part of the Trail passed through the Reservation, there were no markers or signs indicating such. The Trail looked the same. If I had not read it, I would not have known it! Surprisingly, most of the countryside is in forests. The hills and mountains stretch to the horizon and most are fully wooded. Homes and farms seem to take only a small part of the area.

The forests continue to be full and beautiful, but the wildlife is rather nil. Even the birds seem to be on vacation.

The Housatonic River was very close to the shelter that we stayed in last night, and the Trail today paralleled it for about a mile. A white water rafter could have had fun on it today. With all of the rain that we have recently had, the river was really white water material. We would not have wanted to fall in.

Each day, we find one or more deer ticks on us but they are usually dead. Our "Off" spray cannot keep them away, but it sure kills them when they bite. Inasmuch as the ticks have to be on a person for many hours for the harmful effects to occur, the spray is really doing its job.

This morning when we awoke, there was a turkey hen strutting out in the field in front of the shelter. Our moving around did not even seem to bother her. I guess that she got used to activity in the shelter as she paid us no mind. Surprisingly, the days and nights are still cool. It's warmer now than it had been but still is a long way from being "warm". Later on, we will probably look back longingly for these cool days and nights.

June 11, 2002   Stewart Hollow Brook Shelter
Trail Distance: 7.3 miles

On this day, we decided to terminate our hike and go home. It was not a long hike day, but it started out uphill, and Mina was soon exhausted. She seems more tired in the first two hours of hiking than she does later on. She doesn't gain strength; she just seems to gain endurance. At any rate, with the really rough stuff ahead of us, we know that we will not be able to "cut it".

Early morning was rough as we had some more rock paths to go over. At about midday, we had to come down from Caleb's Peak on St. Johns Ledges, a rock face used to train "rock climbers". It was some descent! Again, a hiker had to use super caution as one misstep, one slip, one inattention could spell serious injury. With a full backpack, the descent was way short of being fun.

The view from Caleb's Peak, however, was great. Once down, we got on a little used road that led to a path that was right on the banks of the Housatonic River. At this point on the river, it was full and fast moving but was without the rapids that we had down river. We enjoyed just taking the time to watch and listen to the river performing for us.

We arrived at the shelter before 1:00 P.M. and immediately went to the nearby stream to get our water supply and to wash up a bit. We could not bathe, but at least we could get somewhat cleaner. The river itself is fun to watch, and every turn in the Trail brings a different view. We found out that white water rafting *is* done on this river although we have seen none of it.

The mountain laurel has been coming into full bloom, which really beautifies the Trail. We are also beginning to hear the call of the veeries. We still have not heard their full song but we know that it is them.

The flies are out in force today but seem to prefer me over Mina. I had "Off" on; Mina had none. It was almost as if the spray attracted them.

This shelter is the third of its kind that we have stayed at, and we did not like any of them. The sleeping bag area is only about six feet deep and there is then a two-foot gap down to the dirt. Several logs are then stretched from one side of the shelter to the other side with the top log level with the sleeping area. No one seems to know to what purpose they serve as they really make it difficult for anyone, especially short hikers, to get into the sleeping area. Perhaps we will get more information later. For now, we just complain about it as we cannot change it, and we *do* enjoy the use of the shelters.

June 12, 2002   CT Route 4
                                Trail Distance: 4.4 miles

Sometimes even the best-laid plans can get fouled up. We had been planning on concluding our hike at Salisbury, Connecticut, as we had to make the town in order to pick up one of our mail drops. It was only about twenty-seven miles away, and we could easily make it in three days. A little river stream kind of got in the way. After crossing CT 4 highway, there was the Guinea Stream to cross and it was a lulu. In a little Ravine, it was a raging torrent. There appeared no way to safely cross it. The current was just too strong to cross it, and the large logs across the stream were too far off the water for a safe crossing. Our Trail map indicated that we could go about a mile to our right, hook into the Housatonic River Road, and that would lead us to a trail that would be on the other side of the stream and could lead us back to the A.T.

We had started walking the mile and about midday, we just decided that the detour was not worth it, and we wanted to go home. Accordingly, we hitched a ride to the next town and learned that our driver was going right through Salisbury. The outcome was he dropped us off in the middle of town, right in front of the post office. After getting accommodations for the night in a private residence, hosted by Maria McCabe, we had a nice lunch and checked with the post office to find that our mail was already here. That was speedy service as we had mailed it only two days back.

The next day our hostess, Maria McCabe, gave us a nice breakfast and then drove us to Canaan, Connecticut, where we got a bus to New York City. From there, a short walk got us to Penn Station and a train to Trenton, New Jersey. After a short wait, Noel Brewer (Mina's daughter) was able to pick us up and take us to her home for a few days visit.

Will this end our A.T. hiking? In all probability, it looks that way. Perhaps in the future if we can find some way for someone to meet us at a day's end, carry our food and camping supplies, take us to a nights lodging, we would probably consider continuing. As it is, we simply cannot carry the weight that we are carrying and do the brutal hiking that we are required to do. Forty years ago, perhaps we could have. Now, we do not get stronger; we just get weaker and beaten.

We do not like to quit, we do not like to feel beaten, but realistically we simply cannot continue. We do have utmost admiration for all those, young *and* old, who were able to finish the A.T. Those of us who have done a part of the Trail realize what they had to do and the obstacles that they had to overcome in order to achieve their goal. We tip our caps to them!

— — — — — — — — —

An Unplanned Interlude

— — — — — — — —

June 20, 2002   U.S. Route 7, Housatonic River
                       Trail Distance: 12.1 miles.

We did not change our minds about not finishing the Trail. The opportunity presented itself for us to at least hike to the Massachusetts state line and we will try to do that. Noel and Kevin Brewer had won an "all expenses paid" vacation to a super resort in Virginia. With them gone, we borrowed their second car and drove back to where we had left off the Trail. By "slack packing" we hope to complete our hike of Connecticut.

The raging water had gone down from the stream that we previously had not been able to cross. By dropping me off at the south end of the section, Mina was able to park the car at the north end and then would hike toward me. When we were nearly at the halfway point, we would start calling each other every fifteen minutes on our walkie-talkies until we made contact. Then we would meet, have lunch together, I would take the car keys, and we would continue our hike. As it turned out, I started following the wrong marker and went about two miles out of my way before I realized my mistake. I had started following a blue blaze that was rather faded, it seemed to be going in the correct general direction, but it took me to a parking lot beside a highway. There was nothing to do except retrace my steps and look for the white blaze. Even so, the white-blazed trail was difficult to find. Other than some extra mileage, the day was uneventful with no views and relatively easy hiking. In spite of easy hiking, both of us were bushed and sore at the day's end. Even though we had been off the Trail for only seven days, the legs acted as if we had never been on it at all. We were sore and hobbled around all the rest of the day. Mina had serious reservations about even continuing the next day.

June 21, 2002   CT Route 41, Salisbury, CT
Trail Distance: 10.2 miles

A good night's sleep at Maria McCabe's hiker hostel with a good dinner and breakfast made us ready for this days hike. It *was* a little shorter, and the legs and feet appreciated it more. The first ten miles were along the Housatonic River, and the scenes were worth hiking for. There was a dam across the river that blocked most of the water flow. Below the dam, the virtually dry river bed was all rock with very little water flowing over the rocks. Little by little, other streams flowed in with the result that a couple of miles below the dam, the river flowed at almost full capacity. From a bare rock bottom to a full river took a very short distance. Views, scenery, and hiking were a bit better today.

June 22, 2002   Paradise Lane Trail
Trail Distance: 6.7 miles

Today, we parked our car at a hikers' parking site and walked together up the Trail. It was mostly uphill but the path was gradual and well used. It went over the top of Bear Mountain (*another* Bear Mountain) which had the remnants of an old tower on top. The rock tower was constructed more than a century ago without the use of any mortar. Most of the tower had fallen down but enough remained to give a super view of the surrounding area. Obviously a favorite for local day hikers, we met many going to and from the top. The descent on the other side of the mountain was quite steep, but we had to continue in order to make the Massachusetts state line. This we did! Shortly after, there was a side trail that connected to other trails so that we did not have to retrace our steps over the mountain to pick up our car. Only 2,316 feet high, nevertheless we did not wish to repeat it. Coming up to the top, we were on a stony ridge that gave the impression for over a mile that the top was only about fifty yards away. Fortunately for us, we knew the top to be further so we did not get our hopes up.

The side trails got us back to a parking lot just a few miles from our car. There, we easily got a ride back to our car and a return to our "normal" life.

— — — — — — — — — — —

Another Unplanned Interlude

— — — — — — — — — — —

July 13, 2002   Glen Brook Shelter
                                 Trail Distance: 7.0 miles

It's funny how some circumstances completely change a person's itinerary. Here we were sure that we would never see the A.T. again and the opportunity just presented itself. Mina's daughter is in the process of changing jobs and decided to take eleven days off and visit England *provided* that her mother would join her. That decision did not take too much persuasion! Accordingly, we drove up from Florida, let Mina off in Langhorne, Pennsylvania, and I drove on up to the Trail. I will start where I left off a month ago. When Mina returns, I should be in Vermont by that time, and Mina *may* drive up to meet me at her niece's home. The choice is hers as she may not wish to make the drive. The tentative plans will be for us to do some slack packing in Vermont, but who knows what the next month will bring for us.

The Trail today was not that rough but *felt* rough on feet that had not been on it in almost a month. I was pretty bushed when I got to the shelter. The feet, especially, demanded rest. I had bruised my left heel a couple of months ago, and it still gives me trouble. There were some beautiful views of the countryside today. There were two shelters only about 0.1 mile apart. That puzzled me until I saw them. Each can shelter only four persons. Since I got here first, I had my pick. This shelter is in a grove of Hemlocks, and there is virtually no underbrush. All of the surrounding grounds are clean, and it is quiet.

Tomorrow is due to be a long day. Sure hope that I can get sufficient rest for it. It is also due to be quite warm. As usual, we will just have to wait and see.

With some of the views today, you had to watch your feet as well as seeing the countryside. The Trail frequently was right on the edge of a cliff. You simply could not look and walk at the same time. The views were great as long as you were not hiking. I sure miss my hiking partner. She really adds something to a day.

July 14, 2002   East Mountain Retreat Center
Trail Distance: 16.3 miles

It took eleven hours of hiking to reach the retreat, but it was worth it. A hostel for hikers at $10 a night gives you a mattress, hot shower, and laundry facilities. The only other persons in the hostel are a couple who are also hiking north. With the phone at the retreat, we were able to order dinner to be delivered. That was a nice treat. The town of Great Barrington is four miles away, and that is too far to hike in to go to a restaurant. Our meals were super and really hit the spot.

The hike today was long but not really rough. Some parts were level and downright easy. Other parts required some rock climbing but nothing compared to what we had to do earlier in our hiking.

Again, we had some very nice views. Hikers and birds were few. I was passed by only one other northbound thru-hiker and saw no south bounders. This forest is silent! If you listen real carefully, you may hear a bird or two in the distance, but you really have to listen hard.

This part of the state is very dry, and many streams are dry as a result. Now, we have to check ahead to see if a shelter has water or not. My next shelter is noted for not having water available in dry seasons, so I will have to fill up on water prior to reaching the shelter.

Porcupines are due to be a problem. They crave salt and will eat shelter floors, boots, and anything else that has a sweaty, salty flavor. It can be a problem, but it is nice to know ahead of time so that precautions can be taken.

There were a couple of thru-hikers that stopped in the shelter last evening about 6:00. They refilled their water, cooked and ate their dinner and left by 6:30 P.M. They claimed that they could still hike for two and a half hours. They stated that they left Springer Mountain on May 7 and hiked from twenty-five to thirty miles a day. Now, I would like to be able to do more miles than I do *but* have no desire to cover twenty-five miles in a day. I had passed views this morning that those hikers would not have been able to see last evening. I have paid for those views; I want to see them!

To save on weight, I left my tent in the car. Those several pounds do make a difference. Without a tent, I have to plan around shelters. The next shelter is 5.1 miles, and the next after that is another fourteen miles. Sometimes I may skip a shelter, but I know that I cannot do 19.1 miles. Today was stretching it, and my feet are letting me know about it.

There was a good view from the summit of Mt. Everett yesterday. It has an abandoned fire tower on top that is billed as unsafe to climb. Climbing is prohibited, but some hikers do it anyway. (No, I didn't.)

This hostel can sleep more but there are only three of us here so I get a room all to myself. I passed a southbound slack packer today and stopped for a short visit. "Detour" is section hiking but just any section that may be available. He said that later he would "try to connect the dots." I thought that I would not see him again, but, about an hour later as I was coming to a highway, he was there with his car and was acting as a "Trail Angel". I got a bagel, cheese and tomato sandwich plus a fill-up on my water. He had other goodies but that was all that I needed.

July 15, 2002   Mt. Wilcox North Shelter
Trail Distance: 5.1 miles

It was scheduled to rain last night, but it passed us by. Now, I am hearing thunder so we just may get it later on. This area sure needs it. This shelter has a stream that is unreliable in very dry weather (that means it's dry). I stopped at the Mt. Wilcox South Shelter and got my water supply for today and for tomorrow's hike. Something that we just take for granted at home really keeps us on our toes here. We *must* have water and when the nearest is many miles away, your water bottles had better be adequate. This shelter is very old, but I think the one at Mt. Wilcox South is even older. The logs there are just disintegrating. This shelter looks dry enough, but it is 0.3 miles off the Trail and is in prime porcupine territory. I sure hope that I can keep things out of their reach. As of now, the thunder is sounding closer.

The hike today was short but it had a lot of little "ups" in it. I am still tired from yesterday so those little "ups" didn't help one bit. I got in so early that I treated myself to a hot cup of tea plus some hot soup. That took the edge off. Near the Trail was Benedict Pond, a glacial pond that offers swimming. Maybe on some other day it would have been inviting but my mind was not into swimming today. Besides, it was 0.5 miles to the swimming area.

Tomorrow is either fourteen miles or 11.4 miles. My books all say fourteen, but the Trail marker claims 11.4. Here is a part that does not look reasonable. The Trail comes to within about one mile of the shelter. Then it makes a wide circle of at least three miles and then has a 0.5-mile side trail to the shelter. However, this is supposed to be one nice shelter, and hikers do not pass it up. *This* hiker is looking forward to it.

Many hikers are complaining about the mosquitoes here. My "Deet" keeps them away, but nothing keeps the gnats and flies away. They are pests! Well, the thunder is much closer and the gentle rain has started. As long as the shelter does not leak, I'll be quite happy here.

When approaching the "Ledges" today, I just knew that the Trail would follow the edges. It did! While not too high and offering no views, the Trail just has to see how close it can come to the edges. I'll bet the trail makers used to drive their mothers nuts.

It still surprises me how few northbound thru-hikers that I see. Have most of them already gone by? I would think that most of the April starters would just now be getting up here. Time will tell but at 4:30 P.M., I am still the only one at the shelter.

July 16, 2002   Upper Goose Pond Cabin
Trail Distance: 14.0 miles

Shortly after leaving the shelter, I passed the Shaker Campsite with several camping areas at the site of an old homestead. I am sure that there is a lot of history here but I can only wonder. The area is quite pretty with streams and a nice waterfall for viewing.

This cabin is on a beautiful clear lake furnished with a canoe and invitations to swim. I had really been looking forward to the visit. I left early so that I would miss some of the heat later plus it would give me more time in the water. Leaving at 6:00 A.M., I arrived at 1:45 P.M. I *did* miss the heat of the later day. It never came! With a day cool enough for me to wear my jacket, the thrill of a swim just never came. Suffice it to say, no one else went in the water either.

This is a real, honest-to-goodness cabin maintained by the A.T. along with a caretaker. There is a co-ed bunk room, kitchen facilities, outdoor privy (three of them), tables, chairs, etc. There is no running water so laundry and showers are out of the question.

I have a small mail pickup in Dalton, Massachusetts that I plan on picking up on Thursday. My main mail pickup will be in Williamstown, Massachusetts, and that poses a problem. The post office closes at noon, and I do not know whether I can make it by then. The terrain up to Williamstown keeps getting higher and higher until it peaks at Mt. Greylock, the highest point in Massachusetts. There is about six miles of constant ups, and I get tired just thinking about it.

The hike today started easy enough for about four and a half miles, and then it turned into a typical A.T. Trail with ups and downs, rocks and roots to contend with. I came in tired but not exhausted. However, the feet did need a rest. It's a funny thing about the feet. The first day my left heel hurt, the next day both big toes hurt, but now everything seems to be normal. They get tired and generally ache, but there are no real problems.

There were no good overlook views today, just lots of forests. It is still hard to imagine that there are this many solid forests (and rocks) so close to major civilization points. We are in wilderness and it seems to extend for miles in all directions. Sometimes you can hear road traffic at a distance, but not very often.

This lake is worth revisiting along with some scuba gear. It is warm and super clean. There are some cabins on it and some boats in the water. It *is* a pretty sight!

Dalton is a little over twenty miles away, and I will make it in two days. Most of the hikers here will do it in one day without a problem. I'm not in that kind of hurry *or* that kind of shape.

July 17, 2002   Dalton, MA
Trail Distance: 20.6 miles

What can I say? The Trail was nice, relatively level, the day was cool, and my pack was lighter by three days of food. So, I kept going and finally reached the town. The only really rough part was right near the end where there was a long, unwelcome "up". By that time, I was tired and it almost did me in.

I had really been looking forward to a shower and a nice bed but got disappointed on both. The man who welcomed hikers to stay the night meant in a tent or on his porch. The bedrooms and bathroom were off limits. Three other hikers were staying, and it was already late so I opted to take the porch. The host was really OK. The early arrivals got loaded with ice cream and beer. I could have shared in the ice cream, but I wanted food first.

I had met "Dutch Uncle" at the last shelter, and he remembered Artsy and me from the Four Pines Hostel in Pennsylvania. On the Trail today a south bounder was "Ed" (just Ed) who was section hiking, and he remembered Artsy and me from the shelter near Kent, Connecticut. You just keep running into people that you have met before.

I did have an interesting little episode today. The "Lone Ranger" and I went into a small family restaurant for dinner. I had finished my wine and was starting on my steak and iced tea when I started getting very warm. I started sweating profusely and got so weak that I could not cut my steak. I had been sitting on a bar stool to eat and never fell off but I started to lose it. My friend later said that he was talking to me, but I seemed to be in a daze and didn't respond. The waitress got a cool, damp cloth to put on my forehead, and they called the paramedics. I "came to" when the medics arrived and continued to improve. I was able to answer all of their questions and assured them that my blood pressure of 95/50 was *not* normal for me. They wanted to take me to the local hospital, but I talked them out of it. Within a few minutes, I was back to normal and was able to finish my meal. The medics assured themselves when my color returned and I acted normal. My blood pressure was getting back to where it should have been. I told them that I believed I just over exerted myself today. It was my first twenty-plus-mile day in many years, and I really pushed myself to complete it. I believe that this little incident was unusual. If it repeats itself, I will go to a hospital.

The A.T. goes right through Dalton. Street light posts are used as Trail markers. The town is A.T.-oriented, and restaurants have their A.T. log for hikers to sign.

I took a short jaunt off the Trail to visit the "cookie lady" (Marilyn Wiley) who has been supplying cookies and fresh water to hikers for fifteen years. She was not at home, but her husband was, and he graciously supplied me with some of her cookies and some good conversation. It really made for a good rest stop.

I had really been looking forward to that shower and a Laundromat. It seems that I will have to wait until I reach Williamstown that *now* I expect to reach Friday. I will not have to sweat it out by having to reach there by noon on Saturday. There was one thing that I missed seeing in Dalton. There is a Currency Museum which is operated by the Crane Company, the exclusive maker of the unique paper used in all the U.S. currency. I understand that you can look but they do not give out any samples. Hopefully, some time in the future we will be able to visit this most unusual museum.

July 18, 2002   Mark Noepel Shelter
                                 Trail Distance: 13.7 miles

After a good restaurant breakfast, I visited the Dalton post office to pick up a package that I had mailed to myself. The contents were *still* more than I needed and was able to give some of it away. However, no one wanted any of my powdered milk. I had picked up seven quarts of it and knew that more was awaiting me in Williamstown. I had been using it for breakfast cereal and pudding. Without Mina along, I have not been having these. I suppose that I will just have to drink the stuff. I will not throw it away and, fortunately, I like it.

I was hiking along today and heard a loud noise to my right. A young fawn was racing directly at me. When it was only about fifteen feet away, it saw me and almost turned a flip as it changed course and continued to charge through the forest. I sure hope that its mother will be able to find it as it was much too young to be out alone.

Today was a rough one for hiking. My body and feet were still tired from yesterday and they let me know right away. The Trail starts the climb up to Mt. Greylock, the highest point in Massachusetts. It is only 3,491 feet, but it *is* the highest.

After the Trail went through the town of Dalton today, it passed through the town of Cheshire, Massachusetts. For Williamstown, I will have to get a ride as it is 2.6 miles off the Trail.

As warm as the days are, the nights get cool. I already have on my jacket and will be changing into long pants. We can wear shorts when hiking, but we get cool fast when we stop.

July 19, 2002   Williamstown, MA
                                 Trail Distance: 9.6 miles

It looks as if my Guardian Angel is still on the job. Yesterday when I was about two miles from the shelter (all uphill), the thunder started in two different directions. I was tired but I pushed on. About the time I reached the shelter, the thunder stopped. It "did" give me the impetus to "move it".

Today, there was no thunder so I didn't have to hurry. When reaching State Road 2, a young mother (also beginning hiker) picked me up and took me to the post office to rescue my CARE package. Then she waited for me and drove me to an "inexpensive" motel. She said it had the lowest rates of any around. At $108 per night, I had to take her word for it. That does not come with either breakfast or a telephone. The motel was just across the street from the supermarket but I found that I already had sufficient food for six days. Sometimes you get gifts that you just cannot use.

Once I got checked in and had my much needed shower, it started to rain and it really rained. The fact is, it is still raining.

I have to do laundry but the nearest Laundromat is about one and a half miles up the road on the way back to the Trail. I had been planning on walking up there this afternoon, but the rain short circuited that idea. I think that I will wait for morning, get packed, and get a ride up there. When finished, I'll get a ride further on to the Trail.

The hike today was mostly coming down from Mt. Greylock. I had expected it to be relatively rough going *up*, but it wasn't that bad. Coming down was no fun! There was about two miles of very steep, rocky terrain. I pity the southbound hikers. Even one of the fellows who stayed at the shelter last night complained about the miserable hike down.

I don't plan on a long hike tomorrow so I should have time to do laundry in the morning. At least, I am clean.

Now, I have to start planning on being in some town or near a telephone so that I can call Mina on the 25th. Towns are not always where you want them to be when you want them. Manchester Center, Vermont, can be reached by the 25th, but I may need to take a zero day in order to do it. The next available telephone is something like seventeen miles further on and *that* would be pushing it.

I just noted that there are fifty-eight days to September 15 and 594 miles to Mt. Katahdin. If I can average about ten miles per day, I may be able to finish. I still will not feel bad if I can't do it. There have been some swell people met on the Trail. Hopefully, some of the friendships made will last a lifetime. That is more important than finishing this hike.

When crossing the summit of Mt. Greylock today, clouds set in, and you could not see the top of the monument there. An hour later, everything was super clean, but by then, I was long gone. I did get some good views yesterday when crossing the Cobbles. The view of the town of Cheshire and surrounding valley was well worth the climb up.

I have just about hiked out of Massachusetts. There are only 4.1 miles to Vermont and it is all uphill. What can I say? It *would* be more interesting if my hiking partner were with me.

David's total miles on A.T.: 1,569.8

Mina's total miles on A.T.: 986.7

CHAPTER ELEVEN

July 20, 2002   Seth Warner Shelter
Trail Distance: 6.9 miles

Today, I entered Vermont and began sharing the Trail with the Long Trail which extends from the lower Vermont border to Canada. Interestingly, the Long Trail was the first long-distance trail in the United States and was virtually completed by the time the Appalachian Trail was considered. Things are a bit more crowded now with hikers from both Trails hiking the same terrain and sharing the same shelters. There was quite a group at the shelter this evening, some through hikers, some Long Trail hikers, a few short term hikers, and some scouts. It was a very nice group and super conversation made for a comfortable evening.

The motel last evening was a big disappointment. The room had no telephone, the remote TV control did not work, plus the room must have had very little insulation as the road noise came through loud and clear. To top it off, the room came with a single, small bar of soap. It was just not worth the money. I was stuck, however. My ride had left, and there was not another motel within two miles.

The Trail today was a bit rough on me starting out. It was about three miles of going up, and this rather took my steam away. I had been planning on going to the *next* shelter, but it is 7.2 miles further on, and it was after 2:00 P.M. before I made *this* shelter.

When the sun gets low, it really gets cool up here. Hopefully, it will make for some good sleeping. My new light bag does not work too well in warm weather. It is much better when it can be zipped completely up. It prefers cool but not cold weather. Actually, so do I.

I had been hoping to get a ride down to the Laundromat and

back but had no takers. The result was a longer time to get the job done and an extra mile of hiking. I did not want it that way but was stuck with it.

With the rain yesterday, the Trail was wet, slippery, and boggy. The streams are running well, and this shelter has a nice water supply. It is normally dry in dry weather, but the rain yesterday fixed that good.

My full pack today kind of slowed me up a bit. Each day, the pack should be at least a pound lighter. I sure eat my full daily supply to help it. This place really has room to spare, and Mina would fit in nicely.

| July 21, 2002 | Melville Nauheim Shelter |
| | Trail Distance: 13.1 miles |

I got an early start this morning leaving at 6:20 A.M. I wanted an early start for several reasons. It's cooler in the early hours, it usually rains later in the day rather than earlier, and I like to get to the shelter early to reserve a spot. This part of the Trail can get crowded, and I *do* want my shelter.

When I went over Mt. Greylock, I couldn't see anything because of the fog. Today, I passed by a scenic spot pointing to Mt. Greylock and, as you can guess, it was so cloudy that I couldn't see a thing. Today should have been an easy hike, and for the most part it was. However, the last two miles were a dilly. It was a mile steeply down and then a mile steeply up. It was a real sticky one coming at the end of a hike. By the time that I reached the shelter, I was very ready to call it a day. It looks like there will be only four here tonight, and one of these will be tenting out. Sorry about that as two more just showed up.

The mosquitoes are not so bad here, but the flying bugs are a real pest. They fly on to you and then crawl around. They do not sting but just love to crawl.

Now is the time to start planning on Mina to join me. It will be a bit tricky as telephones and towns are just not where you may want them to be. We'll get it done though.

Rain is predicted tomorrow so I will once again try to get an early start. I do *not* like to hike in the rain. Well, it should not be too long before my hiking partner joins me. I *am* looking forward to that.

July 22, 2002   Story Spring Shelter
                                       Trail Distance: 17.4 miles

This was a long day for me. Leaving this morning at 6:30, I didn't arrive at this shelter until 5:45 P.M. I had passed a couple of other shelters that I chose not to visit. The Goddard shelter was only 8.5 miles, and that was just not far enough. The Caughnawaga Shelter was 12.9 miles, but it was the poorest example of a shelter that I have seen anywhere on the A.T. Very old, it sleeps only five provided that four are midgets and do not mind sleeping with the roof only inches from their head. I have the clearest feeling that this shelter will not last much longer. It just begs to be replaced.

The mosquitoes are really out in force. I am liberally covered with Deet, but they still buzz around and try to get in my eyes, the only spot not covered with Deet. Scenery is still limited with only occasional views of nearby mountains. Hopefully, things will change tomorrow, weather permitting.

I am amazed at the number of bogs and ponds near the summits of mountains. This place has been very short of rain, but there was a fair-sized pond near to the summit of Mt. Greylock. I suppose that some of the rock formations are saucer shaped and just retain the water.

The Trail up here shows a fantastic amount of work. There are many board and log bridges over many of the bogs. The sections of the Trail further south have shown this. This section has rock steps provided up the sides of many of the hills and mountains. These steps had to have required thousands of man-hours to construct over many years. Most of the rocks probably weigh hundreds of pounds with some going over half a ton. Some of the steps are downright massive, and there are hundreds of steps. Thinking back to early hikers, they didn't have the steps or the log bridges over bogs. They probably had to wade through muck up to their knees. I am sure the paths are rockier with more roots now, but I honestly think that we have it better.

This shelter is filling fast and pouring over. The long Trail adds many hikers to it. These hikers are mostly younger than the A.T. hikers. I think that by the time Mina joins me, the scenery should improve. It has not been very interesting so far.

July 23, 2002   Stratton Pond Shelter
                            Trail Distance: 10.5 miles

I really did not look forward to this day and it was for naught. The contour map showed about a three-mile climb to the summit of Stratton Mountain. As it turned out, it was a gradual climb and not difficult at all. There was a great observation tower on top and, as you could guess, the observations were nil. Solid clouds in all directions gave no views at all. It was not a bad hike today and I toyed with the idea of just going on to Manchester Center. A few rounds of thunder put a damper on *that* idea. After the thunder got close, it started to rain lightly. With my rain cover on the pack and just my rain jacket on, I continued on to the shelter. The very second that I stepped into the shelter, the sky opened. We had a very heavy rain for about two hours, and many hikers (twenty-three at one time) came into the shelter to get out of the rain. Fortunately, most hikers left when it stopped raining.

This is noted to be the most popular shelter on the Trail. It sleeps about sixteen, twelve in bunks, and floor space for others. I suppose in an emergency, you could get maybe twenty sleeping bags in the shelter. There is a caretaker for it and a $6 per night fee but it is worth it. The nearby Stratton pond is available for swimming, but the usual thing happens when swimming is available. It turns cold! After the rain today, the temperature dropped about ten degrees. Well, that should make for some nice sleeping weather.

I am not ready for a grocery refill, but must do some tomorrow.

The towns in these Green Mountains are not just where you may want them to be. At least, my resupply should last me to Killington where I will hook up with Mina. Stratton Mountain has a special place for A.T. hikers. The idea for the Trail came to a Benton MacKaye as he sat in a tree on the summit. He published his proposal, and this inspired the imaginations of other dedicated volunteers. Now, we have the benefit of his early thoughts. Sometimes, the "seeds" of thoughts can grow into really large trees.

| July 24, 2002 | Sutton's Place
Trail Distance: 10.6 miles |

After the rain yesterday afternoon, the Trail today was wet, boggy, marshy, and muddy. A person really had to watch every step to keep from getting ankle deep in gook. The clear, dry, and cool day partially made up for the careful footing required. Last night and this morning were cool. My sleeping bag was zipped to the top. Starting out this morning required a jacket. If I had thought of it sooner, the gloves would have been on. Mina would have had hers on for half the morning.

As usual in this part of Vermont, views were quite limited. We had a clear day, but there was nothing to see. Toward noon, there *was* a good overhead view of Manchester Center, Vermont. It took another five miles of hiking to get down *to* the town. Sutton's Place is a respected and coveted hiker hostel in town. Hikers really look forward to stays in places such as this where they can meet other hikers, share stories, visit the "hiker boxes", and sleep in a warm, soft bed. We take these creature comforts for granted in our daily lives but hikers learn to value them, to long for them, and to treasure them.

I still see more Long Trail hikers than A.T. hikers, and they are usually younger. Some are quite young. One of the A.T. hikers has decided to keep going north on the Long Trail where the trails divide in Killington. He said that he has already hiked most of New Hampshire and Maine, does not want to repeat it, and the northern part of the Long Trail looks interesting. An interesting aspect of the Trail in Vermont is the size of the white blazes. They are still rectangular, but the Long Trail rectangles are wider and longer. There is no mistaking them; they are just a bit larger.

This was not scheduled to be a long day so I did not hurry. Getting to the VT 11/30 highway, I had been told that getting a ride into town would not be difficult and it was not. I was taken to the local supermarket where I rounded out three days food supply. A walk down to the Laundromat had me meet three other hikers that I had been cruising with. They had been staying at a location that I had been looking for, so all four of us went to it and I got checked in. Suttons' Place was not that easy to find for me. We had all been planning on going out to dinner at 6:00 P.M., but we couldn't wait and left at 5:30. All of us had some kind of steak. Their homemade grain bread was super, and we consumed two loaves of it.

The manager of the hostel will not allow us to use his phone even with calling cards, and I have not found a public phone that works. Somehow, I must call the Brewers *before* I get on the Trail tomorrow to let Mina know that I will be in Killington on the 25th. I am sure hoping that she will be able to make it also.

I do not know just how Mina and I will work out our hiking schedule once I reach Killington. We may find a way to continue or we may just go home. We'll decide that when we meet. I have the "bug" again now. I want to go on! Those White Mountains in New Hampshire are a challenge that I do not want to turn down. From everything that I have read and heard, those mountains are tough. Gads, I would hate to have to quit now!

It is now cool again. I can just imagine how cool the Whites will be. Sure hope that our clothing qualifies for warmth!

July 25, 2002   Big Branch Shelter
Trail Distance: 16.0 miles

I finally got some great views today. Bromley Mountain had a 360-degree panoramic view extending fifty-plus miles in all directions. It was not noted in the guide books as being a good view, but it was well worth the hike. Only 3,260 feet high, it is also the site of a chair lift terminus for skiers. The views were really great.

Another noted view point was from the summit of Baker Peak. Only 2,850 feet high, it is claimed to have one of the best views in Vermont. Baker was good but covered only about 120 degrees whereas Bromley had a full 360-degree coverage. Baker was interesting in that the final twenty yards to the summit was up a rock face with about a forty-degree slope, and the rock was turned sideways so that you had relatively sharp edges to climb on.

The Trail today was not steep but was not easy. It was not even and had many rocks, roots, and stones to negotiate. It was just not made for an easy stroll. I passed at least five people who were coming to this shelter but never showed up. So far, there are two tenting out and two others in the shelter. As it is getting dark, that will probably be all for the night. Oh well, it is a nice shelter and will be put to good use.

The Lost Pond shelter used to be about two miles further back on the trail but burned down recently. The tenting area is still there and still popular. Water is also there so the ones who prefer to tent have a spot without a shelter to contend with. Another shelter is the Old Job shelter which is a mile off the Trail. I was thinking that few would walk a mile off the Trail when there is such a good one here. So what happens? I passed two young ladies who were going on to the Old Job shelter. Why? I have no idea!

There is a fast moving stream with plenty of water just down from this shelter. I couldn't resist bathing my feet in that cold water. It really felt good. Bathing is permissible but not recommended with the cold water and cool air. It would not make for a good combination.

Porcupines are still a threat here, so everything that can taste salty is put up high. That includes my smelly boots. When you see how they eat the edges off the planks in the shelters, you know to take them seriously. One privy had to have a plastic seat put in as the wooden one was almost eaten away.

I was able to leave word this morning for Mina to meet me in

Killington, Vermont. I had to leave word on a recorder as no one was home at the time. I wished that I could have talked to someone, but the phones and towns are rare in these Green Mountains.

July 26, 2002   Clarendon Shelter
                                      Trail Distance: 16.8 miles

This started out as a very nice hiking trail. Some parts were actually smooth and easy to hike. The Trail passed by Little Rock Pond and Spring Lake, both sites just begging me to bring my fishing rod and get some fresh Walleye and Northern Pike. There were no cottages on the lakes and naturally no boats. I just knew that those fish would be hungry. I had planned on stopping at the Minerva Hinchey Shelter, about 3.8 miles back, but felt so good that I continued on to the next shelter. I'm glad that I did, but it was a rough 3.8 miles.

This Trail was relocated a couple of years ago and does not conform to the map contour. I had not expected to have to cross Bear Mountain, and it was a long way up. Later, we had a steep descent and still later, a rough, steep ascent over and up rocks and boulders. It was no fun going up *or* down.

This shelter sleeps eight in comfort, and there are about a dozen people here. Fortunately, several are tenting. It is a young personable group, and we have the campfire going. Some are on the Long Trail and some are hiking south so we have a good mixture. One lady insisted on mapping out the White Mountains to help Mina and me slack pack through there. The problem is, she has given so much detail that it is difficult to determine just what all the symbols mean. She claimed to have climbed all of the New Hampshire peaks over four thousand feet last year. I met and talked to a young couple with 7- and 11-year-old girls who had hiked to the top of Mt. Washington yesterday. Hearing these people talk makes me feel better about our plans of hiking through the Whites. If they can do it, just maybe so can we.

In addition to the beautiful lakes, there were some nice views. These were not great views, just nice ones. A part of the Trail goes through a rocky ravine. The rocky ravine would be pretty if you didn't have to hike it. Some of these sites are pretty to look at but are just no fun to go over or through.

Another Trail Angel left some treats for thru-hikers. I enjoyed a cold Pepsi with an apple at lunch time. It was a nice treat and had good timing.

I think now that I can make Killington tomorrow. There were some doubts before but now I think that I can do it. Now I'm wondering if Mina will be there. There is no way to know until I get there.

July 27, 2002   Killington, VT
                         Trail Distance: 16.5 miles

This turned out to be a very quiet day. There were no bird sounds at all, no traffic sounds, and no wind. It was just deathly quiet!

Starting out, it was up hill, and that got the blood flowing. After about fifteen minutes, I was about ready to call it a day. As far as I was concerned, it was not a way to start the day. For the next five miles or so, the terrain was relatively level. There were some ups and downs, but nothing serious. The next four miles were billed as "ups" going to the top of Mt. Killington. From the terrain map, the four miles appeared to be a rather strenuous hike. As it turned out, all of the four miles were a relatively gentle rise. The last half mile was something else. It was on the side of the mountain, and the Trail had worn away much of the soil leaving tree roots to walk on, climb over, and stumble through. *That* part was no fun!

Actually, the Trail does not go all of the way to the summit of Mt. Killington. The last 0.2 miles to the summit is virtually straight up. A side trail goes to the peak, but it is one difficult climb up. I made it as I needed to use a telephone and visit the mountaintop restaurant. Both worked out very well. I would not have wanted to do the climb up just for the exercise.

The only way to the top of Mt. Killington is by hiking or the gondola. I suppose that snow mobiles in the winter time could easily make it to the top. The views from the top were billed as fantastic. Its 4,235 feet make it the highest around. Theoretically, you can see views not only of Vermont but of New Hampshire, New York, Massachusetts, Maine, and Canada. When I was on the summit, I was lucky to see Vermont. The clouds, as usual, were super thick.

Coming down from the summit was relatively easy. The slope was gentle, and reaching the highway was not difficult. After trying to get a ride into Killington, I finally broke down and telephoned Mina's niece in Pittsfield. It was probably just as well that I didn't get a ride as Killington was in the opposite direction from where I would have headed. As it turned out, Mina reached her niece just minutes before I did. She had just started her glass of wine when I arrived. Of course, I had to join her. It was really a nice meeting between us. Two weeks can really make a difference.

July 28, 2002   Pittsfield, VT
                                    Trail Distance: 0.0 miles

This was a welcomed "zero" day as I rested, got re-supplied, and it gave Mina and me a chance to tell each other what had happened in the past two weeks. We each had interesting stories to tell. Our hosts were Lou and Elaine Sackrider, Mina's niece and her husband. Truly a super couple, we got along as if we had all known each other for years. My boots, which had seen me through many hundreds of miles of hiking, finally got so slick on the bottom that they were not safe anymore. They were still comfortable, but safety required that I replace them. They will not get thrown away; my conscience would not allow that.

As this day was a Sunday, we were able to visit a small local church and had a very nice reception. This was a church that we easily could have as a church home. During our visits to other cities, we frequently visit churches that we find friendly and fulfilling. After several fine meals and super "visiting", Mina and I were ready to hit the trail again.

July 29, 2002   VT Highway 12
                             Trail Distance: 19.3 miles

This was meant to be an even longer day than it turned out to be. The intention was to make it a 22.4-mile "slack packing" day. Fortunately for me, I bypassed the first 3.9 miles intending to hike them at the end of the day. By the time the "end of the day" came around, I was "hiked out" and couldn't do any more.

Even though I was not carrying a full pack, several things affected my hiking. First, the Trail had been relocated making it 0.9 miles longer. Second, the terrain was just a tad tougher than expected and third, I had on a new set of boots that I had not hiked in before. Even though the boots gave me no problems, the feet still needed time to get used to the new footwear.

Views today were rather limited with one notable exception. About twelve miles into the hike, a side trail leads to an abandoned cabin with an observation platform on the roof. There is a 360-degree view including Mt. Killington with a super clear sky. Mina had tried twice today to drive to the start of the chair-lift only to have to turn back because of low clouds. It seems that neither of us will be able to get a view from the top.

Mina has not been hiking for about a month and wanted to get some practice in before we reached New Hampshire. Therefore, she started at VT 12 and hiked south until she reached me hiking north. She had to hike 4.5 miles to reach me, and I was slow. By the time that she retraced her steps, she had covered a total of at least nine miles with no problems. This, of course, is without a pack, and that is the way we will try to hike until further notice. We have the car with us now, so we will be able to do more slack packing. *Now* the problem will be to find sleeping quarters for the night. If it is not one problem, it is another. For three days and nights, we have been the guests of Lou and Elaine, and they have been super hosts. Tomorrow, we must leave this "control base of operations" and move on. We sure will miss them, but, hopefully, they can visit us in Florida in the future.

July 30, 2002   West Hartford, VT
                                 Trail Distance: 16.5 miles

This was another of those days that was supposed to be easy but didn't quite turn out that way. Actually, it started out easy and I think that kind of softened us up. First, I hiked the 3.1 miles that I didn't do yesterday. By finishing in just one hour, I knew that someone's mileage marker was a bit out of sync. I may have completed two miles, but not 3.1.

The next leg was very different. After hiking for two hours and expecting to have completed about five miles, it was a disappointment to find that only two recorded miles had been covered. It just did not make any sense.

Mina had driven the car to VT 14, parked, and hiked toward me. She was having the same problem from the other end of the Trail. After hiking for three hours at a good speed, she was disappointed to find that only 4.7 miles had been covered. At that rate, she knew that she could not hike all of the way to VT 12 by dark.

I had made arrangements for the two of us to stay at a bed and breakfast for the night. It was located very close to the Trail and about two miles from VT 12. When we had not met by 3:00 P.M., I was going to suggest that Mina go to the B & B rather than completing her hike. When we *did* meet at about 4:00 P.M., Mina decided to join me and retrace her steps, so we continued north together.

There were no great views today, but there *were* some good ones. We had no mountains to cross, but some of the hill tops were bare of trees and gave some very nice views of the surrounding mountains. Mt. Killington was still visible in the far distance.

We are still encountering stone fences. Some are just thrown up and some are painstakingly constructed. They must have served their purpose in their time. Now, they serve no purpose and it would serve no purpose to destroy them. For one thing, what would they do with all of the rocks?

It is nice to have my hiking partner back with me. However, her feet are still a problem. We cannot seem to find a remedy for them.

July 31, 2002   Hanover, NH
                                   Trail Distance: 9.8 miles

Last evening, we stayed at a B & B that was just eight hundred feet off the Trail. However, I had passed that point of the Trail in the morning and later had to drive eighteen miles back to it. The roads take a bit longer to reach points than does the trail. This was *not* a B & B that we would recommend. The accommodations and breakfast were good, but some other aspects were not. The $10 extra a piece for dinner was grossly overcharged. A hamburger patty, a slice of cheese, macaroni salad, cold slaw, and a piece of cake just did not sit well for $10. Then we could not bring our boots or backpacks into the room but had to leave them out on the porch. It was not a comfortable stay.

The hike into Hanover, New York, was easy. The Trail had no large ups or downs, and some Trail Angel had left a couple of dozen cans of pop in a cool stream for the thru-hikers. Small things like that on a warm day in the middle of a forest really does the body and spirit good.

Coming into Hanover posed a small problem. The Trail goes through the town of Norwich, Vermont, and *that* town had a scarcity of Trail markers. They would be lacking for hundreds of yards, and you had to play a guessing game. Hanover, on the other hand, was very well marked and no navigation problems occurred.

Our trail guide informed us that we could get all kinds of information from the Dartmouth Outing Club. Perhaps on some days, the information might be available; this day we got zilch. Accommodations were also supposed to be available, but this too drew a blank. For one thing, today was a day when the Dartmouth female sports teams were amassed in town for indoctrinations, and the town, rooms, dorms, etc. were full of visiting students and their parents. Rooms and information just were not available. We finally got a room outside of town.

· While the white blazes are standard for marking the A.T., there can still be seen some of the orange-black-orange markings that were used on the Trail for many years as it traverses The Dartmouth Hiking Club territory. The "tiger paws" are not used anymore but can still be seen on many trees. It does take many years for the paint to wear off.

Tomorrow, we plan on doing our normal slack packing. Mina will drop me off in town and then drive about thirteen miles out to a point where the Trail crosses another small road. Mina will then hike back toward me. She will give me the car keys when we meet so that I can drive back to pick her up at the point where I started early in the day.

Cars can help a bit on the Trail but can also be a problem. You can't just leave them, and not everyone allows them to be parked on their property. As we continue, the roads get scarcer, less traveled, and it's more difficult to get rides back to the car. We *will* have our problems. Well, we will just have to tackle them as they come up.

August 1, 2002   Goose Pond Road
Trail Distance: 14.2 miles

This was a full slack pack day. Mina left me off in Hanover where I had hiked to yesterday, and she drove to the Trail crossing on Goose Pond Road. We then both hiked toward each other. However, we made a quick hello and went on our respective ways. I had warned Mina about a hiker that she would meet who just loves to talk and does not seem to know when to quit. I had told her to hurry past him or she would be there most of the afternoon. She remembered and did just that! Then *I* remembered that we had forgotten to transfer the car keys, and I had to rush to catch up with her. It took almost a half hour to catch her as she was really moving. She finally heard me yelling and waited for me to catch up. The sounds in the forest carry in different ways, and she had thought I was someone calling his dog. Boy, was I bushed when we finally met. My retracing steps took somewhat longer to cover as many rest stops were in order.

Scenery was very limited today, and only a small garter snake was seen. It didn't stay seen long.

Keeping track of the car, places to stay, and places to eat is getting to be a problem. The average B & B in this area is quite expensive, and motels are few and far between.

Tomorrow, I will be hiking north from Goose Pond Road and Mina will be hiking south from NH 25A. We are to meet on the Trail and spend the night at the Hexacuba Shelter. It promises to be a long, rough day. The terrain is ragged and goes up. It *should* tend to get us in shape for the Whites.

We *did* find a nice B & B at a reasonable rate at the little town of Fairlee, VT. Its rates were about a third of what some others charge. It was clean and comfortable, and the breakfast was excellent.

Our hikes and stops are still under control and should remain so for the next three days. After that, we will be in the White Mountains, and much more information will be needed by us. The days ahead will require careful planning as the Whites are rather unforgiving and supplies are not obtainable. Here is where we need a "director general" to tell us what to do, when to do it, and how to do it. Oh well, it *will* be interesting. We are getting to see the countryside by both car and by foot. It *is* pretty and it *is* rough.

August 2, 2002   Hexacuba Shelter
Trail Distance: 14.5 miles

This was another rather interesting day. Mina dropped me off at Goose Pond Road early in the morning after we spent a most restful night at a B & B in Vermont. Even though we are now in New Hampshire, the Vermont lodgings are closer. Mina then drove to the VT 25A highway, parked the car, and then hiked south to the Hexacuba Shelter.

This shelter is quite unique! Shaped like a hexagon, there is no reasonable manner in which sleeping bags can be arranged efficiently. The bags are all rectangular, and they just do not fit into a hexagon. The shelter is on Mt. Cube, the privy is a pentagon, the bridge below the shelter is based on triangles, and the rectangular sleeping bags do not fit anything! The bridge is unique in itself. It was designed by a Dartmouth student and constructed in 1988. Giving credit to the designer, McGee's Bridge has served the Trail well.

Hiking north in the morning, I came to what I thought was the summit of Smarts Mountain. The views were really nice. Then I looked in my trail guide and it stated that Smarts Mountain had a fire tower on top. After congratulating myself on making such good time to the top, I looked over, *way* over, and saw a higher mountain about a mile away that had a fire tower on top. Needless to say, I was a bit disappointed and was even more disappointed an hour and half later when I finally reached the top to find the views to be quite limited. The clouds, mist, and light rain had come back in. The hike to the top of Smarts Mountain was on the rough side but the hike down was relatively nice.

Meeting some south bounders who told me that water was quite scarce at the shelter, I stocked up with three extra liters (six pounds worth). I later found that water was quite plentiful at the shelter. However, I had to carry those extra six pounds four miles, and that added to an already long day. We had good company at the shelter and everyone turned in early. By 8:00 P.M., the place was silent.

On top of Smarts Mountain, the old fire warden's cabin is now used as a shelter. Now, this one is nice! Rectangular shaped, it is fully enclosed and can probably handle a dozen sleeping bags. It was nice to look at but was just not on our agenda for this day.

I am always a little nervous about leaving Mina to hike alone and do not plan on doing it in the White Mountains. Those are just too wild for either of us to hike alone. I feel confident that Mina can take care of herself; she has proved the point on that. Still, it does not pay to take any unnecessary risks and we have the time and desire to be careful.

| August 3, 2002 | Hikers Welcome Hostel
Trail Distance: 14.7 miles |

With our backpacks on, we hiked north to where the car was parked alongside VT 25A. Getting there rather early, we drove to a nearby convenience store for a snack. Afterward, Mina drove me back to the trailhead where I started hiking north. This part of the trail was very nice and had very few difficult parts. Making good time, I met Mina about a mile and a half from the north end of the Trail. We then drove to Glencliff, New Hampshire, where we made arrangements at a local hostel for sleeping arrangements, laundry facilities, and showers. Finding a nearby diner, we had a super meal with a truly awesome ice-cream sundae.

Tomorrow, we are to tackle Mt. Moosilauke, a peak at 4,802 feet and the first of many to be encountered in the White Mountains. It should give us a taste of things to come. Hopefully, we will be able to meet the challenge. Today was the first day that we were able to get a distant view of the Whites. They will not be taken lightly!

| August 4, 2002 | Kinsman Notch
Trail Distance: 9.5 miles |

This day made up for all of those days where viewing was obstructed by clouds and mist. Mt. Moosilauke is impressive enough when viewed on a contour map. It is downright daunting when viewed from the bottom.

We had made arrangements with the hostel caretaker to drive us to Kinsman Notch where we would hike south over the mountain. This would allow us to hike back to our car rather than try to get rides for the twenty-five-mile trip back. This made for a shorter but much steeper climb to the summit. The word "climb" is well used as the boulder-laden trail had to be climbed rather than hiked. The Trail for the first half mile was beside a cascading creek aptly named "The Cascades". They were truly beautiful! The hike to the summit was uneventful but mostly very steep.

Approaching the summit, we were above the tree line and saw only alpine grass and flowers grew. Along the pathway to the very summit were many rock cairns of which we had to add a few stones.

From the summit, the views were awesome. This was a very clear day and we were informed that we could see five states. Of course, we could not tell where each state was, but we probably could see one hundred miles in each direction. Towards the west, the views seemed to be more civilized as we could see several towns. Toward the east, it was just mountains as far as we could see. Knowing that in a few days we would be on top of some of them looking back to where we stood was more than a little sobering.

We stayed on the summit for a while, took some pictures, and had our picture taken. Actually, we hated to leave the beautiful views. The hike down was longer than going up, but not nearly as rugged.

Back at the hostel, we got our car and then drove to North Woodstock, New Hampshire, to stay at a B & B. There, the hostel manager will drive us back to Kinsman Notch in the morning for the two-day hike back to our car. Mt. Moosilauke was really not all that difficult. The next two days are supposed to make up for it. We can only wait and see.

August 5, 2002   Eliza Brook Shelter
                           Trail Distance: 7.5 miles

This day turned out to be as rough as predicted. There were no major ups or downs but just constant ups, downs, rocks, roots, and tree trunks to navigate. I doubt if there were ten smooth feet anywhere. It was just one major obstacle course. We came over Mt. Wolf at 3,478 feet, but there were no good viewing spots. It seems that when we cross a mountain in good weather, we seldom have good viewing spots. When we cross a mountain in inclement weather, the views are supposed to be fabulous. It's just not fair. Mt. Moosilauke was a notable exception and to that we are thankful.

We had not expected to make good time and we didn't. We averaged only about one mile per hour. Arriving at this shelter, we found it next to a very nice flowing brook. A warm day would have us bathing in the stream. Today was just not bathing temperature.

A group of ten scouts are tenting nearby, and they are surprisingly quiet. Only ten others are in the shelter, and they seem to want to go to sleep early. That is OK with us as we will join them.

We are still amazed at the amount and extent of Trail work done by early volunteers. The work involved in constructing some of the rock steps was enormous. Frankly, we do not see how some of it was done. The results of the work will possibly last for centuries. A person has to see it to appreciate the work and labor involved.

We still see many stone fences. Some are just thrown up, and some are works of art. It would appear that stone fences were common in all of the northeastern states.

August 6, 2002   Franconia Notch
Trail Distance: 8.8 miles

This was the second half of our dreaded two days. Normally, it would not have been that difficult to take. It had plenty of rocks, and many of these were in dry rock streams that were actually paths of the Trail.

Going up or down South Kinsman Mountain, we were informed that we would be indulging in hand-over-hand climbing. That part would be enjoyed by most thru-hikers who ascend it on a beautiful day but cursed by those who go up or down in the rain. As our luck would have it, it rained all day, clouds covered the summit, it was cold, and it was windy. All in all, it was not a very nice day. The beautiful views that awaited us at the summit never materialized, and our efforts went toward just getting down.

For that cold, wet, windy, and miserable place, it took us nine and a half hours to cover this day. Wet rocks and wet roots really slowed us up. We still managed to fall several times, a couple of which were rather painful. We had asked our B & B host to phone in our reservations for four AMC (American Mountain Club) huts that we would like to stay in for the next four nights. We must

have a place to sleep and have breakfast and dinners without having to carry a tent and four days food supplies. We were told that all of the huts were full! There are not many shelters, per se, in the Whites. The main types of shelter are very nice "huts" maintained by the AMC. However, these are frequently reserved months ahead of time by day hikers and tenting is not even allowed nearby. Sometimes, the first thru-hikers can make arrangements whereby they will work for a few hours for their meals and a chance to sleep on the dining room floor. This is great for them as the work is not usually that hard or long and the meals are worthwhile. Many of the thru-hikers are on very limited budgets, and this arrangement is most helpful to them. For us, we cannot simply show up and take a chance that we will be accepted for the night. Meals are served only for the residents. To be honest with ourselves, I cannot carry a tent and four days food supplies through the White Mountains. These mountains are just too rugged, too high, and too much of a change in altitude for me to attempt it. Fortunately, I realize that fact.

Again, the promised views from South Kinsman Mountain were not to be. Rain, clouds, and mist eliminated any chance of views.

Does the Trail end here? Can we continue through the Whites? Tomorrow may tell!

August 7, 2002   Franconia Notch
Trail Distance: 0.0 miles

We tried several times to get reservations at the next three huts in the Whites maintained by the AMC. We all but begged for a place to stay and food to eat. Offering to pay the rather high price for daily lodging was to no avail. They were just full and had been for weeks. The current rate to stay in a hut is $65 per person, and that includes a full breakfast and just as full dinner. Stating that we were rather elderly thru-hikers and really needed floor space, any floor space, got us nowhere. It was with very mixed emotions that we spent the night. The decision to continue or not was tough!

August 8, 2002   Zealand Falls Hut
                                  Trail Distance: 7.7 miles

Leaving early, we drove to Crawford Notch and planned on staying in the well-publicized Crawford Notch Hostel. It was a real disappointment to find that it had never opened. All of the publicity was just a mite premature. As there were no motels or other places to stay, we left the car at the Wiley House which is available for snacks but not for lodging. At the end of three days, we will probably stay the night in N. Woodstock again, and then get a ride back to our car the next day.

Hiking now not only involves planning but the ability to change plans to meet daily needs. The twenty-eight Trail miles in this section involved about forty miles by car. Even so, the views from the car were super. However, they just seem to be more enjoyable when you have to hike for them. How often have we said, "we paid for this view and we are going to enjoy it!'

This was truly a beautiful day, and the views were great. The Trail itself was relatively easy compared to some that we have been on. At first, we had the forests to view, and they remained peaceful and quiet. We heard no bird songs at all. Finally, the Trail opened to a side of a mountain, and we had a grand view of the White Mountains. We were in awe! We had a sight that only a hiker can have. There was no way that any type of vehicle could go where we were.

Making good time, we stopped for a short visit at Thoreau Falls, a beautiful spot about two hundred yards off the Trail. Continuing on, we reached the hut at 1:30 P.M.

Yesterday, we had tried to get reservations at three of the AMC huts. When we kept getting word that there were no vacancies, we then started checking to see if it would be any better for us to travel north to south through the Whites rather than south to north. We found that by changing our direction, we would be able to cover the same distance in three days rather than four and require only one night in a hut. We could make use of a couple of A.T. shelters that would not be reasonable going in the other direction. The outcome was we would just take a chance and hike to Zealand Falls Hut.

We arrived early and found that fifteen persons had canceled their reservations for this night. There were plenty of vacancies and most remained that way. After paying our fees, we each had a big bowl of split pea soup, took our boots off, and started to enjoy the scenery. The views, as could be expected, were grand. Mountains and valleys surround us and pictures simply cannot do them justice. We try to soak them up and hope that some of the memories will last.

While seemingly on top of a mountain, we kept seeing flowing streams coming from one side. We simply could not see higher ground from which the water originated. Obviously, there was land higher, but it sure was not visible.

We had thought that the huts would have private rooms for the prices they charged. Not so! They have co-ed bunk rooms and separate washroom facilities for males and females. I suppose that when consideration is given to the distance that food and supplies have to be brought in on foot, the price and facilities are quite acceptable. We had no complaints! The food was everything that we could have hoped for.

August 9, 2002   Garfield Ridge Shelter
Trail Distance: 9.7 miles

True to form, we had a great dinner and breakfast served by a fine crew of staff members who were all college students. They made hearty meals, provided information, entertainment, and sang a wakeup call in the morning. All in all, they made us thoroughly welcome.

Leaving as soon after breakfast as we could, we started the hike up to the summit of Mt. Guyot. It was above the tree line and gave some fine views. Further on, we reached the summit of South Twin Mountain and had some even better views. There was no mist or low hanging clouds, but the lack of sunshine dimmed the views somewhat. The tree line in this area is about 4,200 feet, and only stunted spruce will grow above that. For most of the area, you have just rocks and some alpine grass and flowers. Needless to say, there is little to slow down the wind.

Hiking alongside of the mountains, we had some fantastic views of the surrounding mountains, valleys, and terrain. There were times when we would stop for several minutes just trying to commit to memory as much as possible. Cameras just could not do it justice.

We could see Galehead Hut 0.8 miles away in a valley. It looked close, but it took us an hour to reach it. Short of cash, they fortunately took credit cards so we enjoyed some minestrone soup and homemade bread. These college kids can really cook!

Hiking on from the hut, we finally reached the Garfield Shelter which is about half way up the side of Mt. Garfield. We had not realized that we had a climb at the end of the day, and the surprise left us winded. This shelter is nice, large enough for about ten persons (we had seven in it), and is maintained by the AMC with an $8-per-person fee for the night. We thought that the fee was a bit much for just sleeping space on the floor, but we suppose funds must be raised for all the fine work the AMC does. We did not object to the fee. (Our guide book claimed only $6-per-night fee per person.)

After a less-than-great dinner cooked by me and good conversations with the other guests, most of us turned in for the night by about 8:30 P.M. When it gets dark, it's beddie-by-time.

August 10, 2002   Franconia Notch
                                        Trail Distance: 10.3 miles

This is the second time that we have arrived at Franconia Notch. The first time was from the south, and today was from the north. It was not an easy day, and Mina came in thoroughly bushed. It's a question of whether she can continue tomorrow.

As our last shelter was about halfway up Mt. Garfield, we continued on to the summit. The hike up was rough and involved much hand-over-hand climbing. We had many, many rest breaks. From the summit, again above the tree line, the views were well worth the climb down and up. Looking down, we could easily see the Galehead Hut which was more than three miles away.

Leaving Mt. Garfield, we had many downs and ups before we started the serious "ups" to Mt. Lafayette. The hike again involved some hard climbing and was rather steep. We could see the summit from our last shelter, and we were impressed. It seemed very high to us. As we got closer, we kept going *down* until the summit was at a forty-five-degree angle *up* from us. Now, it seemed even higher!

When we finally reached the summit (five hours to go four miles), we found about a dozen people there who had come up easier, shorter, side trails. We found even more people at the summits of Mt. Lincoln and Little Haystack Mountains. There must have been about thirty people on the summits, and we think only one other person was a thru-hiker. These locals really like to hike. The views were great and only somewhat dimmed by a cloudy sky.

Coming down from the mountains, the A.T. was rough, rocky, and steep. It was not fun. Mina, especially, had a rough time. We think that the rocks were spaced for six-footers, and her short legs had a hard time navigating them. Many times, I could not step down to the next level; I had to jump. Mina just had to maneuver her way down. Two miles from the end, she was spent, tired, beat and exhausted.

Coming to where the Trail crosses U.S. 3, we were able to get a ride within minutes. Telling our driver that we wished to stay on U.S. 3, he at first said that he was going to continue on I 93 but later changed his mind and continued on U.S. 3 to its junction with U.S. 302. After a few minutes of waiting for a southbound drive, a *north*bound driver turned around and picked us up. A hiker himself, he went out of his way and drove us directly to our car.

Lodging was a bit difficult to get. Most had no vacancies, and one motel made something like eight calls before he found one that could lodge us for the night. With a Saturday night and three local weddings going on, there was not much room in the inns. Thankfully, it was not Christmastime or someone may have offered us room in the stables. However, with friendly and helpful locals, we had no problems.

August 11, 2002   Mizpah Hut
                            Trail Distance: 6.4 miles

We were able to spend a very restful night in an inn about five miles from the nearest town. Breakfast was included in the fee, and it, too, was very well received. Coming in rather late in the evening, we needed to shower, do laundry, and get organized for the next day. Finally, we decided that the laundry could wait until morning. This we did but it gave us a later start for this day. We finally started hiking about 10:00 A.M. and did not reach our hut until about 4:30 P.M. We only had 6.4 miles to do, and it took us 6.5 hours to do it. We had a lot of "ups", some rather steep, and it did slow us down somewhat.

This is a large hut, sleeps about sixty, and the vast majority are day hikers who come up by a shorter trail and just spend the night here. As far as we can tell, there are only three thru-hikers here. The dinner, as expected, was super. No one went away hungry, and I made sure that there was no apple sauce cake left over to insult the cook. Hiking to the hut, we crossed over several named mountains with some super views of the surrounding mountains, *plus* our parking area where we left the car today *and* where we had left it for the past three days. It was rather awesome looking down from three thousand feet to the thin highway and parking areas almost directly below you.

The Webster Cliffs give outstanding views as the Trail goes directly to the edge of the cliffs. This is not a place for the faint hearted or for anyone with a fear of heights. All in all, this was a great day for views.

This is a modern hut with some of the more experimental equipment in use. Solar power plays a great role here. Each privy is modern, and each seems to have a new innovation in use. It's interesting to read just how they work. They are a far cry from the old farm privies of yesteryear.

For the next twelve miles or so, the Trail is mostly above the tree line so we must be careful. We have weather forecasts each day in the huts and the next few days are forecast to be warm and sunny. Of course, this can change at anytime. We are warned that at the very first sign of inclement weather, we should leave the mountaintops and seek shelter somewhere below. The changes can be sudden and dramatic. Hopefully, we will not have any undue excitement.

We are still amazed at the amount of physical labor that went into the making and upkeep of the A.T. The massive stone steps and stones placed so that the hiker is out of the mud must have required countless hours of pure unadulterated labor. We hikers are truly thankful.

August 12, 2002   Lakes of the Clouds Hut
Trail Distance: 4.8 miles

Clear skies along with cool weather made for a nice evening and an enjoyable morning. The only dim part of the day was low visibility. Unlike some days in the past, today was hazy so that some of our views were rather limited.

From the hut, which is 1.4 miles from the summit of Mt. Washington, we can clearly see the cog railroad that operates to there. The forecast for tomorrow calls for clear skies. We can only hope that the visibility does not decrease.

Tonight is a scheduled meteor shower, and the sky is already building up with clouds. Perhaps things will clear up by early morning. At this altitude, over five thousand feet, the viewing would normally be better than average. There are absolutely no city lights around, and the moon sets early. Everything fits in except for the clouds. For that, we will just have to wait and hope. We have absolutely no control over the weather.

We see dozens of hikers on the Trail. As usual, most are day hikers or weekend hikers. Thru-hikers are scarce. This hut is the largest maintained by the AMC and can sleep ninety people. Since it is the closest to Mt. Washington, it is the most popular and is full. The tradition for thru-hikers is to sleep in the Dungeon. That is a small cubical below the main building that has 6 bunk spaces for sleeping bags and is reserved for thru-hikers only. We will not be allowed to have meals in the dining room even if we could pay. Meals are for paying residents only. Our bunk fee is $8 per person rather than the standard rate of $65 per person. This place really looks like a dungeon with the heavy metal door and stone walls.

Most of today was above the tree line, and all of tomorrow will be above. Even so, the gnats and black flies are still with us. As pesky as the flies are, they do have one redeeming feature. They pollinate the mountain blue berries. As there are no bees up here, we would not have the berries without the pesky flies. We do enjoy the berries and stop frequently to pick a few.

As this was a very short day, we will have time for an afternoon nap. Most days do not allow for a nap, so we have to grab one when we can. Mina took her reading light into the bunk with her and tried to do some reading. However, the light attracted some type of insect, and she was constantly swatting them. Finally, she just gave up trying to read and tried to get some sleep. The insects continued to crawl on her. No one else in the dungeon had the problem, just Mina. Finally, after a couple of hours hearing her swat the bugs and keeping *me* awake, I convinced her to join me upstairs on the dining room floor. With our mats, it was comfortable, bug free, and we were both able to sleep the remainder of the night. On our way to the dining room, we tried to see if we could see any of the meteor shower, but the clouds prevented any views.

August 13, 2002   Madison Springs Hut
                              Trail Distance: 7.0 miles

This was not a good day for us. The Trail was mostly brutal and sometimes downright treacherous. We had left at 7:00 A.M. and did not reach the hut until 3:30 P.M. The Trail was mostly rocks and boulders with varying ups and downs. Since all the Trail is now above tree line, we had expected it to be somewhat more acceptable. By the time we finished our hike today, I was really tired and Mina was plain exhausted.

Yesterday, we had arrived at the hut so early that we took a short hike to the top of Mt. Monroe as the Trail had skirted that mountain. We had a decent view from the top, but not great as the visibility was less than acceptable.

Our hike today started with a 1.4-mile trek to the summit of Mt. Washington, the highest peak in the Northwest at 6,288 feet. We had to do some panting to arrive at the peak as the altitude sure slowed us up. We were sorely disappointed at the haze in the air. It brought the visibility down to about ten miles rather than the optimum 130 miles. We arrived a few minutes before the first cog rail car arrived with a full load of passengers. It takes the train about an hour to make the trip from the valley. We have no desire to take the train, but we just may drive up if the opportunity presents itself on a nice clear day. Today, the summit temperature was about sixty degrees and the wind about fifteen miles per hour. These are far more acceptable than some of the extremes that have occurred in the past.

It was rocky going to the summit and rocky and rough from then on. The whole day was rocky, rough, and treacherous to the feet. Mina took a bad fall that bruised her a bit. It was bad enough, but it could have been far more damaging than it was.

Many times, the A.T. just skirts a mountain with loop trails available for anyone wanting to actually hike to the summit. This usually involves about a quarter-mile loop with about a two-hundred- to three-hundred-foot gain in altitude. With rare exceptions, we stayed on the A.T. and bypassed the loop trails. With the haze in the air, we didn't miss many views.

Mina is getting quite discouraged with the hiking. It is rough, and her knees are really giving her pain. Her last fall did not help any. Even if she stops hiking she has quite willingly agreed to help me complete *my* hike. Time will tell just what we will do; we have no firm decision on it yet.

We are quite disappointed with the reservation policy of the AMC huts. They save absolutely no spots for the A.T. thru-hikers except for about two slots for those who would work for their room and board. Many of the reservations are made months in advance where a thru-hiker probably does not know where he will be more than about three days in advance. The net effect is the huts are off limits to thru-hikers unless someone cancels at the last minute. For shelters on the A.T., this policy is just not acceptable to thru-hikers. For what it's worth, the A.T.C. needs to speak out and soon. It probably would not do any good as the AMC was here before the A.T., in fact, many years before.

August 14, 2002   Pinkham Notch
                           Trail Distance: 7.8 miles

We started out the day by hiking to the summit of Mt. Madison. As usual, the hike was rather rough and the views were quite limited because of continued haze. Mina's knees are continuing to bother her, one knee more than the other. She had taken a couple of falls yesterday that banged up her right knee and left her with a couple of scratches and bruises. She is beginning to look as if someone worked her over with a two-by-four.

After reaching the summit of Mt. Madison, we had thought that we would have an easier hike down. How wrong we were! Going down was steep and there was no trail! We had to follow rock cairns constructed over a large, steep, rock field. There were no trail markings except for the cairns. Those rocks and boulders came in all sizes and shapes and were not fun or easy to navigate. Actually, it was kind of a relief to get down to tree level and contend with rocks and roots rather than rocks and boulders. On the way down, Mina took another rather bad fall and banged up her other knee. That took any choice away from us; she just could not hike for some time.

We made out all right last night at the hut. After being told that there were no vacancies and the "work for stay" option for the first two hikers was taken, we were told that we could not stay. We wanted to just put our bags on the floor in the dining area, but we were refused that also and informed that we would have to move on. The manager was nice enough, but rules were rules! We could not stay, we could not tent nearby, and we could not buy any food. What a bummer!

We were also nice but also insistent. I informed the manager that we could not and *would* not be moving on. We were both tired, and Mina simply could not go any further. I informed him that we would be staying, maybe sleeping on the porch (which wasn't there), but we were *not* moving on. It was a kind of stalemate for a while.

While enjoying some cold lemonade, the manager came back to us and said that he had changed his mind, it *had* been a very warm day, and that we *could* put our sleeping bags down on the dining room floor where the thru-hiker workers would be staying. He said that he realized that it had been a hot day, it was rough on us, and we could stay with no problem.

Just as we were getting ready to prepare our evening meal outside, the manager came out to inform us that three others with paid reservations probably were not coming for the night. If they did not arrive by 6:00 P.M., dinner time, we could have their space and meals at no fee to us. Just before 6:00 P.M., we saw two new arrivals and figured that our good luck just turned bad. As it was, those two were *expected* to arrive late so at 6:00 P.M., we began a fine dinner. Later, we slept inside on bunks and had a great breakfast the next morning, all at no cost at all to us. What started out as a real bummer, turned out to be a super stay.

I have lost so much weight that none of my trousers fit. I have purchased two new belts, each shorter than the prior, and am now at the last notch on the last belt. I feel good but haven't seen me at this size since my military days, and *that* was a long time ago. I know that this will not last, but am kind of proud of the way that I look. Of course, without upper body exercise, my chest and arms look like that "one-hundred-pound weakling" we used to hear about.

Today was very rough on Mina. She will take off for a while as the next many miles are supposed to be very rough. Even though the next twenty-one miles are less than some younger hikers complete in one day, our guide book suggests taking at *least* three days to complete. I will try to complete it in three days while Mina bides her time in the area.

I have been trying to find a barber in the towns that we pass. So far, I haven't found one. Two months without shears really does something to one's hair, even when the quantity of hair is not abundant.

August 15, 2002   Carter Notch Hut
                                Trail Distance: 5.9 miles

After a nice "store-bought breakfast", Mina drove me back to Pinkham Notch and the A.T. trailhead. Of course, this was *after* a shower, good dinner, and a fine nights sleep in a local motel. All in all, it was a great rest.

This hut is in a super location. There are high cliffs on both sides, and it is near to two ponds at the base of the cliffs. The Trail comes down from one of the cliffs and will go up the other cliff tomorrow. They are pretty to look at now, but they have and *will* have my unpleasant attention.

The Trail today was billed as a steep climb to the summit of Wildcat Mountain. It was all of that! The first half hour of the hike was relatively flat and easy. Then the Trail got my attention! I climbed for about two hours until I reached a lookout point about a half mile *up* from my starting point of the hike. It was a great view looking down. It then took another half hour to reach the summit of Wildcat Mountain. The local gondola was running so we had some low-landers enjoying the view what there was of it. Actually, my view from a half hour back was better than seen by any of the gondola passengers. On a clear day, the Whites and the Presidential range would make for a fine view, but the haze conditions prevail today. This is in tandem with the ozone level which is also high.

The local ponds are available for swimming, which some of the guests have made use of. Of course, I had neither swimsuit nor any extra pair of shorts so the best that I could do was to take a long nap. After an hour and a half, I felt more refreshed. In all fairness to the locals who made their reservations months in advance, I do not blame them, and this is one fine place to just do nothing except enjoy nature and the scenery. I would really like to bring Mina back here someday as I know that she would love it.

Even though the climb up was steep and rough, it was really

less rough than I had expected. The opposite conditions prevailed at the end of the hike. The Trail coming *down* to the hut was a tad more difficult than anticipated. Also, it took longer than budgeted, but it usually seems that the last expected half hour takes anywhere from an hour to an hour and a half to complete.

This hut does not serve meals but does provide for a bunk with a mattress. There is a $19-per-night fee per person, and this place is full. There had been one cancellation, so I did not have to plead for a spot on the floor of the dining room. Most everyone else had a very easy hike to get here. There is a parking area nearby and an easy Tourist Trail for them to take. We have some older couples here and some very young children. They *all* claimed to have had an easy hike.

Mina and I had seen a snake a few days back that we could not identify, and none of the huts had a reptile book for identification. That was frustrating! This hut had such a book, and the snake was identified as a young northern black racer. It looks nothing like an adult which made the identification difficult. None of the hut managers could identify it from the description given. At least, now we know!

Today, I saw some of the tiniest toads or frogs that I have ever seen. They may have been babies as there were literally hundreds of them near to the pond at the notch. Each toad could easily fit on the fingernail of my little finger with room left over. The body *and* feet could fit there. They were amazing little creatures.

August 16, 2002   Imp Shelter
Trail Distance: 7.2 miles

This was a nice day, kind of cool with a slight breeze, and the views are getting better. From visibility averaging five to six miles, the views are now something like fifteen miles. At least, now a person can see something whereas before it was just haze.

The Trail today was mostly ups and downs with some really wicked downs. When the terrain is almost straight up or down, it is generally easier to go up rather than come down. It may not seem reasonable, but that is the way that it is. Going up, you at least have hand-and-foot holds. Coming down, these holds are not the easiest to see or find. I slipped a couple of times, but the only thing lost or injured was my dignity. Fortunately, there was no one around to even notice that.

I reached the shelter early enough that I could have gone on if I had not already planned on meeting with Mina tomorrow. It would have been a joke to reach town today and not be able to even find Mina. As it turned out, it started to rain a bit in the afternoon, thunder was heard, and I would have been quite nervous if I had gone on. This is a neat shelter and has a grand view of Gorham, New Hampshire. The other guests are comfortable to be with and easy to converse with. Prior crews had built a log "sofa" about one hundred feet below the shelter that has a fine overhead view of Gorham. It "seats" about six if they don't mind being uncomfortable. The logs have no "give" to them.

I have been asking various south bounders what to expect further north. If you know what to expect, it's easier to cope with. The best advice is to take it easy, don't try to go too far, and to relax and enjoy the "ride".

August 17, 2002   Gorham, NH
Trail Distance: 8.0 miles

This section was billed as being difficult, but I found it to be relatively easy. At least, it was easy compared to some of the earlier days. Actually, the last three miles were flat and not difficult at all. The total days hike took just five hours. For me that is pretty good!

Hiking up Mt. Moriah, climbing was not required so that part was pleasant. It was a clear day and views were great until the summit was approached. A thick cloud had settled over it shrouding all but the closest views. It was a bummer!

I had asked Mina to meet me in late afternoon as I did not expect to finish early. She had come to the trailhead early and left a note on the trailhead bulletin board informing me that she had reservations at a motel about two miles away. I got off the Trail at 11:45 A.M. and got a ride to the motel just as Mina was leaving to hike back to meet me. I would say that was good timing!

I tried again to get a haircut in Gorham, but the one barber in town closed at noon. I am beginning to look more and more like other shaggy hikers. To top it off, the battery on my electric shaver is going out, and the shaver works *only* on batteries.

While in Gorham, we checked in at the local post office to pick up the last "CARE" package that we had mailed to ourselves. It wasn't there! The postal clerks searched and emphatically stated that no A.T. Hiker packages had been returned to the senders. We later found that they did not tell the truth. The package *was* returned to Clearwater, and it contained much needed supplies for us. We were able to find other maps but could not get a copy of the *Maine Trail Guide* that we were going to depend on. To say the least, we were a mite irritated. Our package was clearly marked "Hold for A.T. Hiker", the post office has years of experience holding general delivery packages for A.T. hikers, some of the items in the package could not be replaced, and they lied stating that it had not been returned to the sender. After cooling off some, we decided that we would just make do with what we had and "wing it".

After a shave, clean clothes, good food, and a good night's rest, I will be able to hit the Trail tomorrow. Starting on the third day out, I will start to encounter the toughest part of the A.T. Other southbound hikers have told me not to consider it tough, but to consider it as a very interesting, time consuming, adult jungle gym. I hope to be able to keep that in mind.

Coming down from Mt. Madison, Mina had injured her other knee and had trouble just walking much less hiking over the mountains. We decided to let her rest for a few days in order to get some strength back in her knees and to be able to hike with me through the much publicized "one-hundred-mile wilderness". I did not wish to hike that part alone, and I *did* want her to be able to say that she had done it with me.

August 18, 2002   Gentian Pond Shelter
                                       Trail Distance: 11.8 miles

This was not thought to be a rough day, but it turned out to be one. There were really no super rough sections, but there were no smooth sections either. It was just a case of ups and downs, rocks, roots and smooth plank bridges. My feet started acting up with both big toes smarting. I still have had no blisters, although I have lost or will be losing four toenails. I think that was primarily due to the fact that my feet swelled in the old boots. My new boots are half a size larger, and hopefully, that will take care of the toe problem.

The views today were rather limited. There were no peaks with unlimited range. Trees got in the way most of the time. However, there were some good views looking back to Gorham and looking forward to Berlin, New Hampshire. Sitting in this shelter and looking over to Mt. Moriah, a person can see a small forest fire that has been burning for four days. Earlier, a helicopter had been dropping water on it. I suppose that it had some effect as the helicopter stopped what it was doing after a few drops. Smoke, however, continued to come from the site. We later found that the burn was very localized, contained in a canyon of about a couple of acres in size, and was allowed to burn out taking several more days.

Some of the occupants of this shelter just saw a mother moose and her calf stroll by. Somehow, I missed out on that. Oh well, I suppose that a person cannot see everything so you should be happy with the sights that you *are* able to see.

I had thought that it would take me five days to reach Maine 26 and meet up with Mina. By hiking 9.6 miles tomorrow, I can shorten it to just four days. It is kind of hard to judge what you can do by just looking at trail maps. You think that it may be easy, and it turns out difficult and vice versa. For instance, Mahoosuc Notch looks like a "piece of cake" on paper. It is about one mile long and perfectly flat. In reality, it's a mess of huge boulders, and the *better* hikers take three hours to go through it. I *hope* to clear it in four hours. Tomorrow, I should enter Maine and begin the Trail in the last of the fourteen states that it crosses. At this point, I really want to finish and will do my utmost to do so. Mina has offered to help, and I know that I could not do it without her.

David's total miles on A.T.: 1,879.0

Mina's total miles on A.T.: 1,099.9

CHAPTER TWELVE

August 19, 2002   Full Goose Shelter
                            Trail Distance: 9.6 miles

Before leaving New Hampshire, the Trail crossed over Mt. Success, a fitting name for the hikers who came from Georgia. It wasn't meant to be named for them, but the name is appropriate. Now, there is just one more state to cross. The entrance to Maine could have shone in lights, but all we saw was a sign on a tree. I *really* expected more of a welcome!

This was a day of good views, but a person had to pay for them. Some of the climbs to the peaks were rather interesting. That's another way of saying that they were rough and treacherous. Mt. Carlo and the several peaks of Goose Eye Mountain kept a person alert. You would not wish to walk it in your sleep, but the views were great! Gorham is now hidden by mountains and ahead was a great aerial view of Berlin, New Hampshire.

Parts of the Trail today were really dangerous and, as far as *I* am concerned, should not be hiked alone. The chance of falling and getting hurt is high. Hiking is not the problem; climbing and descending over large boulders at about a seventy-five-degree angle is the problem. OSHA would not approve.

I think that some of the rock problems encountered today are a preview of tomorrow. *That* will contain the "Notch", reported to be the roughest one mile of the entire A.T.

Today I saw a garter snake, a cow moose, and a spruce grouse. This grouse is an endangered bird that has no fear of man. The hen was within five feet of me and seemed completely unconcerned. Small wonder they are endangered. A beautiful creature, it was a real pleasure to be able to meet her in *such* close proximity. The moose was a different story. She took off about one hundred feet before she stopped and looked back. Possibly, if I had not been four days without a shower, she may not have moved so far away. I have heard they have sensitive noses.

Something needs to be said about the various kinds of privies utilized on the Trail. There *are* a variety! There is the "two-holer" where you are asked to pee in one side and poop in the other. Still another variety is where you are requested to pee in the woods and only poop in the privy. You are asked to "flush" with a handful of bark to aid in the composting process. Caretakers then will mix the product, let bacteria work its wonders, and eventually obtain a fertilizer. However, the most elaborate process seen was at one of the huts in the White Mountains. At this privy, you could pee and poop together. This was mechanically mixed with mulching compounds; water from an uphill spring was added as needed. The material was allowed to settle in a large compartment, and two years later the material would have worked its way through the privy to become fertilizer. All of this was a natural process and completely contained in the privy construction. There are several variations on the above; a person has to read the instructions before using in order to conform to the requirements.

August 20, 2002   Speck Pond Shelter
Trail Distance: 5.1 miles

This day was one of mixed emotions. I had been trying to look forward to it not as rough hiking but as a challenging game. Regardless, the weather did not cooperate. Rain started in the very early morning and continued at daybreak. No one wanted to get out of their sleeping bags and no one wanted to go through the "Notch" in the rain. Finally, at about 8:30 A.M., the rain stopped and the sun came out. Hoping that the sun would dry the rocks somewhat, I left about 10:30. It took one a half hours of rough hiking just to reach the south end of Mahousuc Notch. It was not quite equal to its billing. Rather than being filled with house-sized boulders, it was filled with boulders of all sizes and shapes up to about room size. They were piled helter-skelter with deep holes and crevices between them. It was not a place for the timid.

The Trail through the Notch was well marked with A.T. markers and arrows pointing out the directions. Many times the thought passed through my mind, "How can they expect anyone to climb up this or get over this hole or cross this ledge?" Somehow, if you looked carefully and studied the possibilities, you could find a way through, over or around the boulders. It may mean hanging on to a root, finding finger holes in the rocks or a notch in the stones to get a toe hold. Sometimes, you had to jump to grab a tree trunk or balance on the rock edges. The rocks were still wet, slips *were* made, cuts and bruises *did* occur, but no major bodily damage occurred. There were three rock tunnels, all short, which had to be navigated. I had to take my pack off twice and pull (force) it through the tunnels, and once I had to take my pack off in order to go through a narrow slit in the rocks. Once, a "controlled slide" down a rock got *out* of control but, again, no injuries resulted. Perhaps leather pants would have given the legs more protection as they looked the worse for wear and tear when it was all over.

The guide book says to allow several hours to complete the Notch. One south bounder claimed that he had "slacked it" in one and a half hours. Another south bounder said that he had met a north bounder in the Notch who had been in it for two hours and still had about an hour to go. I had estimated a four-hour trip, *hoped* to complete it in three hours, but actually took two hours, ten minutes. With dry rocks, I think that I could have finished it sooner. My legs are getting older, but they are still rather agile. Looking back, it was kind of a fun trip. Hopefully, sometime in the future, Mina and I can slack pack it together.

Leaving the Notch and going up to the shelter was almost as rough as the Notch. It was about a seventy-five-degree climb up to Mahousuc Arm. However, the views from the top were worth the trip. The shelter, itself, is nestled between two peaks on the banks of Speck Pond, at 3,500 feet, the highest body of water in Maine. A couple of hikers opted for a swim, but I found the air to be a bit too chilly to suit me.

Some of the views today were great with clear visibility. Being on top of a mountain and looking out over other mountains, many that you have hiked over, is an awesome sight. How many times have we said, "*Wow*, we hiked over *that*!"

It *is* slower going in Maine. The Trail so far has been rocky and rough. The 5.1 miles today took 6.5 hours. That included the two-plus going through the one-mile notch. Other hikers are claiming the same with some claiming only one mile per hour rather than their normal two to three miles per hours. So, we just plan on shorter distances.

August 21, 2002   Grafton Notch
                                      Trail Distance: 4.6 miles

This was a planned short day with tomorrow a zero day. My body is tired, and I really need a rest. Coming down from the shelter, I had to go up and over Old Spock, a four-thousand-foot peak. Again, the views were great with Mt. Washington clearly visible at about twenty-six miles away. Many of the other Presidential Peaks were also very clear.

When I was about half way down the mountain, I met Mina hiking up to meet me. That *was* a surprise as she did not know what day I would return or when in the day I would return. She had taken a chance and figured correctly that I would be coming down at this time. It was a most pleasant surprise, and we were able to hike together for the remaining two miles back to the car.

Our plans are to just clarify our plans for the next two to three weeks, rest, get well fed, and have me slack pack for the next four days. Without a pack, I can cover twice the territory over these mountains and rocks. It will take about two weeks in order to get through most of these local mountains on the Trail, and, hopefully, Mina can rejoin me on flatter ground. This will allow her knees to get better so that once we reach Mt. Katahdin, we can hike to the top together.

August 22, 2002   Bethel, ME
                              Trail Distance: 0.0 miles

With a shower, good food, and a good night's sleep, I am feeling more rested. Finally, after many attempts, I have found a barber. Before, I was available on a Sunday, too late on a Saturday, too late in the day, or the barber was just full. Today, I located a lady barber about seven miles away and had a two P.M. appointment. My hair had really gotten shaggy. However, the beard will have to wait as the battery in my shaver needs replacing. I do not want a barber to tackle the beard as I am a bit fussy about it.

Mina is out doing her good deed for the day. A family of four hikers, who are one day ahead of me, needed a ride from the trailhead to a local town. Mina met the mother yesterday and volunteered to transport them and their packs. By slack packing for four days, I just may catch up to them. They are a nice group, and I had shared the last three shelters with them.

Fall is coming early to the north woods. Leaves are starting to fall and it is cool. I am still waiting for summer to arrive, and already winter is just around the corner. It's going to be a fast year!

August 23, 2002   East B Hill Road
                              Trail Distance: 10.3 miles

After a full day of rest, I thought that I could just breeze through today. Such was not the case. The day started out all right, but the feet started to complain as the day progressed. I found the first seven miles of the Trail to be a bit on the rough side. The last three miles were relatively easy sailing, but by then, I was tired again.

The two peaks of Baldpate, above tree line, gave a great view of the surrounding countryside. As with most peaks above the tree line, the Trail was marked by rock cairns in addition to white blazes.

The blazes are just too hard to see when they are flat on rocks. The cairns, however, are easy to spot and easy to determine where the Trail is going. They are a great help

One of the northbound hikers had spent the night on top of East Baldpate two nights ago in order to watch the stars and moon. He darned near froze! Since he couldn't follow the Trail in the dark, he just shivered and had to wait until morning to continue. I'm certain that he will remember *that* night.

This was a slack pack day as are the next three scheduled to be. On these days, Mina has the habit, very agreeable to me, of going to the end of the Trail and hiking back to meet me. Today, she had to hike about three miles in order to meet me. Then, we hiked out together. Tomorrow, we plan to slack pack the ten-plus miles together. Arrangements have been made for shuttles to and from the Trail.

Mina is still very careful of her knees. There are just too many miles ahead where we plan on hiking together. With some sections, we *must* finish a section together as there is no way out when the section has begun.

The weather is still holding good. The rain, when it comes, seems to come at the right time, and the hiking weather is cool. It will undoubtedly be getting cooler as we continue to hike north.

August 24, 2002   South Arm Road
                            Trail Distance: 10.1 miles

This was another day when we slack packed together. The wild forest scenery is very nice, but there were few overlooks and the views were rather limited. It was only a ten-plus-mile day, but it took 7.5 hours to complete. It seemed as if we were making very good time. However, the distance just was not being covered. The terrain did not make any sense either. The last five miles were shown as being almost all down hill, but a good half of that time we were going *up* hill. It was frustrating! The owner of the lodging house took us to the trailhead at 7:30 A.M. and picked us up at 3:30 P.M. We had actually arrived a half hour earlier and waited for him. A most gracious host, there was no fee for the shuttle service. It was all part of his services.

Mina's legs held out for most of the day. At about the last two miles, one leg started to act up, but it was nothing serious. At any rate, she will take tomorrow off. She may, but is not certain, decide to go to the end of the Trail and hike back to meet me. As can be seen, plans are made, amended, changed and otherwise scrambled to meet the needs and desires at the time.

We like this little town of Andover. There is, however, one thing about it that we do not like at all. The church across the street from the lodging house rings its bell every hour, on each hour, throughout the day and night. Now, just who wants to know when it's two, three or four o'clock in the morning?

August 25, 2002   State Route 17
Trail Distance: 13.3 miles

At first, this looked like a formidable hiking day. The contour map to the top of Old Blue looked steep and downright mean. Actually, it turned out to be gradual and not difficult at all. The views, however, turned out to be somewhat less than spectacular. The summit was rounded without a steep peak. As a result, you could see in 360 degrees, but low spruce limited the views. As with most rocky tops that we have encountered, the Trail was marked by rock cairns, and there were sure plenty of those.

Going to Bemis Mountain, the Trail was very nice. There were no views from Bemis Mountain as it was completely wooded. Coming down from Bemis, there were three smaller peaks that gave good, but limited, views of the nearby mountains.

Mina had driven to the end of the trail and hiked back about three miles to meet me. She had brought her drawing pad along and had made some beautiful drawings. After we met, we then hiked out together. The hike out was far more strenuous to me than the hike to the top of Old Blue. The Trail went steeply down to a valley and steeply up to the road. By the time I reached the road, I was really dragging. Mina seemed to be having less trouble on the Trail than I do; I think that she is getting back in shape.

Later, a shower, clean clothes, and a good dinner put me somewhat back in order. We will be staying in a lodging house that caters to hikers, hunters, and fishermen. It's a weekend, fishing season is in full swing and the town and lodging house were full of visitors.

August 26, 2002   State Route 4
Trail Distance: 13.1 miles

The next thirty-two miles are billed as the most difficult in Maine. Assuming that this is correct, Mina will not be hiking with me and I plan on taking four days to cover the thirty-two miles. My plan is to stay in shelters for the first two nights, tent out with Mina on the third night, and slack pack out on the fourth day. A gravel road crosses the A.T. near to the proposed tent site. Mina will drive up there, meet me, and we will then hike about a mile back on the Trail where we will tent out. In the morning, we will take all of our gear back to the car and I will slack pack out to the main road where Mina will meet me later in the day.

On this day, the owner of the lodge drove to State Route 4 followed by Mina and me. We left our car there and were driven back to the start of today's hike. We then both hiked to our car and drove to Rangeley where we arranged accommodations for the night. Mina just may stay there one or two extra nights.

This was a day that turned out to be fairly close to expectations. The Trail, by A.T. standards, was relatively easy to navigate; there were no mountains to hike up, and no valleys to climb out of. The beauty today was in the pristine lakes and ponds passed. There were few or no cottages on most of the lakes, and they were just glorious bodies of water surrounded by equally glorious forests. There was Moxie Pond, Long Pond, Swift River Pond, and South Pond. They were called ponds, but they were really fair-sized lakes. I suppose when compared to some of the really big lakes in the area, they may be considered as ponds, but to the hiker, they clearly qualify as lakes.

As today's hike was supposed to be relatively nice, Mina did the full hike with me. She is still cautious of her knees and does not want to do any further damage to them. The day ended with good feet and good knees for both.

August 27, 2002 Poplar Ridge Shelter
Trail Distance: 10.7 miles

This was the first day of four through the reported toughest section in Maine. It *was* tough but we have seen it tougher. Actually, the hike to the top of Saddleback Mountain was comparatively nice and easy. It got a little tougher toward the top but, all in all, it was nice. However, it did get frustrating! I thought that I had reached the summit at 11:00 A.M. only to find that the supposed summit was still a couple hundred yards away. Reaching that point, we realized that the supposed summit was again a couple of hundred yards away. This kept up for a half dozen times! The real summit was not reached until 11:40 A.M. I must say that the wait was worth it.

There was super visibility in all directions for upwards of one hundred miles. Mt. Washington was still visible as was Mt. Katahdin. It was my first view of Mt. Katahdin. From this distance, it did not appear too impressive.

On the way to the summit of Saddleback, the Trail passed by the Piazza Rock. It was worth stopping to look at. Imagine a house-sized block of granite balanced on two room-sized hunks of granite. The Piazza Rock had an extension about twenty feet long extending over the forest floor many feet below. A unique display, it was most unusual. Mina, though not with me, hiked and climbed to the *top* of Piazza Rock later that morning.

Coming down from Saddleback was as difficult as the ascent was easy. Above tree line, the Trail stayed above the tree line for almost three miles. How the wind blew and just kept on blowing! The wind chill factor had to be far below the actual temperature. I not only kept my long pants on but put my jacket back on and *kept* it on.

I was able to meet another spruce grouse hen and got to within four feet of it. They really are not afraid of man!

This was a tiring day, and my feet are complaining. Those rocks and roots are just not easy to hike on. Fall is coming to the north-woods. Leaves are falling and can cover the Trail and underlying rocks. They then make things a bit slippery, so extra care has to be taken. In addition, it's downright cool up here.

The shelter this evening has a new twist. It doesn't have planks for flooring but has sawed-off poles. Built in 1961, I hope the habit did not catch with the shelters further north. Rounded poles do not make for the easiest place to sit on and surely not comfortable to sleep on.

August 28, 2002   Spaulding Mountain Shelter
Trail distance: 8.0 miles

I keep expecting the Trail to get rough as reported. Thankfully, the Trail was quite nice and the "ups" were civilized. Leaving this morning at 7:30 A.M., the shelter was reached at 12:45 P.M. I could have gone on 6.2 miles to the tent site but really did not want to. Mina is not expected there until tomorrow, and my feet are beginning to act up. There are no blisters, but the ball of my left foot and both big toes are just begging for relief.

Views outside of the forest were quite limited, but the magic of the forest is beginning to grow. It *is* beautiful!

Tomorrow is scheduled to be a short day both in distance and in time. Mina will drive up a gravel road about a mile from the tent site and just maybe have the tent set up when I arrive. I *am* looking forward to that.

August 29, 2002   Crocker Cirque Tent-site
Trail Distance: 6.2 miles

As hoped for, this was a short and mostly easy day. Except for about one mile, the Trail was nice. I will just skip the one mile un-nice part.

As also expected, Mina had already come to the gravel road one mile south of the tent site and left the car there. She wasn't at the tent site so I kept going on to the road. The car was there, but Mina wasn't! My first thoughts were, "Lost again?" This time I just waited and had a nice snack of peanut butter with Ritz crackers, plus a nice helping of dried fruit.

The tent was missing, so Mina must have taken it. All that I had to do was bring up the supplies for dinner. It was still about a mile uphill back to the tenting site. Going up, I met Mina coming down! She was coming back to the car for more supplies that she wanted. As often happens, sometimes the Trail has confusing markings or duplicate trails, and Mina had gotten on an old trail and was going up while I was coming down. We missed each other in the forest and probably passed within a hundred feet of each other.

This site is nice but really cool. The nights are already getting quite cool, and some would even say cold. There is a small pond near here that we plan to visit when it gets toward dusk and hope to see moose. There are plenty of moose droppings on and near the Trail as they seem to like to travel on the Trail. Mina has not met any yet. If you could see the forests, it is no small wonder that moose like to travel on the Trail. It is hard to believe that those large animals could get through the dense forests. The bucks would seem to have an unusually difficult time with their huge racks but they do not seem to mind. I suppose that there is not much that they could do even if they *did* mind.

August 30, 2002   State Route 27
                             Trail Distance: 7.3 miles

If you were to look at the published terrain map for this day, you'd be impressed by the peaks covered. Actually, the maps do not conform to the Maine Trail so far. According to the maps, we are hiking super steep slopes and descending on even steeper one. In fact, the slopes are quite gentle and respectful. There are a few places where things get a mite interesting but, taking it all together, it was a pleasant hike. Pleasant, that is, by A.T. standards. The average day-hiker would probably claim it to be rough and brutal. A person can look at the terrain map and get really nervous about the hike only to find that it wasn't so bad after all.

The pond that we visited last evening had not fared too well with the long Maine drought. What once covered several acres has shrunk to a little puddle about twenty feet across. There were some old tracks of one moose but nothing current. There *was* a nice stream near to the tent site that had a good flow of water so the local animals do not get thirsty.

The water flows vary from spot to spot. Two days ago, water was scarce all down the Trail. Yesterday, streams flowed very well in many locations. Today, there was water in streams, but not many of them. We still always have to ask south bounders about the water supply further north. We simply cannot take a chance of not having available water. It is one of those things that we take for granted back home, but is so important when you are away from a ready faucet.

We had a nice, gentle rain last evening that made the plants happy but did nothing to help the drought conditions. Fortunately for us, the rain stopped prior to having to break camp so it was not too uncomfortable for the hikers. The rain covers for the tent and backpacks got wet but a little airing in the sun got them dried out very well.

There have been many times in the past, probably every prior hike, when I thought there was little or no chance of every reaching Maine or Mt. Katahdin. Now, I know that I can do it! However, I know that I could *not* do it without the help and encouragement of Mina. She is either driving to meet me at a trail-head or dropping me off at one, helping me to slack pack when I can, or hiking to meet me at a shelter or tent site. Without her aid, I would not be able to finish.

The expected grand views from Crocker Mountain turned out to be quite limited. The elevation and visibility were there but the trees obscured most of the viewing. A peek through the trees did give some fine, limited views of the mountains and valleys.

We are still enjoying our eating. Back home, we really had to watch our intake as the pounds easily accumulate. Now, we eat as much as we wish and *still* want more without danger of gaining weight. This little joy will only last for about three more weeks, and then it's back to a very limited diet. Neither of us seems to be losing any more weight as both seem to have stabilized. I look at my pants waist now and find it hard to believe that the trousers used to fit me. Frankly, it's kind of embarrassing.

We both keep changing our future hiking plans. Circumstances change and plans have to change with them. A casual talk with a Trail caretaker revealed that the Avery Shelter is no longer there. It had been the planned stay on September 1. A call to make reservations at the Harrison Pond shelter on September 2 got the response that they will close for the year on August 31. Now, my plans are to slack pack the thirty-three miles up to the Pierce Pond Shelter. Mina will meet me after seventeen miles and we will either camp out or drive to a town for the night. Then, at the end of the second day, we will get our packs from the car and hike 0.7 miles to a shelter for the night and cook our evening meal there.

Mina is having fun picking up hikers and taking them to their destinations. She is getting better known *off* the Trail than I am *on* the Trail. After the next two slack packing days for me, we should be hiking together all of the way until the end of our hike. From now on, the Trail is mostly level although not destined to be easy hiking. We will just have to take each day as they come and accept the hiking conditions as they arrive.

August 31, 2002   Stratton, ME
Trail Distance: 0.0 miles

This day was Mina's birth date, so we took the day off from hiking. Nothing special was planned; just a day to relax and take things easy.

We had been told where we could possibly see a moose late in the afternoon. So, yesterday we drove the short distance there. By the time that we arrived, there were already about a dozen vehicles there. We did see one moose cow, and she seemed unconcerned about the people milling around on the rim of the parking area. At last, Mina saw her first moose on this hike.

Since we had no big plans for Mina's birthday, we decided to get up early and see if there were any early rising moose at the spot where we were the evening before. Our luck held out! We saw four moose consisting of a bull, a cow with calf, and a cow alone. They kept their distance from each other, and we kept our distance from them. Now, Mina feels that she has really seen wild moose. At this time in the morning, we were the only ones visiting the site.

A nice dinner evened out the day, and sleep time came early. I need an early start tomorrow as I have, at least for me, a long day and a long hike.

September 1, 2002   East Flagstaff Road
                         Trail Distance: 16.7 miles

This was the first of two long days for me. As it turned out, the day was a little longer and a little more rough than expected. It took me almost eleven hours to reach Mina and the car. The paths to the peaks were not that difficult even though two of them were above the tree line. There were just too many of them crammed into a sixteen-mile day. The four peaks covered in the Bigelow Mountain gave some wonderful scenery. Flagstaff Lake, a large man made lake, could be seen in all of its glory. Somewhere under the waters is the drowned town of Flagstaff that was sacrificed in order to form the lake.

When I arrived at the car, Mina had already found a campsite, set up the tent, found a church group that was selling barbequed chicken dinners, had a supply of water, and virtually had dinner ready to serve. As I normally do the cooking when tenting or staying in shelters, I had the night off. There were no complaints from me!

Last night was downright cold! I started hiking this morning with long pants, a long-sleeved shirt, jacket, and gloves. It *still* took me about an hour of hiking before my body and the temperature came to an agreeable understanding. As the day progressed, first the gloves and then the jacket came off. Later, a short-sleeved shirt replaced the long-sleeved one. As the later evening progressed, everything went back on except for the gloves. They can wait until morning.

As this is Labor Day weekend, many day hikers were seen including three from Quebec and three from the U.K. This *is* a popular and well-known trail.

The Trail above the tree line is rather unique. As the Alpine foliage is quite fragile, hikers are requested to please stay on the Trail. Volunteers have lined the Trail with rocks and stones so a person has no excuse *not* to stay on the path. Most do but there are always some that pay no attention to the signs. We like to think these are the day hikers.

We still have not seen that many northbound hikers. We would expect to see an average of about five per day. They are just not here!

September 2, 2002   Caratunk, ME
Trail Distance: 19.8 miles

This was a long-distanced day, but not long in time. I was supposed to meet Mina at the Pierce Pond Shelter, and I covered the 15.8 miles in seven hours flat. For me, that was very good indeed. Actually, the Trail was better than average, and good time could be made without any problems.

When I arrived at the shelter, Mina had not arrived, so I continued on to the road where I found the car. I still did not see Mina! Enjoying some peanut butter snacks, I waited a short time for Mina to appear. When she did appear, she was still wearing her backpack that she was to take to the shelter. Questioning her, she said that she had been looking for the shelter for the past hour and a half and could not locate it. The Trail goes across a rather crude dam on Pierce Pond, and the Trail markings going south are not quite up to what they could be. At any rate, she did not realize that she had to cross the dam and took off on some old Trail blazes that just took her back to the road.

As the day was still early and my feet seemed to be in good

shape, plans for the night were changed. Rather than staying in the Pierce Pond Shelter, I would hike on into Caratunk, and Mina would drive the car around. She had to go about twenty miles south on gravel roads in order to find a bridge across the Kennebec River. I would be ferried across in a canoe when I came to the river. Then, our plans were to meet on the other side, arrange accommodations at a local B & B, have a nice shower and dinner and make plans for the remainder of the trip.

The plans are to leave the car here in town and carry everything that we may need for the final hike to Mt. Katahdin. We will get more food supplies as these are depleted but our clothing will just have to do. The car will not be available anymore until the hike is completed.

The views today were not from mountain tops but from the shores of lakes. We passed several beautiful ones. Yesterday, we had Flagstaff Lake, a large one indeed. Today, we had West Carry Pond (really a large lake), East Carry Pond, and Pierce Pond. All of the lakes seemed to be quite shallow. The water close to the banks was so shallow that you could see the bottom one hundred feet from shore. No boat could approach the shore without hitting bottom a long way out. I suppose that it got deeper further out, but there would be no fishing from shore. No one could even cast as far as would be necessary.

From now until the end of the hike, Mina and I will be hiking together. Her feet and knees seem to be back in shape so we are not concerned. The next and last supply town will be Monson, Maine, due five days from now. From there, the Trail starts the famous "hundred-mile wilderness" section. This section always makes hikers more than a little nervous.

September 3, 2002   Pleasant Pond Shelter
                             Trail Distance: 5.7 miles

A good dinner, a great night's sleep, and a super breakfast got us both ready to hit the Trail again. The Caratrunk House was a fine place to stay, and they served a breakfast better than any that we could have bought in a restaurant. With super hosts, it is easy to recommend it.

The Kennebec River can be quite shallow at times, but hikers are cautioned to *never* try to ford it. An upstream dam can release water without warning, and the water level and current can change faster than a hiker can safely reach shore. Therefore, ferry service is provided free of charge to hikers except that sometimes they may have to help paddle the canoe. I not only wanted to help paddle, but I wanted to be in control of the canoe. My Elderhostel canoe trip last year makes me rather critical of others' canoe expertise. As it turned out, I was only a passenger and did not criticize as I was happy to just get across.

We left our car at a private residence at a fee of $1 per day which we considered more than fair. When we finish our hike, we can either get rides back to the car or we can call, and they will come and shuttle us back. At any rate, we do not expect to see our car again until *after* we climb Mt. Katahdin. Hopefully, that will be in about eighteen days.

The hike today was purposely short and relatively easy. We made the shelter in only three hours. We could have gone 8.8 miles to the next shelter, but this is the first day in a long time that we both are carrying full packs plus a light drizzle is falling. We really *feel* the full packs. We could probably get by carrying a three-day supply of food, will probably need a four-day supply, but are carrying a five-day supply for safety reasons. Rain may keep us in a shelter for an extra day.

Again, Pleasant Pond is misnamed! It is a nice-sized lake with many cottages around it. As with other lakes that we have seen, it appears to be quite shallow with a gently sloping bottom out into the lake. A person could not get a boat ashore without getting his feet wet.

A southbound couple who came over Pleasant Pond Mountain today told us that it was very wet and slippery on top. The man had taken four falls on the rocks so they told us that it was best if we waited until tomorrow to cross so that, hopefully, things would dry up a bit. We then told them that we had not been planning on going any further today.

This is an older shelter, sleeps only six, but is near to water and seems to be comfortable enough. After another cold morning to start the hike, today turned pleasantly warm. We are hoping that the weather, still cool, will hold out for three more weeks. If it does get colder, we have the gear to handle it. However, we would rather carry the gear than wear it.

September 4, 2002   Bald Mountain Brook Shelter
Trail Distance: 9.0 miles

Today started warm enough. We find it rather strange that the mornings usually feel warmer than the evenings. Perhaps it's because we are more tired in the evening. At any rate, we often are wearing long pants in the evening and start out with shorts in the morning.

This day started out with a 1,200-foot gain in altitude in the first mile of hiking. Now *that* started the blood flowing. Once at the top of Pleasant Pond Mountain, the views were limited but appealing. These mountains are not as high as the Whites, but when you are the highest thing around, you still stand out.

We passed the southern tip of Moxie Pond (another large lake) and were able to find rocks on which to cross over. We sometimes have to search for stepping rocks as we do not want to take off our boots and wade if we can avoid it. We know that fording may be necessary later on and have Teva sandals to wet if we need them. If so, so be it but we would rather not. As we climb up from the "pond", we get a better view of it. It is one pretty lake.

This shelter was built in 1994 and still uses an old design that we find rather irritating and cumbersome. Obviously, others have found it satisfactory.

September 5, 2002   Horseshoe Canyon Shelter
Trail Distance: 12.9 miles

We had a cloudy night and just a wee bit of rain fell. Waking up in the middle of the night listening to rain is not a pleasant experience when hiking. It may be a nice sound when a person is safely in a dry room in a warm bed and knows that he will be dry in the morning. However, in a shelter, it is not a sound conducive to good sleeping. You get concerned about wet rocks, slippery roots, and wet leaves on the Trail. Lady Luck remained with us! There was very little rain, and the morning found everything quite dry. We *were* fortunate!

It was a pleasant and scenic hike to the top of Moxie Bald Mountain. Some of the Trail near the summit passed huge squares of granite that appeared as if some giant hand laid them out with small passageways between them. We were rather surprised to find that the Trail did *not* pass through the passageways. On top, the views were super in all directions. It turned out to be a beautiful day, clear, with great visibility.

Coming down from Moxie Mountain, we stopped at the Moxie Bald Shelter but did not stay. We opted to continue on to the next shelter. This shelter was in a nice location as it faced Bald Mountain Pond, another beautiful lake.

The Trail took us past Marble Brook and the West Branch of the Piscataquis River, normally places that we would have to ford. However, with the Maine drought, the water levels were sufficiently low that we could find stepping stones and crossed with dry feet.

We followed the West Branch for over three miles before we reached our shelter for the night. Sometimes we would be near the water level, and at other times we would be one hundred feet above the water. The Trail kept going up and down following the contour of the cliffs. From above or below, the rocky river was a pleasant sight. Too rocky to be navigated in any kind of boat, it *did* have some swell swimming holes. Swell, that is, in warmer weather; it was still cool for us.

This shelter is way up the cliff side, and the spring for water is dry. Rather than going back down the long trek to the river, we located a stream with running water a short distance from the shelter. All of our water gets treated regardless of where we get it so this posed no problem. This shelter sleeps eight, but there is only one other person sharing it with us. Two other hikers chose to tent out.

Continuing on the Trail, we were able to cross the Piscataquis River with dry feet. According to our guide book, this river is normally knee deep and requires the hikers to ford it. We could have done it if we had to, but we prefer it this way. Dry weather does have some benefits. This country is so dry that we could do with some rain, a *lot* of rain, but just not at the time we are hiking.

For the last couple of nights, we could hear the loons calling from the lakes. The sound is not as lovely as their spring time yodel, but it is still a looked forward to event in the night.

September 6, 2002   Monson, ME
Trail Distance: 8.9 miles

This was supposed to be a very easy day, with no mountains to hike up, no valleys to hike down, and relatively easy going. It was all of that but Mina was still very tired after only a few miles. We have only about twelve days of hiking to do, and we are both wondering if Mina can complete it. We will be taking a "zero" day tomorrow in order to get well fed, restocked, rested, and give us time to make that decision. When we leave Monson, we will have about one hundred miles ahead of us with no public roads and no towns. Once we leave here, we *must* go on. There may be a couple of logging roads ahead but no federal, state, or county roads. The "one-hundred-mile wilderness" is well named!

Passing by Lake Hebron today, we saw and heard two adult loons and two young loons on the lake. They are such beautiful birds to be called "Common Loons". There is nothing common about them.

We are staying at Shaw's in Monson, a well-known and well-attended hiker lodge. Again, a shower, clean clothes, a great dinner, and a good night's sleep did wonders for the body. We have met some hikers that we have met before, found out about other hikers that we met in the past, and hikers that we may meet in the future. Shaw's is a great place to stay and we heartily recommend it to others.

September 7, 2002 Shaw's Lodging in Monson, ME
Trail Distance: 0.0 miles

This is a great place for a "zero" day. The accommodations are very nice and quite reasonable. Laundry facilities are right in the lodging house, the supply store is nearby, and the meals are as much as a person can eat with plenty of variety. A hiker just could not do any better. To top it off, our hosts were just wonderful people who thoroughly enjoy their guests.

We were able to replenish our supplies in the nearby store and even found additional food supplies in the "hiker box" that we could use. Most lodging places and hostels available to hikers have a hikers' box. This is nothing more than a box where hikers can leave unwanted or unneeded food and supplies that they have no more use for or find it too heavy to carry. We were able to take from it as needed or desired and leave it items that we did not wish to carry. Since it is all free, it's fun going through the boxes to see what you can find and use. Someone is always leaving peanut butter, and that is something that I cannot resist. It is too heavy to carry, but I can enjoy some while I am resting.

In walking around this friendly little town, we were dismayed to see the number of houses and buildings for sale and others that are rundown and abandoned. The town is right on the edge of beautiful Lake Hebron (not a pond) and seems to be in a great location. Hopefully, someone will have the foresight and ability to bring it back to full life. Of course, it is a necessary spot on the A.T. We just wish that it can be revived so that more than the hikers can enjoy it. The residents are too nice to see their town die.

For the past couple of weeks, we have seen very few northbound hikers. We don't know where they came from, but this place is full of them. Considering that there are two other hiker lodging places in town, there must be at least a dozen northbound hikers here. We are hoping that when they leave here, most will be using their tents as the shelters have very limited capacities and *our* tent is safely back in the car. We will hate to leave this place; the good food and super accommodations can spoil a person.

We have completed most of our grocery shopping to carry us for seven days. We expect to use six days of supplies but want an extra day in case we get hit by a storm, illness, or other mishap. Last night was cold with the temperature down to thirty-four degrees. We left with long pants, long sleeves, and jackets on. Gradually, we took off the gloves, long pants, jackets, and changed to short sleeves. The days warm up nicely, but the nights can be quite chilly. The mornings would be a little warmer if we slept later, but we like to get an early start so that we can reach our destinations by early afternoon. Leaving at 6:30 A.M. is not unusual.

September 8, 2002   Wilson Valley Shelter
Trail Distance: 10.4 miles

This was a day of many, many small ups and downs. Nothing was ever level for very long. Fortunately for us, each of the ups and downs was never very long. There were never any mountain top views but the many ponds had great views from the lower levels *and* from higher levels.

After a zero day and four super meals, one would think that today would be rather easy. Such was not the case. Mina was just tired! I was also somewhat tired but had two feet that were giving me a problem. They both bloody hurt! It seems like if it is not one part of the body that gives concern, it is another. Perhaps we should be thankful that all parts do not complain at the same time.

We are now officially in the "hundred-mile wilderness", but it looks and feels just like any other part of the Trail. This was a warm day. It started warm and stayed warm well into the evening. That was part of the problem with Mina. She was not only tired, but she got overheated. We were lucky that we did not have too far to hike. Tomorrow is supposed to be another day like this one. If so, we will just take it easy, not try to see how early we can complete our hike, and take rests as needed.

We could hear the Little Wilson Falls long before we came to it. It is a sixty-foot waterfall in a slate gorge, reported to be one of the highest on the A.T. Further on, we easily crossed the Big Wilson

Stream that many hikers had to ford. We had programmed ourselves to fording some streams but have managed to make use of the dry weather and get across on rocks and stones in the streams. Our Tevas were specifically brought for the purpose of wading through water, but we just do not like to do it.

September 9, 2002   Cloud Pond Shelter
                                   Trail Distance: 8.7 miles

We are now feeling about how we felt when we left the Trail in Massachusetts. We are exhausted! We start out tired, and it doesn't get any better. Today would normally have been a short day, but our many rest stops didn't allow us to reach the shelter until 3:20 P.M. That was with a 7:40 A.M. start.

My left foot is giving me problems, and I am glad that the hike will soon be over. We have scheduled nine more days of hiking before we reach Mt. Katahdin. From where we stand now, that looks like nine days of exhaustive, painful foot wear.

Going over Barren Mountain gave us some good views of the countryside. The Trail, for us, was rather rough. We feel certain that the younger hikers find it easier. They just breeze by us. We still refer to them as "gazelles", a name that we give to them with a certain amount of envy.

Our shelter for the night is neat and comfortable. Several hikers elected to tent out on the shores of Cloud Pond, a very attractive lake high up in the hills. The nearby spring is dry but there is plenty of water in the lake.

Mina has already gone down to the lake to bathe and wash some clothes. She is begging me to do the same. If I know what's good for me, (and I do) I will do the same. There are many bushes near the shore line and many little coves that allow a person to have some privacy when bathing. Since no one lives on the lake, the only other people around are other hikers, and they are screened by the trees.

Starting out with seven days supply of food, I *am* carrying a heavy pack. After today, I will be two days of supplies lighter. *That* should help me a bit.

All of a sudden, Maine has turned warm. Both yesterday and today were quite warm. Last night was so warm that we both slept outside of our sleeping bags. That was a first for us since we started back in April. In the summer, we had a hard time just getting warm, and now we would like some (not all) of that cool weather. Who knows what the next nine to ten days will bring. It could be hot and it could be too cold for comfort. That "unknown" always makes for some interesting things to look forward to.

September 10, 2002   Chairback Gap Shelter
Trail Distance: 6.9 miles

We had an interesting event happen to us last night. I had a "call of nature" about 2:00 this morning. While out, I noticed the light from a flashlight passing through the trees up the hillside from the shelter. I kept watching and it kept going back and forth, shining up in the trees and through the bushes. This went on for several minutes, and I was really curious as to what was going on. Finally, I heard Mina call for me. I had not noticed that she was missing when I got up. She had gotten up earlier for the same purpose and, without her glasses, could not find her way back to the shelter. She had been out for almost a half hour and was getting more than a little nervous about the whole episode. There were many trails around the heavily bushed area, and Mina had somehow gotten up the hill from the shelter and could not see it in the dark. She could have yelled and gotten all kinds of help but she figured that eventually I would notice her missing.

This was another elevator day. It was ups and downs all day in the Barren Chairback Range. Outside views were quite limited, but the constant forest is quite nice to be in. Hiking can be slow and somewhat rough, but we were in no hurry and made the shelter by 2:00 P.M. We had earlier been told that the shelter spring was dry so we filled up with water at a stream about two mils back.

Just to be certain, we checked the spring, and it was bone dry. Hey, they were telling the truth for a change.

Others have reported seeing moose and bear on the Trail but, so far, they have eluded us. For one thing, we are so constantly looking at our feet and where to put them, that we could have passed many wild animals without seeing them. We *did* see another spruce grouse hen, and like the others, seemed completely unafraid of us. These are truly beautiful birds. Remembering our chickens when I was a child, no chicken would *ever* allow anyone to get as close as these birds allow.

It continues warm today, the warmest that we have seen. Another hiker reported it to be ninety-five degrees in some parts of Maine. The nights stay warm, also, and we continue to sleep outside of our bags. We sure hope that this continues for a while. We sure go through more water when it is this warm. We go through a *lot* more water, but being cold just to use less water does not thrill us. Most all of the pictures that we have seen of hikers on top of Mt. Katahdin show them in winter gear. We hope that is not what we will have to do. However, we are somewhat prepared. We had stopped in a thrift shop back a ways and purchased some heavy duty sweat shirts for use in cold weather. They are heavy, but we would rather carry them and not need them than need them and not have them. We have been cold before, and that is no fun!

We are well into the "one-hundred-mile wilderness" now and hear no sounds of civilization except for an occasional airplane. We once heard a sawmill in operation at a distance from us. This section of Maine sure seems wild and primitive. We love it!

September 11, 2002   Carl Newhall Shelter
Trail Distance: 9.9 miles

Taking everything into consideration, this was one miserable day! However, it was not a surprise as we had been warned. Last evening, Weather Man, one of the thru-hikers, told us to expect rain today. The probability was 100 percent. Now, that is a rather high percentage. As a retired weather man, we believed him and tried to get an early start. The first part of the day was nice, and we were able to cross the West Branch of the Pleasant River by walking on rocks rather than fording it. From then on, things went rather downhill.

Shortly after crossing the Pleasant River, we passed through The Heritage, a beautiful grove of white pine trees which are protected by the Nature Conservancy. Back in our colonial times, the best and straightest of the white pines were selected for masts for the sailing ships and warships. These were considered to be the property of the English Crown, and anyone stealing one was hanged. It may seem a high price to have to pay for a tree, but that was the law the colonists had to live with. This prohibition and resulting punishment was a major factor in the rebellion of the New England colonists. The complaints about the English tea tax were only a secondary factor in the rebellion. Today, The Heritage is pretty to look at but no camping is permitted in the preserve.

We would have loved to take time off to travel the Gulf Hagas Trail. This would have involved a five-mile loop that would have passed the "Grand Canyon of the East". There would have been five major waterfalls and a gorge five hundred feet deep to view and marvel at. However, the threat of the oncoming rain just would not allow us this luxury. As much as we wanted to "smell the roses", we had to pass this one by.

The first rain drops had us put our pack covers on. When it started to shower a little harder, I put on my rain jacket, but Mina decided not to put hers on. Then the rain really started, got harder, and continued to rain very hard. After about two hours of rain, the temperature started dropping and dropped about twenty degrees. By then, we were both quite wet, our boots were wet, and Mina put her jacket on just to get some warmth. It took us another hour to reach the shelter, and it was a miserable hour. We were cold, shivering, and could not stop for shelter anywhere. We just had to continue. Once in the shelter, we did what another hiker had done. We stripped, dried off, put on our ski underwear, and dove into our sleeping bags. Even so, it took us a long time to warm up as we got just a bit too close to hypothermia. "Chilled to the bone" is another expression that fits. Even after we had warmed up in our bags, we both continued to shiver until the bodies came back to proper temperatures.

I did not bother going for water. I just cooked what I could with the water that we had. This shelter sleeps six, but seven, all drenched, were in for the night. It was most cozy. With everyone trying to get dry and warm, most were in their sleeping bags by 7:00 P.M. Wet clothes and wet boots were hanging from every available line, nail, hook, and cranny. It would be a wonder if everyone got all of their gear back. It is a royal mixture, and many of us are wearing the same kind of hiking socks. Tomorrow could be interesting!

September 12, 2002   East Branch Shelter
                            Trail Distance: 10.8 miles

It was a cold, restless, and uncomfortable night. No one could turn over without disturbing the two people on either side of him. It was just plain crowded, but no one complained. We were glad to be dry.

We woke up cold, and no one seemed particularly anxious to leave his bag. Finally, the "call of nature" got me up, got me moving, and started to get the morning organized. After a late start, we moved out toward the next shelter. The Trail today crossed three mountain peaks. Although none were like the Whites, the views from the first three were limited or nil but White Cap Mountain gave fine views in all directions. The day was sufficiently clear that we could see Mt. Katahdin and, even at sixty miles away, it was impressive. Of course, the Trail miles will be somewhat longer as they do not even come close to being in a straight line. That mountain is akin to a magnet. You are not content to just look at it; it draws you to it with some kind of irresistible force. I have heard of it for so many years that I just have to visit it.

We were not sure of just how far we would hike today. Mina had injured her foot in the morning and consideration was given to stopping at a shelter only 7.2 miles in. However, by the time we reached there, Mina felt that she could carry on, and she did. She is some woman! The feet gave her no lasting effects.

White Cap Mountain will be the last mountain above the tree line that we cross before Mt. Katahdin. We are scheduled to continue to have our ups and downs, but nothing like we have had in the past.

Our shelter for the evening is right beside the East Branch of the Pleasant River. Needless to say, there is *plenty* of water for our needs. In a sharp contrast to last night's crowded shelter, we have this one to ourselves. We were able to get our boots sufficiently dry to walk in, but our other clothes are still wet. We try to dry them when we reach a shelter, but it sometimes takes a couple of days for them to be really dry. When you are hiking, you have to leave behind some of your natural modesty. All kinds of undergarments can be found hanging from any nail or peg in a shelter. It makes for an interesting variety.

September 13, 2002   Cooper Brook Falls Shelter
                              Trail Distance: 8.1 miles

After a good night's sleep, although a little cool, we were not in a hurry to leave the shelter. The weather looked good, and we did not have that far to go. Why rush when there was no reason for it?

We had our usual ups and downs and made several stops to put rain gear on, take it off, put it back on, and finally took it off for the day. It would threaten, sprinkle a bit, the sun would come out, it would get cloudy and sprinkle some more. When it first started, we both stripped right in the middle of the Trail and put back on the semi-dry clothes that we had worn previously that had not quite completely dried. By wearing them, they dried out. As we were carrying only one change of clothing, we could not afford to get everything wet.

We made good time to the shelter as the last three miles were an ideal hiking trail. Others were to join us later. The rain was not quite over and gave us a good shower before it quit.

This shelter is ideal. It sits right beside the Cooper Branch, and there really is a small waterfall and a large deep pool that, in warmer weather, would be great for swimming or bathing. With the air temperature what it is, neither is an option. A most peaceful and serene location, whoever chose this site could not have done better.

Tomorrow, we hope to cover thirteen miles to White House Landing, where we expect to get supplies and lodging for the night. To do that mileage, we *must* start early. Without a weather report, we can only hope that the day turns out at least dry and hopefully warm.

September 14, 2002   White House Landing
Trail Distance: 13.9 miles

All in all, this has been one great day. The Trail for the first several miles was just a "walk in the woods". It was really a joy to be able to hike and not worry about rocks and roots under feet. Then we had a few miles of rocks, boulders, and many hundreds of feet of log bridges over marshy and boggy areas. These bridges are nothing more than a log split down the middle and nailed to a short cross log so that hikers can cross the underlying muck. Maine has many hundreds of feet of this type of bridge, far more than any other state. As with many other aspects of the Trail, much labor went into the construction of these.

Many lakes and ponds were passed, each beautiful in its own right. Our favorite was Remadumcook Lake, which had a grand view of Mt. Katahdin overlooking the lake. Sure hope that our pictures come out, but they could never come up to the standard of an actual view. It was a view that we would have gladly gone out of our way for but it was right on the Trail. This was a definite "plus".

It seems rather odd that we are getting so close to the end of our hike. A dream of fifty-five years, many hikes over the past eleven years where most ended with the thought that it was the end, and now the true end is literally and figuratively in sight. Just a few more days of decent weather should do it.

Hikers, in general, are super neat people. They pack it in and pack it out. Garbage of any kind is just not tolerated. Yesterday, we encountered two short term hikers who did not fill the bill. They left food, a peanut butter jar, and a pair of long underwear right in the middle of the Trail simply because they did not need it anymore. I will not shame the state from where they came by naming it. I *will* say that their mothers should be ashamed of the sons that they raised, and I do hope that these men are not married. Their wives would deserve pity.

Even though most hikers are extremely neat, most are quite negligent on their common courtesy Trail responsibilities. Basic hiker duties require that hikers remove dead limbs and branches from the Trail, remove loose rocks from the Trail, and break off any offending twigs and branches that would hit another hiker in the face or eyes. Almost without exception, hikers ignore all of these. Limbs could rot on the Trail without any hiker removing it. Sure, there are volunteer crews that do these things, but it would be so simple and courteous for the actual users of the Trail to do *some* of it.

We have had some high winds during the past couple of days and have seen many branches and some trees blown down. Trees do have a hard time here. The topsoil, where there is any, is frequently only a couple of inches deep covering solid rock. Most trees do not have a tap root or any kind of root system going down to give them support. All they have are shallow roots spreading out from the base. It's a wonder that some even stand upright. It is no surprise that a good wind will push them over. The real wonder is how so many stand at all. Sometimes you can see where the roots have encircled a boulder giving the appearance of giant fingers gripping on for dear life.

We will be staying at the White House Landing on the shores of Pemadumcook Lake. We had to hike 1.2 miles off the Trail to the lake and blow an air horn to summon a boat to pick us up. For this night, we *will* have a warm, dry bed to sleep in. Although their dinner menu was quite limited, neither of us had ever seen such a huge cheeseburger as we had. They are a classic on the Trail. The half pound of meat made it a truly "two-fisted burger" and that was just for *half* of it. It was really a "full meal" burger.

We will be staying in a cottage with several private rooms and a common kitchen and living area. A wood burning stove gives heat, and it is most efficient. One stick of wood keeps the place warm for hours. There is no outside electricity here, and lighting is from butane lamps. When we asked about the availability of laundry facilities, our host pointed to a wash tub, hand wringer, and the nearby lake. Well, they worked!

Shortly after we came in, a family of four joined us. The father, mother, 6-year-old son, and 11-year-old daughter had started out in Georgia in March and had come this far. We were quite impressed with them, and we all got along fine. They seemed to be one happy group and actually covered ground faster than we did. The kids kept up without any complaints.

September 15, 2002   White House Landing
Trail Distance: 0.0 miles

Sometimes our days are just not planned. This was one of those. We were packed and ready to travel after a wonderful breakfast. However, the local weather report changed that. For a state with an extended drought, Maine has sure seen some water in the past week. We already had a light shower this morning, and the forecast was for rain all day and night with scattered thundershowers this afternoon. As we are dry, warm, and happy, we saw no reason to change the situation. Besides, we would just love to tackle one of those cheeseburgers again.

If the rain slackens a bit, we would like to take one of the canoes out on the lake. We are on a small, long cove, and a moose or two may be just around the corner. Many have been sighted here, and we are definitely in moose country. This place is beautiful but difficult to get into. It is on a private logging road that other cars may not enter. Our hosts have a key to the gate and can pick people up at the town of Millinocket, but it is a well-known place, and people do come. There are the hikers and fishermen in the warm months and hunters in the cold months. I had been thinking that this would be a good spot for northern pike and walleyes but was told that Maine has neither. This *was* a surprise! There are landlocked salmon and trout, but none of what I would have been fishing for.

I am getting more than a little concerned about my weight. I did not accept the last scale reading in Monson that had me down by thirty-five pounds, but the scale here confirmed it. I went from 180 pounds to 145 and I had not been that low since my early Navy days when I was 18 years old. In the Navy boot camp, I shot up to 150 pounds and have not seen that weight or anything close to it since. It's no wonder that I am always cold and weak. I must have very little body fat left. Perhaps a couple of days of heavy duty eating will make my clothes fit better.

We *were* able to do some canoeing on the lake but were not able to see any moose. The lake is interesting enough, but a person does have to be careful in a boat. Huge boulders are sometimes just inches below the surface, and it is very easy to run into them. A boat with a motor had better have a guide aboard or there just may be some bent props. It was an interesting and scenic canoe trip, and we were able to use some of our learned skills from last year.

September 16, 2002   Wadleigh Stream Shelter
                              Trail Distance: 7.6 miles

For a while, we thought that we would be staying at White House Landing for another day. We had mixed emotions on this. We would have enjoyed the stay, but we really wanted to complete this hike. The rain continued until about noon so we left at 1:00 P.M. If the rain had continued longer, we would have stayed longer. We were just too comfortable to go out slogging in the rain. Bill, from the lodge, motored us over to a spot about 0.2 miles from the Trail. When we had first arrived, we had to hike further to reach a spot where we could call to the lodge, but they were able to bring us back to where it was closer to the Trail. From there, we took the wet, slippery Trail on to the shelter. This part of the Trail was quite nice so we made good time. As it was, it was getting dark by the time that we reached the shelter.

We came to the southern end of Nahmakanta Lake, a large, beautiful true lake. They did not even try to call this one a pond. Several miles long, we had great views from many angles and from many levels of viewing. I had been aching to do some Walleye and Northern Pike fishing back at White House Landing. When told that there were none in the lake and none in Maine, I really doubted it. On request, I was presented with a Maine anglers rule book to see what a fishing license for a non-resident, senior citizen would cost. It was $9 for a one-day license, *but* the Maine book clearly indicated that there were no Walleyes or Northern Pike in the state. Most all of the lakes were stocked with landlocked salmon and lake trout. Well, so much for a Walleye dinner!

The forests here are beautiful but quiet. Hopefully, spring time will hear birds singing and making the kind of bird calls that make forests more interesting. Fortunately for the birds, flying is the easiest way to get around in the forests. Unlike forests that I wandered through as a child, *these* are not designed for easy traveling. These forests are thick, rocky, moss covered with broken limbs and fallen trees covering the area. After every high wind, we find freshly fallen trees on the Trail. Off the Trail, the area is a northern jungle. Stepping is also rather hazardous as there are many hidden, deep holes between many of the rocks. We don't think Daniel Boone would have liked it here, and we just know that his horse would not. We still find it amazing that the moose, especially the bulls, can get around in here. We just shake our heads in wonderment.

Our cool weather (cold at night) has dampened the spirits of local flies, mosquitoes, and gnats. They are not bothering us anymore. We both have carried our mosquito head nets to Alaska and to Maine and haven't used them once! I suppose that we would rather carry them and not need them than need them and not have them. It *is* a small consolation.

September 17, 2002   Rainbow Stream Shelter
                             Trail Distance: 8.1 miles

We had expected, as we had been told, an easy hiking day. It was not too bad, but we had expected better. There were many ups and downs mixed in with rocks and roots, all wet, so the travel was rather slow. A couple of miles of the Trail were near to Rainbow Stream, and *that* was scenic and melodious. There were the continuing sounds of water cascades and many were in sight as we passed near. The shelter is located only about thirty feet from the stream, so we will listen to the sound of the water all night. It *does* make for easy sleeping.

The Nahmakanta Lake is several miles long, and the Trail followed the shore line for about four miles. It *followed* the shore line but was not on it. Sometimes it was near to the shore and then would go up about one hundred feet or so, come back down, and then go back up. In all, there were many fine views of the lake including a great view of Mt. Katahdin looking down on the lake.

Even though there are no towns, no houses, and no public roads in the one-hundred-mile wilderness, there are many logging roads, and some are open to the public. As a result, there are cabins on some of the lakes and parking areas where day hikers can have relatively easy access to the A.T. and to local trails. Once in this stretch, there is no easy way out, but a person *could* get out in an emergency. However, he or she may have to wait a day or two for a ride.

We shared the shelter last night with two men, one going north and the other south. The north bounder has already passed us, electing to tent out about four miles further north. Two young men are tenting out, and at 5:00 P.M. we have the shelter to ourselves. This is *not* our favorite shelter. It is referred to as a "baseball bat" shelter. The flooring is made up of round tree trunks, each about three inches in diameter. In addition to being cold tonight, we can look forward to being downright uncomfortable. I feel certain that the additional cost of lumber would more than make up for the trouble and labor utilized in the cutting, trimming, shaping, and laying all of these long "baseball bats".

September 18, 2002   Hurd Brook Shelter
                              Trail Distance: 11.5 miles

This was to be the next to last day of hiking before we started the climb to Mt. Katahdin. Circumstances may change that a mite. We had not gone four miles today before Mina complained of being very tired. As we were on relatively level ground, it gave us concern about the planned thirteen miles tomorrow and the climb to the peak of Mt. Katahdin the next day. We are fairly stuck with the thirteen miles but *could* break it into two days. As there are no motels or hostels around, there is no place near to take another zero day. Mina is tired, very tired, and needs more rest and more good food. We had several options and after much consideration, we decided on one. We will hike 3.5 miles tomorrow to Abol Bridge and try to get rides back to our car. That may take a while. As a last resort, we can phone the Caratunk House, and they will come shuttle us for a nominal fee. To us on our little adventure, hitchhiking will be more fun, we hope!

Originally, we had planned on getting back to our car after completing the hike and driving to New Brunswick, Canada. Our change in plans will not require many more miles plus it will both allow Mina more rest and allow us to slack pack the ten miles on which we would have carried a full pack. In addition, it will allow us to use our tent, if desired, and give us more options of campgrounds to stay in. We have been informed that many of the tent sites and shelter spots have been reserved by hikers months in advance. We *may* find a spot in our desired location, but there is no guarantee. For that, we will have to enter Baxter Park and see what, if anything, is available. For special consideration *only* to thru-hikers (we qualify), there is a shelter at our desired final location that is available *only* to thru-hikers, but only to the first twelve on a first-come, first-served basis. At any rate, with our car, we are not tied down and can fit into the park's reservation policy and into the whelms of the weather. Today would have been a great day to climb Mt. Katahdin, tomorrow is supposed to be good, the day after is questionable, and who knows after that.

We have been informed that about one-third of the expected thru-hikers have not shown up. Now, that is a bundle! We would like to stay ahead of them as we would not want the shelters full when *we* needed them.

About four miles of the Trail today kept us in view of Rainbow Lake. If you consider that out flowing streams from the lake form several other lakes called Rainbow Deadwaters, and flows from these form the headwaters of Rainbow Stream, we had about eight miles of lakes or runoffs from it. Several times, we could hear and see pontoon planes taking off from Rainbow Lake. Somebody else was having a different kind of fun. Oh well, we can't do everything that we would like all at once. We still have this one to finish.

Rainbow Ledges was not particularly high but *was* higher than the surrounding forests. It gave us some good views of the surrounding countryside, distant mountains, and particularly good views of Mt. Katahdin. The closer that we get to that mountain, the bigger and higher it appears.

Now we are getting nervous. We are so close to the end and want to finish and do not want any snags or long delays. Time will tell!

September 19, 2002   Abol Bridge
Trail Distance: 3.6 miles

We are so close, and Mina is just running out of steam. She is tired, her legs and back hurt, and she is fairly shot by midmorning. I had been planning on a 13.4-mile hike today over fairly level ground to put us at the base of Mt. Katahdin. We changed that to a short hike to Abol Bridge and travel back to our car. If we are going to take a short day or a zero day, we can at least make use of it and bring our car up. We will not be wasting much mileage.

I am super appreciative of Mina really doing everything that she can to make this hike possible for me. In return, I had mentioned the possibility of visiting the Bay of Fundy. I knew that she would enjoy it, she had not been there before, and it was not that much further on for us. It would be a kind of "thank you" for her efforts.

In getting back to our car, we met some super people. We did not even stop at the store at Abol Bridge but stuck our thumbs out and tried for a ride out of the park. Traffic was scarce, but about the third vehicle stopped and made room for us. A fisherman (they are nice also) returning home with a van full of equipment stopped and rearranged his gear so that we could fit in. As it was, Mina had to sit on the floor in the rear along with all of his gear. After a few miles down the road, the driver stopped and offered us some cheese and rolls, smeared with jam. Of course, we accepted and enjoyed the short respite. He then took us to Millinocket and left us at a good corner for a ride. It felt good just sitting and enjoying the scenery from a moving vehicle.

An electrician in a company truck then stopped and gave us a choice. If we would accompany him to a particular site, he could take us even further than where he would have had to let us off. We agreed and went a couple of miles off the main highway to a spot where a tree had fallen on a power line. He got the tree cut down, sawed it into sections and then drove us to another town further on our way.

Shortly after sticking our thumbs out, a lady in a tiny Celica stopped and said that she could take us as far as her friends' house down the road. She then drove us many miles further and dropped us off in Milo. She really went out of her way for us.

In Milo, a man with a pickup stopped for us and said that he could take us as far as where the route changed. However, if we would go with him to his house so that he could pick up his dog, he could take us a little further. To this, we agreed and a happy hound joined us but sat in the pickup bed where he wanted to be. *This* driver was not satisfied to just take us a little further but drove us forty-five miles to our car in Caratunk, Maine. We were most appreciative, but he would not even take any gas money. He enjoyed doing a good deed and, needless to say, we enjoyed it also.

We had enjoyed our last stay at Caratunk House, and this was a repeat. With a good shower, good dinner, good night's sleep and a super breakfast, we took off the next morning back to Abol Bridge.

Mina had a rest, but it did not seem to help her much. She *still* felt tired.

September 20, 2002 Katahdin Stream Campground
Trail Distance: 9.8 miles

There was some discussion and outside factors that determined our hike today. We *would* be slack packing, and the terrain was basically level. In addition, this day and the next were due to be mild and dry. The following two days are to be rainy. With that, Mina decided to "go for it"! We then drove from Caratunk, and she dropped me off at the Abol Bridge about noon. I then hiked north, and she drove to the Katahdin Stream Campground and hiked south. Unknown to us, the old road from Abol Bridge to Baxter State Park was closed, and she had to drive many miles south before turning north to the park. It took her over an hour to make the drive, go through the long line at the entrance, and then find the campsite.

Today, Mina saw her first moose on the Trail. A cow moose strolled not twenty feet in front of her, completely ignoring her, and then continued to stroll into the forest. Mina was not quite quick enough with her camera and missed the shot. Well, at least she saw a moose on the Trail.

After reaching the campground, we found all sites full, and we could not get any kind of site in the park. *Everything* was full! All shelters and tent sites were filled by reservations, the vast majority by day hikers or just campers. Since most thru-hikers do not know many days in advance just were they will be, there were twelve sites reserved *just* for thru-hikers on a first-come, first-served basis, but these, too, were filled. When I reached the car after a very pleasant and scenic hike along the Penobscot River and the Nesowadnehunk Stream, I drove back to Abol Bridge Campsite and made reservations for a tent site there. As it was getting late, I then hiked back up the Trail to meet Mina. We met after about a mile of hiking and then hiked out together. She was dead tired but gamely came on. She insisted on hiking all the way back to the campsite and would not consider a lift in the car. Some gal!

The Trail today followed the stream for about seven and a half miles, either as a river full of small rapids or as a cascading stream. The water views were great, and many of the rapids and falls just begged for a swimmer to hop it. Unfortunately, lack of time would not permit it.

Unlike many past nights, this one was fairly warm. With our tent, it felt downright comfortable. For Mina, this was her second good night's sleep. She just cannot handle the "baseball bat"-type of shelter flooring, and two in a row were not welcomed.

Tomorrow, we will see if we "go for Katahdin" or wait for a better day and a better-feeling Mina. A day off does not seem to help her; several days off are needed.

September 21, 2002   Mt. Katahdin Peak
Trail Distance: 5.2 miles

Mina decided to go for the top and just hope that she could do it. To save time, we left as early as we could and just left the tent up. By making the long drive around, we arrived at the park entrance just in time for them to put up a notice that *all* parking lots in the park were full. Since parking is permitted at only designated spots, we felt crushed. Nevertheless, we were determined to climb Mt. Katahdin even if it meant coming back to the park in several days. When our turn came to go in, I explained to the attendant that we were thru-hikers and this climb was *all* that remained of our A.T. hike. She was sympathetic, stated that they gave special consideration to A.T. thru-hikers, made a call to the ranger at the Katahdin Streams Campsite, and got permission to pass us through. We were greatly relieved!

On arrival, the ranger showed us where we could park, got our personal data, and wished us both well on our hike. He, like many others, asked us our ages. We think that we may be impressing them. The Trail started easy enough, and the first mile went fast. The second mile required a bit more work, and the next three miles were extremely difficult for us. Many younger hikers just blazed past us, but *we* passed many younger hikers who did not even make it to the top. We believe that all of the thru-hikers made it even if they had to crawl. We made it, but it was a rough, tough, difficult, and challenging climb. Finally reaching the peak, we found about twelve people there and all were in a joyous mood. We had several pictures taken of us at the "End of the Trail" poster and hope that some of them turn out. Views were limited as we were in the clouds, but the weather was warm, and we finished still wearing shorts and short sleeves. Carrying all of our heavy duty sweat shorts, long pants, and long-sleeved shirts was just a wasted effort. However, we would much rather carry them and not use them than need them and not have them.

Today, I fulfilled a 55-year-old dream of mine that began when I was 17 years old and did not get started until 1991. I truly could not have completed it without the full support and uncomplaining help of Mina. I owe her for being able to complete my hike. As promised, I will help her complete *her* hike of the Trail if she so desires.

It took us almost five hours to reach the peak and another four to come down. Coming down was almost as rough as going up. It is rather difficult to describe this mountain. There is just no easy way up. The peak sets on top of almost vertical cliffs almost 1,500 feet high. The easiest way up requires hand over hand climbing, stretches using both hands and feet to go up "V" notches, and many approaches that require inventing ways to manage them. Once near the summit, there is a half-mile segment that is a knife edge with vertical drop-offs on both sides, and *this* segment has an edge of large boulders that require the utmost care to navigate. To say the least, this climb and return taxed us to the limit. We came down dead tired with the knees, especially, begging for relief. Obviously, the younger hikers did not fare so poorly. For us, giving considerations to all aspects, we were quite proud of our achievement, and only others know what we had to do to complete our hike. How many times in the past did I quit, give up, say it was not worth it, and decide just not to come back? Probably after

each hike in the past, something like that was said: "Well, I *did* finish the Trail, it *was* worth it, and I have absolutely *no* intention of doing it again."

Why do we hike? If you discount the super people that we have met, the people to whom we have given unrestricted invitations to visit us, the fantastic sceneries that we have witnessed, and the friendliness of small towns and trusting drivers who have given us rides, the only thing left is it's a great way to lose weight. Hopefully, I will be careful about putting some of my thirty-five-pound weight loss back on. Mina did not lose as much but, still, she did not have much to lose!

Springer Mountain, Georgia—Mt. Katahdin, Maine 5/1/91-9/21/02

David's total miles on A.T.: 2,164.8

Mina's total miles on A.T.: 1,303.4

Official A.T. total miles: 2,172.8

APPENDIX

References:

Appalachian Trail Maps (fourteen states)
Appalachian Trail Conference
Maine Appalachian Trail Club
Appalachian Trail Guides (eleven books)
Appalachian Trail Conference
Keystone Trail Association
Potomac Appalachian Trail Club
Maine Appalachian Trail Club
Appalachian Trail Data Book
Appalachian Trail Conference
The Thru-Hikers Handbook
Center for Appalachian Trail Studies

BVG